CELEBRICITIES

 INVENTING WRITING THEORY

Jacques Lezra and Paul North, series editors

CELEBRICITIES

MEDIA CULTURE AND THE PHENOMENOLOGY
OF GADGET COMMODITY LIFE

ANTHONY CURTIS ADLER

Fordham University Press   *New York*   *2016*

THIS BOOK IS MADE POSSIBLE BY A COLLABORATIVE GRANT
FROM THE ANDREW W. MELLON FOUNDATION.

Copyright © 2016 Fordham University Press

All rights reserved. No part of this publication may be reproduced, stored in a retrieval system, or transmitted in any form or by any means—electronic, mechanical, photocopy, recording, or any other—except for brief quotations in printed reviews, without the prior permission of the publisher.

Fordham University Press has no responsibility for the persistence or accuracy of URLs for external or third-party Internet websites referred to in this publication and does not guarantee that any content on such websites is, or will remain, accurate or appropriate.

Fordham University Press also publishes its books in a variety of electronic formats. Some content that appears in print may not be available in electronic books.

Visit us online at www.fordhampress.com.

Library of Congress Cataloging-in-Publication Data
Names: Adler, Anthony Curtis, author.
Title: Celebricities : media culture and the phenomenology of gadget commodity life / Anthony Curtis Adler.
Description: First edition. | New York, NY : Fordham University Press, 2016. | Series: Idiom: inventing writing theory | Includes bibliographical references and index.
Identifiers: LCCN 2015045242 (print) | LCCN 2016013044 (ebook) | ISBN 9780823270798 (cloth : alk. paper) | ISBN 9780823270804 (pbk. : alk. paper) | ISBN 9780823270811 (ePub)
Subjects: LCSH: Materialism—United States. | Mass media and culture—United States. | Popular culture—United States. | Heidegger, Martin, 1889–1976. | Marx, Karl, 1818–1883.
Classification: LCC B825 .A3155 2016 (print) | LCC B825 (ebook) | DDC 306.01—dc23
LC record available at https://lccn.loc.gov/2015045242

Printed and bound in Great Britain by
Marston Book Services Ltd, Oxfordshire

18 17 16   5 4 3 2 1

First edition

for Hwa Young Seo

CONTENTS

	Exordium	ix
	Introduction	1

PART I

1	The phenomenology of television	13
2	The life not ours to live	21
3	The celebrity and the nobody	40
4	Being(s)	51
5	The life of things	59
6	Ideology and truth	64
7	The truth of the commodity	71
8	Value, publicity, politics	76
9	Reproduction	100
10	The gadget	121
11	To the things themselves	132

PART II

12 Methods · 137

Concepts of criticism; Language is the . . . of being; Satanic laughter; Techniques of writing; Vita contemplativa; The raccoon trap

13 Celebrity · 141

Epic form; Celebrity and singularity; Innocence; Of celebricity, or: toward a phenomenology of Madonna; The strange celebrity; The Uncandy; Candy Candy; What percentage of the American population are celebrities?; Specters of Spector; Excrement and enterprise; The dissociating pleasure of things; Abstract pleasures; Experiences; The theory of suffering; Advertising; The next top model; Television and celebrity; Politics and humor; The visionary; Things; Listening to Radiohead for the first time, 17 years too late.

14 Television/Gadget   176

It's bicycle repairman . . . ; Dialectica gizmotica; The Trojan horse; The personal computer; Terror-vision; The Joker; Gigi; Nip/Tuck; The Following; The Ring; House; Disjecta membra Dexteri; Boogie Nights; Man or Muppet; The sweatshops of Hollywood; Muppetation and mediation; Demectomy; Action figures; Liberal Arts; Glee; Bunheads; Breaking Bad/Elective Affinities

Epilogue   213

How I met my mother (French Theory, by François Cusset)

Notes   *215*

Bibliography   *233*

Videography   *241*

Index   *243*

Acknowledgments   *249*

EXORDIUM

Here I am. I find myself, once again, watching TV. *I would like to learn to live finally.* I would like to learn to live, to teach myself to live, to teach, to live. But I can't. Am I even watching? This is the worst thing. Life is not here, I think, life is elsewhere. I cannot follow what is going on, here or elsewhere. I am watching with others. We are watching. This is the worst thing. Living, not living, not together, together. But now we are rarely bored. Life is fun. It's interesting. My parents once kept me from watching more than half an hour a day. Always *The Muppet Show*. No coca-cola; sugar cereal only on my birthday. Limits drawing a limit separating our suburbia from others. Suburbia nothing but these limits. Limit folded within limits, without limit. A perverse monadology. Every space private to a degree, with its own special rules. The line that divides the bedroom, even the bed, in half. The television at the heart of it all. Every limit collapses, save one. A monadology of perversion. My parents split. Their vigilance faded. My father, who never watches TV, allowed me to watch. Soon we had cable. To my shame. Far beyond all the small hidden transgressions. Adolescence is the endless process of trying to escape one's adolescence; the shame of adolescence. One adolescence traded for another. Books for television. This music for that music. Wagner for rock. Berg for Wagner. Handel for Berg. Marx for Heidegger. Heidegger for Marx. Poetry for Philosophy. Hölderlin for Hölderlin. *I would like to learn to live finally.* Here I am. I find myself, once again, watching TV.

CELEBRICITIES

INTRODUCTION

Friedrich Schelling once wrote, "Just as walking [is] a constantly *hindered* falling, so life [is] a constantly hindered extinguishing of the process of life."[1] It is hardly surprising that this elementary truth of walking and of life escapes us in our everyday lives, even though we are born incapable of the very form of mobility that will distinguish us from other mammals. But eventually we overcome our impedency no less than our infancy. At first blessed with neither a stride nor a voice, we become walking, speaking animals. We no longer give a second thought to the daring act by which we shift our weight from one foot to another, falling away from stable ground with each step; falling into the abyss; almost beyond the point of no return; and yet somehow hindered, impeded, held back . . . And it all happens so quickly, so heedlessly and unthinkingly, that this effortless grace, from which all the grace of dance is born, seems as nothing.

If walking on two feet is perhaps the least of our human accomplishments, it is thinking, so the philosophers have always reminded us, that is our greatest. Yet thinking is in the end nothing but an intensification—a potentiation, as Schelling himself might say—of living and walking. Thinking also has its stride and its gait, its grace and elegance and flow, and its faults and faltering and clumsiness. And we might add, almost categorically: the unthought in thinking, thinking's own unthinking, is the necessity by which each step itself falls into the abyss—and by which it recovers. Pedantry, at once the antagonist and complement of thinking, is perhaps nothing else than the insistence that, so long as one follows certain steps and rules—a certain formula—one can stay safe, remaining on solid ground.

What makes me think of all this is not only a recent misadventure (stepping onto fresh ice, my foot slid out beneath my weight, twisting my ankle around and fracturing my fibula), but the peculiar challenge of writing an introduction to the work that will follow. Having read it over several times, hoping to discover the key that would allow me to lead the reader into and through it, I've become ever more convinced that an introduction, properly speaking, would be out of order. To lead the reader into one's own work presupposes a certain posture of mastery and self-mastery, indeed a certain pedantry; one must suppose that its steps can be taught and followed. One poses as the master of one's work, and of oneself. Yet I feel, more than ever before, the strangeness of my own path of thinking, which indeed seems like a kind of self-estrangement; as if I were myself carried away, convinced, in a way, yet also somehow exposed more than ever before, ashamed; embarrassed by my own lack of pedantic cover. This is not to say that the reader can expect to find no cohesive argument, only a mélange of haphazard insights—*Einfälle* as the Jena romantics would put it. There is, I cannot but believe, a consequence in these thoughts; a certain logic pulls them forward. But this consequence stares back at me from across a crevasse just wide enough to give pause; it is no longer quite my own. For I cannot pretend that the argument will consist in a series of steps so small and so comprehensible—so *nachvollziehbar*, as one says in German—that each will lead easefully into the next, and it will never be necessary to feel the transient groundlessness that distinguishes thinking from ratiocination. Thus, rather than lead into the argument and show the way out of it, I can do no more here than anticipate the peculiar trajectory and cadence of the steps away from the ground and their, as yet groundless, recovery. Even so, it is necessary to stress not only that these will be steps rather than leaps (where both feet leave the ground) but also that there will be a recovery: it is not a question of abyssal thought as an end in itself but rather what we might describe, through a Heideggerian terminology that it will never be entirely possible to abandon however much we twist it around and turn it against itself, as the disclosure of a new horizon for thinking; a new field of truth—though, properly speaking, there is no thinking apart from this disclosure, even if it has only recently stepped forth into the center stage of theory's *theatrum*.

This disclosure involves a certain repetition of phenomenology. It will be necessary not only to repeat, but indeed to recuperate it, to regain it, since phenomenology, especially in the radical and transitional sense that it assumes in

Being and Time, seems to have become in some fundamental way impossible—or at least impossible for *me* and, I dare say, for *us*: for all those who grew up surrounded by television, celebrity culture, gadgets. The problem, which is at once the ground of the necessity and the impossibility of phenomenology for us, is that we cannot even begin to *find ourselves* or figure out what our situation is. If phenomenology, as understood by Heidegger, is first of all the task of opening up the horizon for the question of being by showing what we ourselves are in ourselves as the being whose own being, even though it is always in and most often lost in the world, is "at issue for it," then the problem we now face is that neither we nor the world seem to be given in such a way that they could even potentially show themselves as they are in themselves. It is not merely that the world and our own being are first of all mistaken for something worldly, but that the world, in the sense that we have been seeking for it, barely seems to be there at all, no longer showing itself—and that we ourselves are somehow hopelessly, irreparably lost to ourselves.

The problem to begin with is that the world experienced in and encountered through phenomenology, while itself issuing from a far-reaching and profound challenge to the obfuscations of the philosophical tradition, is no longer my world. To do phenomenology, even if with a view to its deconstruction, it has been and would again be necessary to achieve an adequate philosophical-phenomenological point of departure by taking seriously the way in which my intellectual horizon and scholarly activity has been constituted by my "lifeworld." Yet what I finally came to realize, as a child of the seventies and eighties who, seduced by deconstruction just as its star had begun to fade, had turned toward Europe, away from America, away from the guilty televisionary pleasures of my childhood, is that the "high theory" in which I had been schooled as a doctoral student (indeed at one of its last and most austere outposts) was itself incapable of realizing its most radical theoretical intentions unless it achieved a "subject position" and theoretical horizon that is, for want of a better expression, truly its own. Or indeed truly my own. This attempt to renew the project of phenomenology demands taking seriously almost everything that, in trying to fashion myself an intellectual in the European style, I had repressed, and most of all that televisionary accompaniment that, following a strategy I had been taught by my parents and that is perhaps quite typical of my class, I had regarded not only as fictional, spectacular, but as a kind of experience that, for all its obvious seductions, is unworthy of being experienced; cannot even be called experience—a nonexperience and nonlife in the very heart of life. But coming home to the TV—not by watching more TV but by refusing not to experience it, refusing either to banish it from life or to subordinate it to life—means experiencing a kind of break and doubling of the self and of life, and thus the impossibility of phenomenology as it has been classically conceived even by those thinkers, such as Derrida, who, through an internal transformative critique, call the project of phenomenology into question by bringing it to its limits and exhibiting a quasi-ultratranscendental structure of temporal and logical difference.

This then is the first step: a phenomenology of television—repeating, recuperating, rethinking the project of *Being and Time* in terms of *televisionary life*. This first step must appear as a kind of parody, in a literal sense, of Heidegger's masterwork. The analytic of Dasein will be rethought starting out not from the toolshed or the workplace but from the couch, face-to-face (sort of, at least, since we might well be lying down, and are probably also doing something else at the same time) with our uncanny life companion and paramour. This is the task of the first three chapters of the first part of this book. Chapter 1 ("The phenomenology of television") will venture a step out into televisionary life, showing that television, as the tendency to unworldliness inhabiting Dasein as being-in-the-world, stresses the project of phenomenology to its limit, posing the condition of both its possibility and impossibility. Living with television we find ourselves not only in two different places at once, not only here and there, but at once in a place and a nonplace; within the everydayness of our world but at the same time in another everydayness that in some essential way is before us, that we are constantly faced with, but is not for us. The second chapter ("The life not ours to live") takes this analysis further by conceiving of televisionary existence, with its complex schedule of moods, as the rhythmic organization of a life, or indeed a multiplicity of lives, that are *not* ours to live and yet in a certain sense still ours *not* to live. Rejecting the premise that there is fundamentally just one life to live not only calls into question the opposition of authenticity and inauthenticity that structures Heidegger's analytic of Dasein, but indeed undermines a presupposition that remains latent even in many deconstructive and poststructuralist accounts of television, and also in every attempt to conceive of the logic of television through a romantic dialectics of irony. Here I propose that the reality show and the cartoon exhibit the defining limits of television, while so-called quality television, with its insistence on compelling dramatic structures, seeks to restore a moment of authenticity that, moreover, has a narcotic dimension. The drug indeed itself promises a kind of pseudoauthenticity—the real enjoyment of televisionary enjoyment—whose possibility is itself promised by televisionary advertising. The third chapter ("The celebrity and the nobody") turns to the question of the *who* of televisionary Dasein. Just as life with television is a double life, having always already *split*, the *who* to whom this life belongs is also disarticulated in such a way that authentic resoluteness is no longer possible. The celebrity is not the "authentically" existing nobody. Rather, the nobody always exists next to the celebrity without ever being able to overcome its nobodiness, even though at the same time the celebrity is never anything else than a "staging"—or we might say, a celebration—of the nobody. And ultimately, by shattering Dasein into the nobody and the celebrity, television irrevocably disjoins the middle-voiced self-reflexive logic of self-showing on which phenomenology depends.

This first step, and each of the many steps of which it is composed, cannot but appear as so many missteps. For if Schelling is right, the proper step is always on the verge of being a faux pas. The formulations I will use to screen televisionary life are not rigorously self-evident and self-validating, nor will they be developed as mere readings of other texts, but instead serve as formal indications gesturing toward the prospect of *another* horizon of experience; another truth. Televisionary life is not what we always already are in our ordinary everydayness; it is not even a possibility of what we are or could be. It is something else: it is preontologically strange and foreign to us. Nor is it the abyssal strangeness and difference that always already inhabits the self. But in just this way, television cancels the premise on which the project of *Being and Time*, and Heideggerian phenomenology, rests. Ontological knowledge can no longer arise from preontological familiarity. And while we might still maintain that televisionary life is constitutively related to the question of being, it is clear that we cannot approach this question by interrogating the being that we ourselves are, the life that is ours to live even if proximally and for the most part we are not living it. Television explodes the entire framework of ontological questioning. It points toward the collapse of ontological difference itself.

The second step (chapters 4 through 8 of part I) takes its departure from the thought of this collapse. The event of television, chapter 4 will claim, involves a purely contingent occurrence that not only discloses a radically new ontological horizon, but indeed initiates ontological collapse. The world of television is a world of beings that are also being itself. The televisionary event in this way does not just disclose a new ontology, but the very possibility, grounded in nothing else than the being-there of its beings, of ontological multiplicity. This rethinking of ontology, moreover, points toward a concept that for the most part seems to belong to a different domain of discourse: the commodity. For as chapter 5 ("The life of things") will argue, the Marxian and Marxist theorization of the commodity itself gestures toward the ontological collapse that stands at the limit of Heidegger's thought. And while the theorization of the commodity remains caught up in metaphysics when it fails to think the commodity in its ontological radicality, phenomenology itself cannot do without a certain "materialist" turn, which ultimately amounts to nothing less than the recognition of history as ontological contingency. Chapters 6 and 7 will argue, moreover, that the horizon for thinking this precarious confrontation of Heidegger and Marx—the destination of this second step and misstep—is the convergence of the Marxian/Marxist problem of ideology with Heidegger's extraordinary rethinking of truth as disclosure and unconcealment. Finally, as chapter 8 ("Value, publicity, politics") will seek to show, the commodity, and the ideology that is constituted in the commodity, should be conceived as that which shows *as* value. The commodity institutes a manner of showing in which all beings appear in terms of their relations of value. This is the radical ontological significance of the event of commodity production. In this way, the nature of the tense relation between Heidegger and Marx, the basis of any possible dialogue between them, becomes clearer: while Heidegger brings into view the sense of being as that which is *beyond* value, he refuses to think the commodity as the site of the production of value. And while Marx does think the commodity in this way, he remains largely within the epistemic horizon of metaphysics, and is thus incapable of thinking the *alethic* sense of production itself—that production is the production of a truth-horizon.

The third step, comprising chapters 9 and 10 ("Reproduction," "The gadget"), begins with this impasse, and it will not be abusing the metaphor of stepping to remind the reader that the complete step is a two-step: landing first on one leg and then the other. And indeed it is only by stepping out into a double abyss, the fractured life of television and the value-truth of the commodity, that we can find our way back—or rather fall back onto—the new ground. Starting out from a reading of Althusser's essay on the ideological state apparatus, I will argue that this famous theorization of the reproduction of the ideological conditions of production must be taken even further to encompass what I call the alethic conditions of production. If production is of essence alethic—the bringing forth of an entity into unconcealment—then it must itself be capable of producing and reproducing its own mode of alethic productivity. This in turn opens the way toward an account of the distinguishing characteristics of contemporary capitalism: now, in an unprecedented way, the reproduction of the alethic, phenomenological conditions of production can no longer be taken for granted. If bringing forth beings into unconcealment presupposes a horizon in which they can "show up," if production, as it were, demands a world in the phenomenological sense, then contemporary (late, postideological) capitalism finds itself in a peculiar predicament: the demand for production has outstripped our familiar world and its ontological underpinnings. Production must bring forth its own alethic horizontality. This is the "work" of the gadget: the gadget is the commodity that has taken alethic production upon itself. The gadget brings with it its own world, even its own Dasein. Or rather, and more precisely, it appropriates our world, our existence, our very being the being that has its being to be, our authenticity and inauthenticity, our temporality, our moods and disclosedness and truth, perhaps even televisionary Dasein itself—even the life that is not ours to live. It makes these its own. This has nothing to do with mere commodification or reification; it is not that we become commodity-like, thing-like, or gadget-like but that the gadget becomes, plays, runs and runs away with *we*.

With this our path has come *almost* full circle: we began by encountering television, and we end with the gadget's pluripotent televisionary screening and "self"-screening. This circling, however, is not exactly hermeneutic: the gadget does not simply "work out" the horizon anticipated by television. Rather, the theorization of the gadget will suggest the fundamental ambiguity of the project of phenomenology, even—indeed especially—in its most radical reformulations. Rethinking truth as the play of disclosure and concealment, even as the deconstructive play of the signifier, may itself play into commodity-truth-production. Yet we also cannot simply deny the gadget. The truth of the gadget must *also* become our truth; another world, touching on yet somehow beyond the world of the gadget, must come into being as our world. The truth of the gadget, becoming our truth—recuperating an *us* and a *world*—must be set off from gadget-truth. We must be careful, however, not to think of this principally as an appropriation or reappropriation, and least of all in terms of a dialectics of alienation and its overcoming. The aim is not to gather gadget-truth back to what was there before it, an everyday life before television and modern teletechnologies, as if we were still there and needed only to recover ourselves. Rather, it is a matter of bringing forth a screen beyond the screen, a television beyond television, a gadget beyond the gadget, perhaps even a celebrity beyond celebrity. Or better and more simply, since the image of the beyond already leads us back and thus misleads: another television, another gadget, another celebrity, revelatory and revolutionary in their alethic play.

The eleventh chapter of the first part ("To the things themselves") calls attention to this task and marks a transition to the second part, which indeed starts out from the very situation—the truth-horizon—toward which the first part awkwardly points the way. Between the two parts we will have crossed a threshold, yet each leads to the other—they are, as it were, the opposite sides of a Möbius strip—nor will it be necessary to begin with the one rather than the other. Yet if the first part, despite the abysses of its several steps, approximates a sustained argument, leading toward a certain destination, indeed imploding into the commodity, the second bursts apart into a multitude of pseudoimprovisational initiatives, each with its own ductus, mood, and characteristic gesture. Repeating the themes of the first part, these fragments will seek to catch the drifts, waves, eddies, and swells that arise as the furtive combinations and clandestine assemblages of the truth-play of gadget-commodity-life. Scattered and random as these might at first appear, they are not without a certain development, an overarching movement and momentum, a texture of cross-resonances. And with the mounting prospects comes ever greater risk of undertow.

I can hardly hope to conceal that, for all their critical tendencies, an enthusiasm is at work in these fragments; indeed a certain rapture and ecstasy: I have often felt carried away by the things that they seek to screen and surf. The things will come to show themselves through the theorizations, the critical gestures, the fluid networks of meaning, the truth-plays that they themselves call into existence. The result will often be vertiginous, and may seem idiosyncratic and eclectic if not arbitrary, and always somehow willfully, avowedly "personal." Yet while there is no way to get to the things themselves apart from the singularity of an encounter that can never be cashed out in generalities, it is never a question of mere subjectivity as an end in itself, let alone a fetishized critical sensitivity, but of the ecstatic disclosure of what we might call without hyperbole the most radical objectivity, the most extreme *Sachlichkeit*. Moreover, this enthusiasm is the late-born issue of a thinking that broods obsessively yet soberly over its objects. In the words of Rousseau: "I see well only what I recall, and I have intelligence only in my memories."[2] This is itself a point of the greatest methodological significance. Though it seems to promise pure immediacy, television will never really be watched in the present but rather through a fecund afterlife of sporadic, spontaneous recollection.

Despite these obsessions with televisionary objects, I am not after a theory of television, or, for that matter, celebrities, gadgets, and popular culture more generally. Television is not first of all an object to be theorized but rather a mode of experience, and indeed a form of living—and unliving; existence and in-existence. Thus I will make no attempt even to begin to do justice to the complex history of American television, let alone television's various regional and national histories. Yet there also can be no posture of naïveté: watching TV is of essence a theoretical experience. It is not just one phenomenon among others, but a phenomenon that, even though always facing us as an *other*—a houseguest that we can never find it in us to ask to leave—is itself constitutively phenomenological. Thus televisionary theory cannot be forced. There can be no claim to mastery: it is always a kind of happy coincidence. Television escapes us as soon as we refuse to submit to its casualness.

Nor should this book be taken as a televisionary deconstruction of phenomenology, or a phenomenological deconstruction of television. A certain deconstructive tendency is at work, to be sure, and we will strike upon more than one self-effacing, self-undermining, aporetic formulation. Yet the value of these will not consist in exhibiting a certain inexorable, ultratranscendental logic, or a-logic, of textuality, language, and thought, but rather in pointing to a new positivity of experience and truth that is (and this is the most crucial point) irreducible to a purely formal structure. Perhaps nothing else is at stake, indeed, than becoming open to the contents, or better the form-contents—the historically emergent ideas—of the media-driven, media-haunted, and media-haunting popular culture of late capitalism. Yet by insisting on a phenomenological point of departure, we also part ways with speculative materialism, speculative realism, and object-oriented ontology. For indeed, to suppose that, rejecting the "correlationism" of Kant, Husserl, and Heidegger, one could regain access to the things themselves, allowing for a glorious new epoch of speculative ontology, is to play into the gadget-commodity's dreams.

It might seem peculiar, given the role that Marxian and Marxist theories of the commodity and ideology play in the first part of this book, that I should begin by attaching such privilege to thinking. Has the question of praxis simply been abandoned? I am certainly not trying to do Marxist political philosophy through some torturous Heideggerian detour. Something else is at stake. Yet I would also claim that, at the present moment, concrete political praxis demands taking up once again the question of theory, thinking, and truth. The critique of ideology must give way to the interrogation of what we might call *alethology*: the truth-play that plays out in the gadget-commodity. Praxis reveals itself and constitutes itself as alethic. An account of praxis that does not acknowledge this turn must prove at best ineffectual. At worst it will play into the very order that it seeks to overcome.

I have tried whenever possible to cite existing translations of foreign-language texts, though in the case of Heidegger I give the pagination of the standard German editions when these are cross-referenced by the English translations: John Macquarrie and Edward Robinson's version of *Sein und Zeit*; Richard Rojcewicz and Daniela Vallega-Neu's recent English rendering of *Beiträge zur Philosophie (Vom Ereignis)*; and various other volumes published by Indiana University Press. I have not followed Macquarrie and Robinson in capitalizing "being" when translating the nominalized verb *Sein* and usually render *das Seiende* as "beings" rather than "entity." For the sake of terminological coherence, the English translations of Heidegger have been silently modified accordingly. Following the practice of Macquarrie and Robinson, *Dasein*, a perfectly ordinary German word, is left untranslated. The reader should keep in mind, though, that Heidegger's *Dasein* is not something occult or strange but is nothing else than the being that we ourselves are. *Seyn*, the archaic variant spelling of *Sein* deployed in *Contributions to Philosophy*, is rendered as "be-ing" in contrast to "being."

Translations that are my own and modified translations are so noted. Unless otherwise indicated, quotations follow the emphasis of the original.

PART I

1
THE PHENOMENOLOGY OF TELEVISION

When Heidegger was named to an unchaired professorship at the University of Marburg in 1923, television was little more than the dream of inventors and science fiction hacks. By the time he had published *Being and Time* four years later, in the spring of 1927, it had already become, with Philo Farnsworth's demonstration of the first working all-electronic television system, an effective reality.[1] There is perhaps little reason to suppose, in a century that had witnessed so many momentous discoveries and technological innovations, that this is more than a coincidence. Having served as a radio operator during the First World War, Heidegger was certainly no stranger to the innovations in the remote transmission of sound and text that had already decisively transformed both warfare and commerce. Two decades had already passed since, with the laying of a transpacific telegraph cable, the nearly instantaneous transmission of information around the world became possible. Yet these extraordinary technological transformations leave few traces in *Being and Time*: Heidegger's analysis of being-in-the-world and everydayness is presented, following a distinction he will later disavow, as systematic rather than historical in character, and for the most part seems of indeterminate historical reference, as if valid for any Dasein—any form of human existence—that, having reached a certain fullness in its articulation, could no longer be characterized as primitive.[2] Yet there is at least one moment in which the question concerning technology begins to take shape in a form that anticipates the striking role technology will play, beginning in the thirties, in Heidegger's thought.³ In section 23 ("The spatiality of being-in-the-world"), having just introduced *Ent-fernung* (de-severing, dis-tancing, or more literally, dis-distancing) and *Ausrichtung* (directionality) as fundamental characteristics of the spatiality of Dasein—the way in which it is *in* the world—Heidegger, clarifying the meaning of the first of these terms, explains that it involves a "bringing-close" achieved either through actually procuring something and "putting it in readiness" or in a "purely cognitive manner." He continues:

> *In Dasein there lies an essential tendency towards closeness [Nähe].* All the ways in which we speed things up, as we are more or less compelled to do today, push us on towards the conquest of remoteness. With the "radio," for example, Dasein has so expanded its everyday environment that it has accomplished a dis-distancing of the "world"—a dis-distancing which, in its meaning for Dasein, cannot yet be visualized.⁴

The phenomenological method of *Being and Time* demands carefully regulating the movement between ontological and ontic perspectives. Only by this meticulous control can he keep the fundamental-ontological inquiry rooted in the analysis of Dasein and the concreteness of everydayness, avoiding the "worldlessness" that, having afflicted metaphysics from the beginning, led to the absurd conjecture of an isolated epistemological subject that must somehow leap out of itself into a relation to the world. Yet precisely this caution and patience, as if overwhelmed by the urgency of an insight occupying the limits of *Being and Time*, breaks down in the passage cited above, which moves in rapid succession from the italicized characterization of one of the innermost tendencies of Dasein to the increasing speed that marks the present moment and then to the concrete example of radio.

It is as if the phenomenological method—itself the supreme practice of a kind of theoretical patience, letting that which shows itself be seen as it shows itself by dismantling the constructs that force the phenomena into a mode of comprehension foreign to their essence—had to be abandoned, indeed to abandon itself, under the pull of the phenomenon of radio and the culture and technologies of speed it exemplifies. If we are more or less compelled to participate in, to "make with" or "get with" (*mitmachen*) this increase in speed, it is not only a matter of the difficulty of "slower" forms of life surviving in an ever-accelerating world. The compulsion seems to seize hold of thinking itself, which, for this brief moment at least, cannot resist submitting to the vertiginous tendency to nearness and speed just as it identifies it: as if that which showed itself in the radio, this particular technology, could not but show itself impatiently, with a kind of urgency. It is as if it were precisely what could only show itself not as itself, such that the very question of the source of this compulsion—does it come from "within" Dasein or somewhere out there in the world or even from a thing that is not like Dasein—becomes at once urgent and irresolvable. Perhaps tracing the problem of technology back to a tendency of Dasein and the history of being, enforcing the distinction between ontic and ontological, is itself an attempt to bring the problem of technology home to us and close to us. Precisely here we seem to find an intimation in Heidegger of what Derrida will come to refer to as teletechnology—a term encompassing not only radiological broadcast media, the telegraph, the telephone, the gramophone, but also the technique of writing itself.[5]

Yet perhaps we should not go quite so far—not just yet. A marginal note in Heidegger's own copy of *Being and Time*, included without date in the complete edition of his works, suggests that Dasein's tendency to "nearness" is deeply bound up with the ontological problematic and that his invocation of technology and speed would not contest the primacy of the phenomenological method. Asking "to what extent and why?," Heidegger answers, "being *qua* constant presence has priority—making present [*Gegenwärtigung*]."[6] Dasein, in its ceaseless striving to bring near, grasp hold of, and secure in "constant presence," undermines and destroys the very world in which, as being-in-the-world, it ex-ists, and from out of which alone the question of the sense of being opens up. Yet precisely this tendency also cannot be banished from Dasein. The very spatiality of being-in-the-world is characterized first of all by *Ent-fernung*: the dis-distancing that involves bringing near what is distant as distance, in its distance; opening up the space of a world in which things can have distance from each other. It is thus that dis-distancing, as existential characteristic, discovers distance (*Ent-ferntheit*), a categorial determination that refers to things, both ready-to-hand and present-at-hand, that are laid out in space, though even this distance need not articulate itself in mathematically precise measurements.[7] One could even argue in this vein that the entire problematic of *Being and Time*, and perhaps of fundamental ontology itself, is bound up with this essential tendency of Dasein. That Dasein tends essentially toward "bringing near," constituting distance by bringing distance itself near, is really but to say that Dasein, in its existence, understands itself: that it "stands out" in the "there" (*Da*) of disclosedness; that it is "out there" in a world. This tendency, in other words, has everything to do with the fact that Dasein is "in the truth"—that Dasein is the site of the originary truth of disclosure, of dis-concealment. What Dasein "brings near," brings into the opening of the truth in this way, is first of all its own being. Yet in thereby explicitly and thematically bringing its own being near to itself, it brings it near to it in the way that things in the world are brought near to it. It treats its own being not only as a thing or a being (*ein Seiendes*) and indeed a worldly being—something ready-to-hand, bound up in a context of applications (*Bewandtnisganzheit*) and meanings (*Bedeutungen*)—but as a substance with properties, torn out from its worldly context to be present before the theoretical gaze. It gets near to its own being by turning this being into "constant presence." Bringing not only the beings of the world and other Dasein, but its own being and the being of beings that are not like it near to itself—opening up the possibility of both ontic and ontological truth—Dasein necessarily also strays from the truth. Dasein is, hence, both originally in truth and in untruth. It strays from its truth, falling into untruth, to the extent that it refuses to abide with the concealment residing within disclosure; the darkness inhabiting the clearing (*Lichtung*) of the truth. It errs above all when it seeks to get too near to itself; forgetting the original ontological distance of itself from itself by bringing it near to itself in the same way as beings out there in the world, which are ontically more distant but ontologically closer. Everything hinges on Dasein learning, once again, to respect distance—and, first of all, the distance between being and beings.

The same point of departure has thus brought us to two very different, seemingly irreconcilable, conclusions: on the one hand, television, which barely yet existed as *Being and Time* was written but found a harbinger in radio and film, marks the impossibility of phenomenology—or at least of the form of phenomenology as which alone, following Heidegger's dictum, ontology would be possible.[8] For indeed, if phenomenology, at least as understood by Heidegger, has everything to do with the play of proximity and distance, indeed with the careful control of their interplay—if the showing of that which shows itself as it shows itself ultimately comes down to allowing this very interplay between proximity and distance, as which the truth takes place, to play out in all its subtlety—then television, fluctuating wildly and without mediation between a proximity that has become infinitely distant and a distance that has become infinitely proximate, would spell the end of phenomenology, or at least of phenomenology as we know it. Living *with* the TV, we are not, as Jonathan Crary would have it, arrested and immobilized by a disciplinary, "anti-nomadic" apparatus, with "hundreds of millions of individuals" suddenly beginning to spend "many hours of every day and night sitting, more or less stationary, in close proximity to flickering, light-emitting objects."[9] We are, rather, always at once there and not there, living at the threshold, in the words of Richard Schickel, of an "electronic limbo—that nowhere that is anywhere and everywhere," having entered into a relation to "intimate strangers" who, even though removed from us by an insurmountable distance, become as familiar to us, in their "tics and blinks and glances," as our most intimate companions.[10] This might suggest why after the Second World War, when television began its invasion of everyday life, phenomenology finds itself ever more concerned with radical alterity and difference, becoming, as François-David Sebbah puts it, a phenomenology of excess in a double sense.[11] Postwar phenomenology, the phenomenology constituted by phenomenology's self-deconstruction, is, as Derrida intimates in an interview with Bernard Stiegler, of essence televisionary.[12] The specificity of television vis-à-vis other teletechnologies consists in the fact that "the greatest compatibility, the greatest coordination, the most vivid of possible affinities seems to be asserting itself, *today*, between what appears to be most alive, most *live* [in English in the original], and the différance or delay, the time it takes to exploit, broadcast, or distribute it . . . . A maximum of 'tele,' that is to say, of distance, lag, or delay, will convey what will continue to stay alive, or rather, the immediate image, the living image of the living: the timbre of our voices, our appearance, our gaze, the movement of our hands."[13] Television, by bringing *différance* and the claim of absolute presence into the greatest, most uncanny and spectral proximity, thus forces on us the thought of deconstruction. Yet on the other hand: phenomenology, even as understood by Heidegger in *Being and Time*, is already itself of essence a *Fern-sehen*, a seeing of what is far, of what is ontologically distant, just as television itself is not simply *Fern-sehen*, a distanced seeing, but *Ent-fern-sehen*—a dis-distancing seeing. The danger of television is not only a danger that defines Dasein in its fallenness *into* the world—and hence conditions the possibility of phenomenology as the attempt to come to terms with, rather than evade, this fallenness—but is the very condition of the possibility of phenomenology and of Dasein itself, which is inauthentic before it is authentic, captivated by and distracted into the world before it has taken ownership of its ownmost possibility in the moment of resoluteness.

Television, this is to say, is the tendency to unworldliness inhabiting Dasein in its being-in-the-world. But it also takes us up to, and pulls us beyond, the limit at which the world has been, irreparably, shattered. If television is the possibility of phenomenology, it is also its impossibility. It comes down to the question whether television can still be seen to belong to Dasein, to be a possibility of Dasein in its own relation to its possibilities, or whether it is something completely other and alien: a voice and vision from beyond. Strikingly, Heidegger speaks of radio almost as if it were the sacred vessel through which Dasein sought to accomplish the project of dis-distancing the world by way of "extending" and "destroying" the everyday environment. But if radio is the vessel of Dasein, Dasein will become the vessel of being and its history (*Geschichte*). But perhaps being is nothing else than this otherness announcing itself through the radio as a voice to which the only response is silence.[14] And perhaps the most fundamental project of Heidegger's thinking is nothing else than to turn the stupefying silence greeting the radio broadcast into the resolute staying-silent (*Schweigen*) of the one who can speak but would prefer not to. It is perhaps in the resonance of this voice and this silence that we can begin to approach the question of Heidegger's "greatest stupidity": his Nazism.

If television takes us beyond the perspective that radio, in its urgent anonymous address, has already disclosed, it is because it no longer allows silence as a response, and thus offers a far more radical challenge to the strategies through which Dasein seeks to handle and defuse, and appropriate as its own possibilities, the world-shattering tendencies of technologies of instantaneous communication and contact. We cannot confuse television with the voice of authority, of leadership, of *Führung*. We cannot take it for a voice that leads us somewhere.[15] We might also understand this in terms of the second "characteristic" of Dasein's spatiality: directionality (*Ausrichtung*). Because radio's disembodied voice seems to come from everywhere and nowhere, hence from beyond the regions of the world, it can still orient us. If it brings us to the threshold where distance and proximity coincide in their absolute opposition, it can also restore a kind of orientation amid disorienting worldlessness by having us hearken to *One* voice. It is here that the project of fundamental ontology and fascism converge. Television, in contrast, takes dis-distancing to the limit but refuses a compensatory, orienting directionality. It shatters the world into pieces but returns these pieces to us as a "pseudoworld," a phony world, another world—a world that sort of "takes place," having its places and spaces, but never such that we could put ourselves, and find ourselves, to rights in it. It is hardly surprising, then, that in the opening paragraph of the "hint" (*Hinweis*) introducing the Bremen lectures—Heidegger's first public appearance after the Second World War—television marks the culmination of the shrinking of distances in time and space brought about by aviation, radio, and film. "The pinnacle of all such removals of distance [*Beseitigung aller Entfernung*] is achieved by television, which will soon race through and dominate the entire scaffolding and commotion of commerce."[16]

Radio holds open a prospect that television forbids. The rhetoric of authenticity, through which Dasein finds its way back to itself and its most radical possibilities, is of essence radiological—just as radio, despite its novelty, may still be regarded as an extension of classical rhetoric, holding open the possibility of a radically democratic participatory politics (a politics founded, as in Rousseau, on the constitutive presence of the people to itself) beyond the physical confines of the classical *polis*. Yet television does not eliminate the radiological but takes it up within itself, so that it remains there as a possibility holding back television from its outermost tendencies.[17] Hence it would be a disaster for theory to think it must choose between the possibility and impossibility of phenomenology. Even here, at this most critical point, the very last thing that television can want from us is for us to make a choice. If television has become the privileged, ideal medium for advertising, it is because it gives us choices without making us choose. Having to choose, spending one's own money, is not so much the direct effect of television advertising as the futile attempt, falling back to earth as it were, to hold onto freedom and choice in a realm in which, in the excess of choices, choice has been suspended. Advertising is precisely *not* simply rhetoric in the classical sense, even if it also does not exactly exclude rhetoric but brings it to a peak of subtlety. The point of advertising is not to make us choose but to give us choices. While it may be true, as Bernard Stiegler has noted, that Freud's nephew Edward Bernays played a crucial role in the development of marketing strategies in the early twentieth century, his propagandistic and rhetorical conception of media power can hardly make sense of more contemporary practices.[18] Nor are we justified in regarding television advertising as the culmination of a strategy of the *"generalization of the availability of brains"* that leads merely to universal fatalism and the destruction of spirit.[19] Advertising, this is to say, neither creates the desire for the product to be consumed nor directs desire toward this product. Rather, it discloses the brand that, with its unchanging logo, stands in the same relation to the infinite multitude of televised images and mass-produced commodities as the Platonic Idea to the things that imitate it. Whereas the capitalist economy, like every restricted economy, itself consists in the distribution of finite resources, and thus is organized around a strict principle of finitude, without which both exchange value and use value would be incomprehensible, advertising, playing such an essential role in the ideology of capitalism, is indeed ideology in the most literal sense: it refers the finitude of real things back to the realm of eternal, unchanging brands—the heavenly "eternal life" of the commodity—that, just like the Platonic Good, and in strict contrast to mere earthly goods, we can all partake of.

The great challenge of a phenomenology of television, if we can still speak of such, is to enter into a thoughtful relation to this nonchoice that opens up between the possibility and impossibility of phenomenology. The danger is always that we merely either reduce television to an aspect of everyday life—

conceiving of it ontically in terms of sociology, cultural studies, anthropology, and the like, or even ontologically as an extreme expression of "the dictatorship of the 'one'"—or collapse everyday life into television, turning it into a "society of the spectacle." Television takes place (and time) at the threshold between the operativity and effectivity of everyday life, which continues to be governed by putatively real needs and real desires, and the order of spectral, simulacric virtuality. It will be a recurrent, revenant theme for us that in just this way television hauntingly, uncannily doubles the playful labors of deconstruction.[20] The trick is to think how, living with television, we are not only two places at once, here and there, but also at once in a place and a nonplace; within everydayness, with the prospect of the moment of resoluteness and hence also of phenomenological insight and entrance into the question of being, and simultaneously outside everydayness—or, rather, in another everydayness that is no longer *the* everyday everydayness in which we can live. If television viewers take such delight as the law closes around the criminal with a relentless inevitability, discovering the one trace that will betray an otherwise perfect crime, it is because television, whose experiences are constantly disappearing without a trace, offers the perfect alibi for an endless, gothic sea of wayward desires.

It is in this sense that, reading him against the grain, defying the *telos* that governs his own analysis, we might credence McLuhan's characterization of the television medium as cool rather than hot, participatory rather than passive, process rather than product-oriented, tactile rather than visual or auditory, synesthetic and synthetic rather than analytic, involving an active relation to depth rather than the passive reception of a well-defined surface.[21] Yet the depth of television, doubling the depth of our own life, cannot be understood as an extension of our sensory-motor apparatus, a prosthesis of the self. It cannot be received through a teleologic of appropriation. We are participating in television, constantly reaching out into it, touching its depths, tarrying with it, but without ever reaching it or touching it—without the rapture of synthesis. It is not participatory but a-participatory: we take part, absolutely, by taking ourselves apart; or, rather—exposing ourselves to a procession of improper parts—by never taking part. While the medium is the message, it can never be the whole, or even the most important, message: in its "contents"—its particular, ever different, changing, historical messages—television exposes, imparts and a-parts, that improper irreparable part that resists appropriation and instrumentalization.

2
THE LIFE NOT OURS TO LIVE

I remember watching an episode of *Beavis and Butt-head*.[1] The two protagonists, adolescent reprobates and ironic television junkies, find a card in an ATM, guess the pin code, and, withdrawing thousands of dollars, run back to their home and their couch, only to watch on television—their misdeed, it turns out, had been captured on a closed-circuit feed—as the police break through their door to arrest them.

I found myself laughing. I was laughing at their foolishness, their stupid criminality, to be sure, but I was also laughing at them laughing in their muted, hideous fashion at the TV, at themselves, without recognizing themselves *as* themselves, and suddenly, in this moment, I was also laughing at myself—for I too, like them, was laughing at myself as not myself. Thus I became the object of my own laughter to the very extent that I did not see this.

Few moments expose the nature of the television medium with such devastating force. Yet if the force of this laughing epiphany is lost on us, it is because we still tend to grasp it through the weary dialectics of irony and self-referentiality that continues to guide the theorization of television.[2] Even the subtlest attempts to think postmodern mediality, such as Lawrence Grossberg's work on MTV, take recourse to concepts such as "authentic inauthenticity" that remain rooted in the conceptual framework of romanticism.[3] Theatrical irony and self-referentiality depend on, and reinforce, the prior presupposition of an identity of the "world" and the "stage"—a presupposition that finds its fulfillment in philosophical subjectivism. Irony is the extreme moment in which reality becomes identified with a spectacle that the subject and spectator posits for itself.

It assumes, in other words, that there is, at least at any given moment, only *one life to live*—such that the very authenticity of life consists in taking ownership of this one life, of owning up to the responsibility for the one life that it has been given us to live. That we can live in the *essence* or in mere *appearance*, in accordance with the *logos* or without *logos*, authentically or inauthentically: the very possibility of such decisions depends on the ultimate unity of the *one life* that may be lived differently. This in turn demands that the dualisms of philosophy—appearance and reality, for example—remain somehow bound to each other such that each is *of* the other. The reality must be *of* appearance, and appearance *of* reality; the one *of* the many, and the many *of* the one; being *of* beings, and beings *of* being. The presupposition that there is one life to live remains in effect in Heidegger, who conceives of Dasein as having to choose between authenticity and inauthenticity, and indeed understands authenticity as nothing else than owning up to the "mineness" that binds my singular existence to my choices. Nor does he abandon it with the so-called turn in his thinking, as countless passages from the *Contributions to Philosophy*, regarded by many as the key text for understanding his later thought, would attest.[4] Likewise, Debord's "society of the spectacle," which Agamben has sought to revive and develop, and Baudrillard's simulacric hyperreality continue to operate within the presupposition that the spectacular or simulacric constitutes a homogeneous plane of experience substituting for reality. Even Derrida's *exappropriation*, the "double movement" that desires to appropriate something while "knowing at the same time that it remains—and while desiring . . . that it remain—foreign, transcendent, other, that it stay where there is alterity," retains a trace, perhaps more than just a trace, of a logic of authenticity.[5] Yet it is in psychoanalysis that the *one life* finds its most tense and paradoxical formulation: the unconscious—the strata of thoughts that do not present themselves to the subject in the mode of consciousness, that do not offer themselves in a perspicacious self-evidence—would still belong to the one life we have to live, and would still need to be appropriated as such, even if we must renounce the hope of bringing its contents to consciousness.[6]

The presupposition that there is only *one life to live*, even if this *one life* is characterized by an internal fracture, is of essence tragic. The power of the tragic stage, indeed of all conventional staged theatrical dramas, has to do with the dignity that decisions and their consequences, joy and suffering, good fortune and bad, assume in light of the monstrous responsibility of living this one life. Tragic above all is the conjunction of character with plot, action, fate. If the Greek gods enjoyed such a blessed existence, it is because their character, if you could still call it such, always transcends their action and their suffering: they could—one recalls the final scene of the first book of the *Iliad*—always laugh. For us it is otherwise: we become defined, and finished off, by our choices, and even by things we did not choose. This is what it means to be mortal.

Self-reflexive theatrical irony in no way marks a rupture with this tragic logic, even when it passes over into the purest comedy. The subject that produces its own reality and reflects upon itself, and even must be given over to itself in infinite self-reflection in order to secure the first sense of itself, remains consigned to its own one life, even if this is not something that it can ever actually secure for itself as the point of departure for really living. But the comic moment in *Beavis and Butt-head* points in an entirely different direction. Laughter happens when the cartoon and the reality show collide. It is this collision that exposes the being, and life, of television.

That the ATM serves as the vehicle of this collision might still seem to reveal a romantic dialectics of irony at work. The identity card and the notion of a money based on the power of pure signification rather than the seeming concreteness of gold, as the writings of Fichte suggest, belong to the idealist discourse that, by trying to found subjectivity on an algebra of signs (I = I), opens the way to the paradoxes of infinite reflection.[7] Yet the bank card already marks a rupture with the logic of self-identity. Whereas the uttering of "I" could still be said to *express*, or at least seek to express, a self-identity that is then confirmed by one's physical presence (the corporeal givenness of the body of the one who says "I"), the bank card *indicates* a self-identity (the fact of being oneself) that, to the extent that it exists only through this indication, is exposed absolutely to the risk of expropriation, and indeed can really only be said to exist as this risk. Identity itself can now be stolen—it has paradoxically become the property of that by which it indicates itself rather than of the subject whose identity it is.

The cartoon and the reality show, while both dispensing with "real" actors, stand in a diametric and symmetrical opposition to one another, and indeed together represent two extreme possibilities that emerge, remaining structurally dependent on one another, with the dissolution of the acted and fully scripted TV show that inherited the *dramatic* structure of Western theatricality. The cartoon presents a world that never changes, returning after each episode to the same state. Themselves exempt from time, its characters (think of Tom, Jerry, Fred Flintstone, Bart Simpson) appear, much like Barthes's wrestlers and the archetypes of the commedia dell'arte, bound up with a "situation" but absolutely without a life fate.[8] This results in an existence that is neither blessed nor sacred but in a radical sense free from guilt, punishment (or reward), and death: like the limbo described by Agamben in *The Coming Community*, where children who die unbaptized undergo a punishment that consists not in affliction but merely privation, "the perpetual lack of the vision of God"—a lack that, not even felt as lack, since the very capacity for supernatural knowledge granted to the soul at baptism is lacking, turns into a "natural joy." "Irremediably lost, they persist without pain in divine abandon."[9] To the characters in the cartoon belongs an innocence beyond the innocence of those who have merely been found not guilty, or who are saved, redeemed, pardoned: the innocence of those who never felt the shadow that law and judgment cast over life. The sign of this is a physical comedy whose humor depends on the laws of natural cause and effect remaining in force, yet without ever leading to those consequences—injury and death—from which recuperation is no longer possible. Even extreme sadism, seen thus, can appear as play.

The reality show, in contrast, knows nothing of a character that transcends life and fate; nothing of a form-of-life that could exist in an innocence from judgment. Now human life appears only through the modalities that characterize its subjection to the law: it is judged, punished and rewarded, and subject to disciplinary regimes; pursued and arrested by the police; tortured and forced to labor, held in captivity and under surveillance. And thus it is sacrificed on the altar of its own all-too-human needs, ambitions, desires. This is the case even when the reality show seems to seek nothing more than to apply documentary realism to everyday life. As Baudrillard observes in his brilliant analysis of *An American Family*—the 1971 experiment in reality television—the chosen family is doomed by its very statistical perfection: "Ideal heroine of the American way of life, it is, as in ancient sacrifices, chosen in order to be glorified and to die beneath the flames of the medium, a modern *fatum*. Because heavenly fire no longer falls on corrupted cities, it is the camera lens that, like a laser, comes to pierce lived reality in order to put it to death."[10] Archetypal, situated but fateless character dissolves and only life events and actions remain, and winners and losers alike must submit to the joylessness of a life conceived only as competition. The sign of this, the counterpoint of the effectless violence of the cartoon, is the joyless sexuality, obscene in its very lack of pornography, of shows like *The Bachelor*, a long-running dating reality show in which a crowd of women vie for the hand of a single eligible man: sexual exchanges appear bereft of all play and all pleasure; they have a purely instrumental meaning, serving to promote the intentions of the contestants and help them achieve their ultimate aim. If every cartoon is as it were broadcast from limbo, the ideal site for the reality show would be a prison or concentration camp. Nothing less could satisfy the interests of a viewing public that already delights in witnessing others submit to surveillance and selections, forced to eat insects and worms, stressed to the limit of their physical and mental capacities, hectored and humiliated, and subjected to arbitrary and changing regimes—"rules of the game" that vary at the whim of the producer. Yet living under the constant threat of expulsion, even paradise would become hellish.

Occupying the threshold space delimited by cartoon limbo and the carceral reality show, television orchestrates and organizes a kind of everydayness, though fundamentally different from Heidegger's *Alltäglichkeit*. For even now we do not exactly live in television, but instead it accompanies the times and seasons of our lives. We still also exist in everydayness, between life and death, but now *we* (one, they, *das Man*), while living, watch TV, which has become the constant accompaniment to a life beyond work, organizing it through a complex system of rhythms (interstitial, hourly, daily, weekly, yearly) that, in contrast to the schedules that govern monastic orders, the military, schools, factories, and hospitals, no longer have any sacral, political, or even purely instrumental and productive rationale.[11]

Television is without the violence of direct compulsion: you can always change the channel. You can even turn it off. It is the purest achievement of a perfectly *willing* submission to power. What child has not wished to stay home from school and watch TV all day, only to find himself or herself exposed to an even greater tedium than the tedium of school? This is why television is so often despised by those who cling to a more conventional sense of human dignity: it uncannily avoids the very resistance that faces everything that appears compulsory. For the political imaginary of liberalism, being compelled to watch TV—one thinks of *The Clockwork Orange*—is the sinister essence of totalitarianism. But being *able* to watch TV and having the freedom to change the channel, even if only just a few channels remain, is a privilege still sometimes afforded even to the convicted and condemned: practically the last human freedom granted them. Perhaps someday there will be living wills describing in meticulous detail the programming that one will be able to, and have to, watch if one should become "locked in," or that will at least name, in a sanctified juridical language, the trustee of the remote. Will this be viewed as a medical decision or as the last freedom, even political freedom of the one who has lost all freedom of movement, speech, and self-expression, retaining only a perfect, and perfectly monstrous, freedom of thought? Here, at least, compulsion and freedom enter into a state of perfect indistinction.

Yet the lack of overt violence, exemplifying the freedom in passivity of consumer capitalism—that television touches life loosely and lightly; there like a friend but never intruding—is precisely what allows television to dominate everyday life as never before: dominating it in and as its everydayness.[12] What distinguishes this domination from almost every other is that it demands nothing of us: it presents us with possibilities, but it does not make us do anything, let alone any work; it does not demand our attention. You can watch TV while sleeping, while dining, while doing housework—you can even watch without watching, without listening or even without hearing.[13] It can just be on. There are exceptional cases: the televangelist, the home shopping network, audience participation and voting. But these prove the rule: being asked to do something, being "called on" if even without being named, becomes a surprising and extraordinary event, and one that nevertheless always lacks force. If we are still inclined to understand the efficacy of television in terms of subliminal messages or affective manipulation, it is only because we wish to hold on to a model of domination and exploitation based on active repression and coercion, on making someone *do* something. But with TV, this model, ultimately based as it is on *work*—if only the televangelistic *opus dei*—breaks down utterly. Nor does television function principally as a means of representation, an ideological conduit. Not only would this still involve a kind of operation and work, with the value of ideology still understood in terms of its role in reproducing the conditions of production, but it fails to appreciate the extent to which television, in its most exemplary manifestations, no longer needs to be understood, comprehended, synthesized, or digested. This explains why television, which might seem the perfect vehicle for education, has so little pedagogical value. Even if people can learn this or that from watching TV, it fails almost completely, at least in liberal democracies where it is not endowed with authority, to turn us into subjects of ideology. TV is almost completely divested of the power of interpellation. It never calls on us to be present; it rarely even identifies us as members of the audience, and can never demand a certain behavior from us, as even the cinema still does. We watch TV from our space—from the small privacy still left to us—or even from the transient cocoon that TV erects around us in public places: no one tells us to be quiet, or turn off our cell phones, or throw out our trash as we leave the theater.

The dominion of TV is neither coercive nor ideological, representational, mythological. It is not even, in its core, affective: if TV ever makes us feel something strongly—if we cry or hate—it feels a bit shameful. Embarrassed for ourselves, we become painfully aware of how stupid it really is to be watching.

Television does convey certain moods with a peculiar efficacy, and by means of these moods it organizes our existence—moods that, even if touching us lightly and infrequently, become intercalated into the rhythms of everyday life. But these are not really encountered, not felt and experienced, as *our* moods, but present themselves as the moods of a life that accompanies and organizes our everyday life, and yet that is precisely the life that *I*, me myself, in my own existence, however lost in the world and consigned to inauthenticity, do not ever actually and really participate in. It is the life that is *there* but is never my life to live—not even the life that I live so far as I am not really authentically existing as myself. This life that is *there* is a "disclosedness" (*Erschlossenheit*) that is not of my existence: that is not my own being-in-truth. We could think of this *other life* as the life that remains subtracted from Dasein—indeed outside of it—in both its authenticity and its inauthenticity. It is a life without relation to *bios*, with no *biography*, but it also has nothing to do with our merely biological existence, even if to some degree it mimics our cycles—even giving us the time, between shows and scenes, to defecate. It is what we might call an *afterlife*, though not in the sense of an eternal life that would supplement and fulfill our *bios*, nor as a remnant that survives this life, but rather as a kind of *metazōē* and *metabios*, an after-bare-life: simply *besides* the life that we live and the truth of that life. TV is the phenomenology of an everyday life that can never be turned around from inauthenticity to authenticity; an everyday life that never calls us, that never names us, that lacks even the prospect of a mineness that is continually evaded—the life that we do not live; the life that is at once no living, vegetative as the couch potato, but at the same time something more amazing and extraordinary than our lives. It is in just this sense that it shows both the possibility and the impossibility of phenomenology: the showing that it shows is precisely what can never be appropriated by us as the path to insight into the being that is at issue for us.

Every TV show presents a kind of space, time, and disclosure (truth) that belongs to a life that is not ours to live. Each has its *mood*. The morning news introduces the new day with a feeling of levity and novelty that has little to do with the monotonies, the challenges, the tedium and excitement that await us at work, at home, or at school. The game shows begin—this is how I remember it from my childhood—around midmorning: a sense of possibility and excitement that will never really be for us, even if some trivial and sad attempts are made to bring us in; even if one could travel to California and to Hollywood and join the studio audience, waiting to be called to come on up and be the next contestant on *The Price Is Right*. Then the soaps, with their strange insufferable heaviness of the eternal repetition of the same joys and the same miseries: *there is one life to live, as the world turns,* with *all our children,* in the *general hospital* that Rilke first named in the opening lines of his *Notebooks of Malte Laurids Brigge.* More game shows. Syndication. Evening news. More game shows—better, cleverer game shows: words and trivia for those who are still alert; not just prices and shopping for retirees and housewives. Prime time. Syndication. The late show. Sometimes the programming ends: a silence that is also programmed. Or the shows for the restless, sleepless, unhappy: infomercials promising a new life; strange, gothic movies. Prime time has its own rhythms as the week progresses. The weekend comes. Sports and then religion. And *Saturday Night Live*: a party for those who have no parties to go to. A life of last resort—sociable, comic, edgy in its way, slightly adult—for those who, having no life, need to "get a life."

The moods of everyday life have everything to do with the fact that while each of us has been consigned to the one life that we have to live, we are, for the most part, always evading this responsibility, losing ourselves in the distractions of the world. The moods of television, in contrast, belong to an *afterlife*, a *paralife*, that has nothing quite to do with our own life, though touching it incessantly. Whereas the moods of everyday life originate in the *indifference* of the one life that can either decide for authenticity or keep on evading the decision, televisionary moods issue from the noncoincidence, indeed the absolute, originary, unbridgeable difference, between cartoon and reality show; characters without events and events without character. Each mood involves a conjunction of these possibilities, yet the conjunction always gains its sense and its resonance as mood from there being, in the last analysis, no relation possible between character and event. The two are always already disarticulated. This is why the concept of theatrical irony cannot explain the effect—one hesitates to still call it comic—of the episode from *Beavis and Butt-head* and why it must ultimately fail to make sense of television. The basis of theatrical irony and self-reflectivity is the hermeneutic circularity of Dasein as the being for whom, in its being, its being is at issue, is of concern to it. The concept of irony seeks, in a philosophically inadequate (subjective and still metaphysical) manner, to articulate the condition of possibility of Dasein as being-in-the-world. Indeed, irony is an experience of this possibility—the possibility of having one, and one's, life to live. When we think of television, or postmodern culture, as suffused by irony, ironic to its core, we still seek to reassure ourselves of the possibility of truly living. Irony, in the vulgar sense, is an evasion of commitment, sincerity, action, and genuine politics.[14] But even as such an evasion, it is still an evasion *from* and thus brings about the possibility of finally entering into a relation to the genuine life that it shadows and dissolves. Hence the tedium of discussions of *Seinfeld*'s irony: a Jedediah Purdy, child prodigy of sanctimoniousness and future legal scholar, is always ready to jump in, reminding us of common things. To deride or glorify the irony of television is always to turn it into a sort of homeschooling for life. The episode of *Beavis and Butt-head*, in contrast, does not bring us before the possibility of television, let alone life, nor does it initiate us into the truth of the society of the spectacle. Rather, by choreographing a collision of cartoon and reality show, forcing these into an impossible conjunction, it exhibits with shattering force that television-life can never be our everyday life. I, to be sure, am sitting on the couch—perhaps alone, perhaps with a friend. We laugh *like* Beavis and Butt-head, as they laugh—themselves, on a TV that is now itself on TV. But even with this laughter we in no way become identified with them. Rather, our laughter, like the smile of the Cheshire Cat, lingers on as the symptom of a mood that can never belong to me or to us, to the one life that makes each of us *one* but is also the foundation of our community. It exists purely as the tension, the radical dissonance, between cartoon and reality show, character and event. In this way, it exemplifies the moods of television: it brings us before the impossible conjunction that is the source of every televisionary mood, none of which can ever belong either to *me* or *you* or *someone* or *they* or even to *no one in particular* or *no one at all*.

The moods of television involve the rhythmic organization of a life, indeed a multiplicity of lives that are not ours to live but also not ours not to live, and yet somehow in each case ours not to live. Each show shows its own time, space, and manner of truth (disclosure)—each opens onto its own life and its own world—and yet these are all fused to a clock and calendar time that presents itself with an almost perfect mathematical precision. While the clock and the calendar are tools organizing the activities of everyday life, this mathematically precise time elicited by the television is precisely not the *time of our lives*. It exists as it were at the limit of our lives as a time that imposes itself on us but that we can never actually inhabit. It is at this limit that television touches our life, but we should never suppose on this basis that the rhythms of television have anything to do with the everyday life that we live. And as we watch the usual television we will not easily err in this way. Television nevertheless also constantly seeks to go beyond its own limits, and take command of our time. This is especially true of prime-time television—the weekday television set aside for those who still work outside the home and do not have the luxury of watching television (even if in the course of arduous or tedious domestic labors) during the day. Prime-time TV is meant to be watched with a certain attentiveness. In it we seek to recover from the demands and stresses of the workday by discovering a meaning in work. Hence it so often either presents a work that is tragically meaningful (law, politics, police, medicine) or comically senseless (*The Office*) or reminds us of the good things for which we sacrifice ourselves at work: family, friends, sex, adventure, status, clothes, toys. And then there is the really good television—the so-called quality television. Quality television often returns to more explicit and elaborate epic, dramatic, theatrical conceptions, yet forced to confront the specific mediality of television, it also must innovate, and thus, in contrast to a derivatively highbrow fare—such as that of television's first "golden age" from 1947 to 1960—it stresses existing genre conventions to the limit.[15] It seeks to restore the tragic dynamic between character and event by creating a sense of time that holds together life in its totality; a time in which we can once again find ourselves. The privileged vehicle for quality television is a series extended over the course of many seasons, combining an "epic," world-building scope with "dramatic" plot lines that unfold rhythmically not only in each episode and throughout each season, but over the course of the entire series.[16] In this way the characters come to their destiny.

Yet we must be suspicious of quality television. To the very extent that it appears most plausible, realistic, dramatically powerful, serious, effectively stylized, it seeks nothing else than to destroy the afterlife of television and restore us to our one life to live. When there is nothing fanciful, cartoonish, absurd, when one never has to feel even the least bit ashamed at watching, when it is almost entirely true to life, then it shows us the least about television as such.[17] The deep intention of quality television, which can be achieved through a multitude of different aesthetic means and can even sometimes dispense altogether with vulgar naturalism and enter into the realm of fantasy and science fiction, is to create a fictional realm that has its own autonomy and dignity, and that we enter into not merely with the obsessions of the fan—who tears every element away from its context as if a religious relic and barely acknowledges the limit between fiction and reality, actor and character—or of the connoisseur with his minute value judgments, but with the sensibility of a dedicated spectator and critic, who seeks internal coherence, epic fullness, and even a correct vision of life. Quality television, this is to say, presents us, by way of a fictional and stylized world, with an image of our life in its fullness, its totality. The other life becomes a microcosm, simultaneously epic in scope and tragic in concentrated intensity, of this life; the story of others restores *our life* to its wholeness. Quality television thus involves a limit experience that stands at the threshold between inauthenticity and authenticity, everydayness and being-toward-death.

The death of the hero can substitute for my death only when his death, like my death, is fundamentally unsubstitutable: it is the hero's experience of the unsubstitutability of death that makes his death able to stand in for mine. And the existence of the hero becomes bound up with the comprehensive existence of a world, so that his death is also the death of this world, allowing us, by way of this vicarious exchange, to take in our world as a whole.

This is why drugs have emerged as the preeminent theme of quality television. Much like tragedy itself, drugs allow a kind of authenticity within everydayness. For the drug user, being-toward-death, without assuming the genuinely authentic form of becoming open to the call of conscience, nevertheless takes on the dignity of real experience—of a pleasure laden with the heavy seriousness of finitude. Addicted Dasein, as Ronell shows in a remarkable analysis, is drawn toward the experience of its finitude, and yet addiction at the same time blocks "the opening for which anxiety is properly responsible."[18] Moreover, whereas the death of the tragic hero becomes capable of substituting for my death in its unsubstitutability, drug use becomes unsubstitutable in its substitutability. Not only are drugs the quintessential mass-produced commodity, affecting everyone through identical biological mechanisms and thus transforming the singular moods and pleasures and suffering of life into the mere consequences of generic chemical, metabolic, and neurophysiological processes, with elemental moods available "on demand" for a certain price, but all addicts become, through their addiction, fundamentally the same addict with the same addiction, treatable in the same way, with the same steps to recovery. But precisely this generic aspect of drugs lends a particular pathos to the life and death of the addict, which appears in all its irreducible uniqueness to the very extent that it takes upon itself, as its own death, the mass-produced, mass-distributed death par excellence. It is not surprising then that the celebrity must die of a drug overdose, though, in a pinch, a traffic accident will do.

Drugs, epic, and tragedy form the elemental constellation of quality television. Ideally, as in *The Wire*, it has all three. *The Wire* indeed has the appeal of heroin itself: it promises grit, authenticity. It gets under the skin. The junkie throws away *his life*. The damage he inflicts on his own body, the damage the drugs do to the body, is the last refuge of the authenticity of experience that television forbids. The pleasure of the junkie thus gains the gravitas of finitude. Whereas the drug provides the model for ideology during earlier stages of capitalism—the pleasure of drugs are delusional, numbing us to the suffering that follows from real social relations and relations of production—now the exemplary moment of ideology, to the extent (and this will become the question in what follows) that we can still speak of such, consists in thinking that television could itself be regarded as a kind of drug. What is most unsettling is that television asks nothing of us, nothing of our bodies—that it is simply there. The addict can still enjoy his pleasure because he knows that ultimately he is paying the price for it with his one life. Hence the drug also remains the privileged metaphor for advertising and consumerism in general. Advertising is ultimately where television comes back down to earth, where it again touches our life and, despite never doing more than just giving us choices, does in fact ask something of us—if only by way of the most delicate forms of suggestion. If television *were* in fact a drug, then it would never be able to make this last, vital appeal. Whereas the print advertisement appears as a charming diversion from the content of a magazine or newspaper, and indeed is a source of much of the aesthetic pleasure—and even social utility—that these provide, television advertisements stand in a more complex, fraught relation to the medium they support. Television offers another life alongside the life we live: it should be able to entertain absolutely without demanding any commitment or sacrifice. It should simply be on and be there—granting absolute enjoyment without even asking for our attention. But if it were to succeed absolutely at this, it would negate the very conditions of the possibility of mass consumerism and hence, in the case of commercial television, its own condition of possibility. The enjoyment provided by television must have a limit, since it is on the basis of this limit—the structural limit of the enjoyment of a dissociated watching—that the claims of advertising assume their urgency. This limit consists in nothing else than the sense that television-life is not real life and that the pleasure of television is not real pleasure—that it lacks the actual fullness and satisfaction, the savor and flavor and spice of life itself. It would be wrong to think, though, that television advertising succeeds by recalling us to our life, reminding us of the unreality of television and of the things that we need to live, to really live our one life and to live it well. Television advertising, rather, introduces us to a realm of druglike real enjoyment that exists not as the reality of our one real life but as the real enjoyment of television enjoyment. It invites us—advertising is inviting, not coercive or dictatorial—to "where the flavor is," to a sensory realm that still cannot be televised. But this land—barren and strange and stark—is found nowhere in our everyday lives. It is, rather, the relation to our mortality, the relation to death, that, peeled off from everyday life, is grafted onto the other life of television as its shadow, the trace of what it lacks. If it is true, as Baudrillard claims, that "what advertising bestows upon objects, the quality without which 'they would not be what they are,' is 'warmth,'" then television is itself a perverse duplication of the hearth (I recall from my childhood how each year, on that one most special day, the television would broadcast a fireplace), granting warmth to things with its coolness. And here too, perhaps, there are gods.[19]

Real pleasure and real suffering involve the convergence of *character* and *event*. The character becomes real, no longer cartoonish, as the one who can only enjoy and suffer so much—the one who has a limit. Bringing the promise of an unlimited pleasure back up against the limit of the body and its mortality, drugs stand at the threshold of both everyday life, with its potentially authentic inauthenticity, and the other life of television, the life for which authenticity and inauthenticity are no longer at issue. Advertising thus allows this life and the other lives to touch. But it would be a mistake to think that advertising brings the two kinds of life into a real relation, such that an effective causality could exist between them. Rather, the very limit at which the touching occurs itself divides into two separate limits that are at once parallel yet different: the commodity-drug on the one hand and the advertising-drug on the other. The commodity-drug is the sense of everyday life: the mortal pleasure, rooted in the body and its exposure to its own finitude, in which everyday life, under the conditions of capitalism, finds its sense and purpose. The advertising-drug touches on everyday life by giving sense to its sense: by incessantly reaffirming the belief in the possibility of finding satisfaction through a true experience of the commodity. But it also gives a sense to television-life by bringing it into a relation to the one thing it lacks: an end. The entire constellation of lives—this one life that we live and the television-life that we never live—are held together in this way by a kind of experience. But this experience—and precisely this is the decisive point—is never unitary. It is never the one experience that brings the one life before its truth. Rather, it is always at once the experience of the one life and the experience of the other life, the life that is not ours to live and always indeed ours not to live; lives that touch each other only in and as the experiences of the difference that divides and disarticulates them.

Suppose we are watching the advertisement for an automobile: driving, which is for the most part a means to an end, presents itself as the experience of the commodity itself. But this experience belongs to television; it is the experience of television. It is perfectly satisfying save in one respect. It is not for us since we have not paid for it. The advertisement tells us that the life on television, wondrous as it is, is not really life, and certainly not our life, since we have not paid for it. And it also tells us that our everyday life can and must have meaning; but we must be willing to pay.[20] It can and must be filled with experiences: we can find sense in the tedium of driving to work or driving our children around by driving *this car*. These two messages will seem almost identical, yet they can never coincide. Otherwise we would fall down to the earthy reality of our everyday lives or float up into the stratospheric pleasures of television. But we must remain floating between both realms, and this demands that the two messages pull us in opposite directions—toward the commodity and toward television—at the very instant that both seem to be telling us exactly the same thing. The experience that is one, that is the very experience of unity and limitation, must never be one.

It is precisely for this reason that legal pleasure-inducing drugs form a kind of dangerous limit of the commodity-drug/advertising-drug complex, and often must even assume a spectral status whose strangeness is seldom fully appreciated. Permitted to exist as commodities but prohibited from being advertised, these become truly obscene: they are allowed to exist, as the shameful orifices of the body are allowed to exist, but are kept from public view. What must be hidden is precisely what already *hides* itself demonstratively, what could never be shown as such since it is nothing but an exposed retreat from exposure. This is because these obscene commodities come too close to allowing a rapturous contact between everyday life and television-life. You can smoke while watching people smoke on TV, appropriating their pleasures as your own, just as you can masturbate while watching pornography. What must be kept from view is the moment of contact—the point at which the one life and the other life open up to each other. All advertising must refer back to these moments but with the greatest discretion, since they must be forbidden to ever actually take place.

This throws light on the success of *Mad Men*, a recent incarnation of quality television. We watch them smoke and drink—it is almost sexy—but we are certainly not smoking or drinking with them anymore, just as we do not sleep with our secretaries, who have gone the way of the IBM Selectric typewriter. Our gadgets allow us to internalize the mechanical manual dexterity that was once their privileged domain. We now have a distance from advertising with its commodities and its pleasures. We look down on this world, of skyscrapers and executives, like gods looking down on heroes. If this extraordinary distance is possible—and we might compare it to Homer's vision of the gods, his poetic revenge on their delight in our suffering—it is because the obscene commodities, the commodities around which the entire system of advertising turns, have lost their allure and their charm. We have finally become disinterested spectators to the spectacle of advertising. The impossible promise of a contact between the two lives no longer makes its claims on us. *The Wire*, for all its narrative virtues and its gritty realism and rigor, sought to force television-life into a relation to everyday life by granting it the sublime dignity of the junk and product by which we throw our lives away. Thus it served a radically ideological function. By contrast, *Mad Men*, with its stylized pseudorealism—a realism that corresponds only to a phantasmatic memory mediated by the commodity-advertising that is its ultimate concern—exposes the fact that television-life has itself disintegrated, though without restoring everyday life to its dignity. Just as the owl of Minerva flies at dusk, epic is only possible when the epic world has already disappeared. Epic always seeks to recapture a world that has fled. And thus an epic of advertising, in which the adman appears as much larger than life as the commodities he celebrates, is only possible when the world of advertising is somehow no longer possible. There will, of course, still be things to buy and ads to sell them. Advertising and marketing will still matter. They will continue to influence consumer behavior and support mass media. Perhaps, in an empirical sense, these will matter more than ever. All the elements, and all the interactions between these elements, will continue to exist as before, just as the elements of the heroic world continue to exist in all their glory scattered about certain sub- and underworlds. But these elements will no longer constitute the world that, existing as the membrane between everyday life and television-life, held them together in such a way that the former would be illuminated and transfigured by the latter, and the latter in turn granted substance and reality through the former.

Put another way: what is no longer possible is the illumination of the commodity by a myth that wraps it up in desires, fantasies, and dreams: the superposition of everyday life and dream-life. The commodity can no longer bask in the light of sexuality, exteriorizing the organs of erotic desire as if to bring forth sexual difference, and the pleasures of intercourse, as a secret language of things that nevertheless remains indexed to real life and hence bound up with a logic of possession and with the singularity of the object of desire despite its mechanical proliferation, as if the playful appropriation of the commodity were itself to promise a nostalgic return to origins that could heal the rift caused by the traumatic separation from the womb. In a telling scene from the first season of *Mad Men*, Don Draper pitches a campaign for the Kodak Carousel, a slide projector whose circular tray allows slides to be shown in endless rotation. While the technology itself, reinventing the wheel, is new, his pitch explicitly summons nostalgia as a force in the soul that is deeper than the desire for novelty. The Carousel not only summons by its name the nostalgia for the simpler pleasures of childhood, but allows for the repetition of repetition itself, the temporality of everyday adult life, as if transfigured into an imagined—indeed purely fantastic—temporality of childhood. ("It lets us travel the way a child travels. Round and around and back home again, to a place where we know we were loved.")[21] Everyday tedium, marked by the repeating mechanical click, becomes the rapturous time of dreams, and the moments of everyday life, remembered on film in all their banality, finally discover, as the object of repetition, the joy that had always escaped as they were being lived—as if the melancholy that penetrates everyday life as the faint sense of its inadequacy, incompleteness, and transience were transformed into the joy of taking pleasure in the fleeting sense of loss; taking pleasure, from out of a future time where all has been lost, in the very sense for time and its transience—for our human finitude—that always evades us in the more ordinary pleasures of the moment. The alchemy of advertising turns childhood and youth into the ultimate objects of enjoyment, yet only by way of a detour through the feelings of loss, destruction, and futility that shadow their own simpler pleasures. Here Don Draper shows himself a master of the Freudian insight that, in the very first episode, he rejects: the opposition of novelty and nostalgia, the two guiding desires summoned by advertising, suggests, in veiled fashion, *Eros* and *Thanatos*, love and death. Yet the manipulative powers of the adman depend on denying the *truth* just as he comes closest to it: nostalgia is the death drive veiled as desire for a return to the simplicity of childhood and the absolute assurance of the mother's love, or indeed the radical negation of the trauma of birth and emergent sexual difference.[22] The commodity becomes the site not of psychoanalytic truth but of fiction: or indeed the most literal reenactment of the subterranean Platonic puppet show—the theater of memory as the dream-projection-system to which, with the commodity, we willingly submit ourselves.

The Carousel exemplifies the dream-commodity and dream-advertising, the commodity that, suffused with the potential for phantasmagoric productivity, gathers together everyday life into a dream-life in which it finds its ultimate sense and purpose. Novelty and nostalgia are the two characteristic modalities of a sphere of affect that reveals itself with purity only in dreams. In everyday life, nothing is ever truly old or new; things differ from before only by degree. Yet now the dream-commodities and dream-advertising are themselves no longer possible: the Carousel, long condemned to obsolescence, appears in *Mad Men* as the object of the nostalgia for a kind of nostalgia and novelty that is itself no longer possible. It exemplifies not only the nostalgia of advertising, but the nostalgia *for* advertising, a nostalgia for nostalgia and for the novelty that is its counterpart. It is no longer possible for us to be taken to the place where we ache to go again.

The features of the Carousel, to be sure, have been taken up by a multitude of gadgets that are now the constant companions of our everyday lives. We can take digital photos with our smartphones or tablets and play them back in an endless looping virtual slide show. We can use a special digital flat-screen picture frame or integrate these images into our laptops or Smart TVs as a background. Miniature projectors can be plugged into our gadgets, and PowerPoint has become a ubiquitous feature of the academic and corporate workplace. We are forever presenting ourselves to our circle, if not to the entire world, as a montage of slides, personal and borrowed, with laconic, often cryptic commentary—as if the vacation slide show forced on dinner guests, once the butt of jokes, has become the principal form of social interaction, replacing dinner and party alike. Rousseau's words have never been so true: "they live not to live but to make others believe they lived."[23] And perhaps it won't be long before smart glasses, enabled by facial recognition, extend our memory, offering an immediate recall of all we have ever seen and prompting us with information about those whom we encounter. Yet while image and remembrance have become woven into everyday life as never before, they are less and less capable of speaking to our dreams and desires. For if the image is now as mundane a part of everyday reality as the milk container, and we find ourselves constantly at work manipulating the images constituting our public persona with the sophistication and resourcefulness of the adman, our images have at the same time been taken up into the World Wide Web, where they coexist without order or distinction as a dreamlike phantasmagoric life that no longer has anything to do with *our* dreams and desires but serves only to express the omnipotence of the gadgets, information processors, and data clouds whose relentless novelty, formulated by Moore's law, organizes the flow of everyday life by punctuating it, with the periodic announcement of new products becoming an annual festival. Whereas the dream-commodity illuminated everyday life from within with the splendor of those deep desires that belong to dreams, the gadget *has begun to dream on its own*—to dream its own powers into existence. And as a result, advertising has already begun to lose most of its allure if not its effectiveness. It no longer augments the commodity, enveloping it with fantastic possibilities, but collapses the potentialities of the thing into the simplicity of a form that can fit perfectly with every lifestyle. Trying to be clever, Microsoft took aim at the iPad by having Siri admit her own limitations—as if a sense of limit were not the last charm that advertising can still conjure for the ever more pluripotent gadget.

In more ways than one it must now be clear that we stand at the end of an epoch. If the advertisement, which allows television-life and real life to touch, has become impossible, it is ultimately because television-life, the life that we do not live, has taken on a new, even more scattered and distracted form. It has passed over into the Internet, which replaces the orderly schedule of television-life with the absolute simultaneity of possibilities. The past coexists alongside the present, or is forgotten utterly, and the future is no longer the prospect of the new day and the new year but the constantly abiding expectation of something different showing up for us. While the Internet does seem to return a certain agency to the once completely passive television viewer, this agency is itself always split between two functions that no longer have anything to do with each other: we live our lives *on line* and at the same time the Internet lives through us. The constellation that I have worked to identify in the previous pages—everyday life/television-life (with its moods)/advertising/drugs/obscene commodity/dream-commodity—characterizes a perspective that remains, if in an extreme and unprecedented sense, phenomenological, even as, indeed precisely because, it *shows* both the possibility and the impossibility of phenomenology. What is fundamentally at stake in all this is still a system of modes of coming to appearance, of the showing forth of ways of showing. With the end of television's dominion and the rise of the Internet and the gadget, this phenomenology is itself brought to the limit of its possibility—and its impossibility. For indeed, it is not exactly that phenomenology, even as the *showing* of its impossibility, will become impossible but that it will cease to be either possible or impossible *for us*: the life that is not ours to live will no longer even be ours *not* to live but will become something else entirely—gadget-commodity-life. The theorization of this will come. For now it is enough to note merely that an explicit analysis of television is itself possible only because the phenomena in question are themselves on the verge of passing into oblivion. For just as the disclosedness of everyday life cannot be conceived apart from being-toward-death as the authentic relation to Dasein in its totality, the phenomenology of television necessarily involves a relation to a certain *limit situation*. This suggests what the reader must already suspect: in showing little or nothing about TV itself—in failing, for all its medial self-reflexivity, to show the showing of the TV show as such, to show TV in the constitutive limits of its possibility—quality television also shows everything. Demanding too much of the viewer to be watched simply as television, quality television reaches the apex of its possibility when television itself, as a scheduled organization of the life that is not ours to live, has already fallen into irrelevance. Indeed, one can hardly imagine the present so-called golden age of quality television, perhaps a third golden age following the second, were it not only for the rise of cable television but also for the development of such media as the VCR, DVD, and VOD that, by allowing for shows to be consumed in sequence beyond the strictures of conventional broadcast media, precipitated a fundamental change in the market forces at work in television production. Quality television shows the *possibility* of television only by bringing it to the point of dissolution. Hence it must expose the obscene commodity and disillusion the dreams of advertising.

3

THE CELEBRITY AND THE NOBODY

What was it that Mark David Chapman said after he shot him? It was like "All of my nobodiness and all of his somebodiness collided."

    Criminal Minds, Season 8, Episode 12

I felt nuisanced and stupid in the presence of small children. They reminded me of miniature celebrities.

    Ryan Ridge, *Hunters and Gamblers*

In *Being and Time*, Heidegger asks about the *who* of everyday being-in-the-world. His answer opened the way to an extraordinary analysis of everydayness: it is not me or you or anyone else, not even the "everyday Joe" or the German or Frenchman or the citizen or the subject, but *das Man*, a paradoxical expression, combining the indefinite pronoun with a neuter definite article, that can only be rendered imprecisely and inelegantly into English as the "they" or the "one."[1] The "one," which prescribes the being of everydayness, is Dasein precisely insofar as it is not itself, and does not exist in the mode of authenticity, failing to take ownership of the "mineness" that essentially characterizes its existence. Rather, Dasein has lost itself in the others, become dissolved in the others, such that it no longer is a "self" at all. The others have taken its being from it. And these others are no longer even distinct others, but exist in a kind of radical, "neuter" indefiniteness, indistinguishable from one another or from Dasein "itself." Thus "the real dictatorship of the 'one' is unfolded": we do (enjoying ourselves, seeing, reading, judging) as one does, are shocked by what one finds shocking, and are even repulsed by the masses as one is repulsed.[2]

It is precisely the "one" with its everydayness, and hence its unremitting dictatorship, that becomes impossible in the face of television. The "one" is characterized by a fundamental symmetry: *we* is each one of us; each doing as the others do. It involves the radical effacement of the very "mineness" of existence that, by making my existence (and my death) incapable of substituting for the death of others, introduces an asymmetry into the relation between different Dasein, not by exposing the "I" to the radical alterity of the Other, but rather by drawing the self into the singular, individuating experience of its *own* being-toward-death. The dictatorship of the "one" is in this sense the latent essence of a popular sovereignty—the rule of public opinion: the Rousseauian general will (which always expresses itself in the categorical generality of the law and never touches the individual in his singularity) so far as this has not explicitly taken ownership of itself through an act of legislation.[3] It is precisely this symmetrical inauthenticity, which in turn allows for resolute authenticity, that television has exploded. In being-with-television, the "one" of everydayness, living as one lives and watching what one watches, finds itself with another life that is not its own to live or to be but is also not simply the life of the other—a life that it cannot follow, cannot imitate, and from which it has nothing to learn, and yet which accompanies it somehow and is there with it. Hence it is no longer possible to give a simple answer to the question: *who* is it that lives this life that is always already divided and disarticulated between the *one life* and the *other life*—everyday life and television? The who is double: the celebrity and the nobody.

We discover intimations of this other life in those works of literature that brought the tragic paradigm, at least as traditionally conceived under the influence of Aristotle's *Poetics*, to its breaking point, even if one might argue, especially with a view to *Antigone*, that Greek tragedy itself already began to anticipate televisionary life. Thus Penthea, in Hölderlin's *Empedocles*, observes that the philosopher's demise (*Untergang*) could never be her own.[4] And in Goethe's *Elective Affinities*, Ottilie, inimitable in her mock martyrdom, shows up as the first televisionary celebrity, even as the theatrical Luciane, the last actress, pretender (like Wilhelm Meister) for a world stage that no longer exists, passes on into irrelevancy. The death of the tragic hero can no longer be the object of emulation or imitation. With this is called into question not only the dominant European conception of tragic drama but also the possibility of the resurrection of tragedy that, half a century later, the young Nietzsche will seek to advance as the condition for the cultural renaissance of German and European culture.

We again recall *Beavis and Butt-head*: it turns out that the bank card belongs to Michael Jordan, at that time the celebrity of celebrities. His password, jeopardizing the identity that it should protect, is "balls." The double entendre at work and at play (athletes' celebrity, after all, has everything to do with the perfect unity they achieve between play and work) is not just obscene: balls are at once the exposed container of masculinity (a masculinity that is of necessity put at risk, turned out from the enclosure of the body)—the source of phallic potency—and those things that, following the rules of the game, must never be held, must be kept in motion, always and forever dribbled, passed on, thrown. Here crime assumes its paradigmatic form in televisionary capitalism: it is the identity theft in which the nobody and the somebody—the celebrity—collide by way of the very technologies that allow celebrity to exist in the first place.

The celebrity and the nobody, so conceived, are neither personality types, nor sociological types, nor general descriptive characterizations of people whom we might encounter. They correspond to no given reality out there in the world. They are modes of existence, or, better, forms by which the *who* of existence, the one *who* exists, articulates—or, rather, disarticulates—itself. Just as Dasein for Heidegger does not switch back and forth between authentic and inauthentic selfhood in a succession of moments—the time of authenticity (the moment of resoluteness) is a fundamentally different kind of time from the time of everydayness—the nobody and the celebrity are not two possibilities that are open to us at any given time, nor are they two "social positions" we can occupy. Televisionary Dasein is disarticulated into these two "subjects" of existence, which together preclude both "being just somebody" (*das Man*) and being authentically myself.[5] These two sides of televisionary Dasein share neither a single time nor a single world, and moreover there is never a choice to be made between them. I am nobody, and I *am* not a celebrity—but this "am not" does not mark a disjunction between two possibilities. The "am not" does not simply negate either predicative determination or the attribution of existence, but means rather that *I exist by way of my negativity vis-à-vis being a celebrity*. I exist in not having this life to live, in not being a celebrity, and yet for this very reason I also live with and toward the possibility of being a celebrity. The celebrity, to be sure, is what I am not—and yet I constantly also project myself into this possibility *as what I am not*. It is in precisely this sense that celebrity life is not only not mine to live, but always and in each case mine not to live. It is the being that is at issue for me, that concerns me always and intimately, as the being that I *am* not, and indeed never, to be.

But what about the celebrities? They also exist, after all. The celebrity is also divided against himself or herself, and always also relates, though in a different way, to the possibility of being a nobody. It is not merely that, as Rojek observes, "celebrity status always implies a split between a private self and a public self," a disturbing bifurcation between the "I" and the "me," since "public presentation of self is always a staged activity, in which the human actor presents a 'front' or 'face' to others while keeping a significant portion of the self in reserve."[6] Rather, being a nobody is the very source of the possibility of being a celebrity: it is not the I of authentic selfhood but nobodiness itself that is the reserve power of the celebrity, who becomes a celebrity by "staging" the nobody for nobody, whether through impersonation or by projecting the nobody's desires (and above all, the desire for celebrity), or, as with Oprah Winfrey, by making us intimate with the celebrity that we ourselves are—the celebrity hidden within us, bathed, like the Platonic-Christian soul, in the lambent residue of withdrawn transcendence.[7] Richard Dyer, in his study of the Hollywood star system, describes this aspect of celebrity with acuity, arguing that stars "articulate the business of being an individual, something that is, paradoxically, typical, common," embodying the social categories (gender, race, ethnicity, religion, sexual orientation, etc.) in which people are placed and through which they make sense of, and indeed constitute, their lives.[8]

The celebrity, this is to say, disarticulates and makes manifest the very conceptual determinations through which Dasein exists in the publicness (*Öffentlichkeit*) of the "they"; the explicata through which it conceives of itself as at once a unique individual and just like everyone else. The celebrity is the nobodiness of the nobody; the nobody is the celebrity of the celebrity. Thus we can also hear in the celebrity the faint echo of celebration and the Latin *celebrare*, which means "to frequent, throng, fill," and, by extension, "to practice, engage in, say, use, employ, repeat"; to go in great numbers to a celebration and hence, to celebrate, solemnize, keep a festival; to honor, praise, celebrate in song; to make something known, proclaim, publish abroad. It is as if *celebrare*, overflowing its first overflowing sense, thronged into a range of meanings that together express the essence of a phenomenality grounded not in calm, rational political assembly but in an exuberant, overflowing, thronging, chaotic, passionate confluence that, passing beyond all restricted communities and spatial limitations, cannot but proclaim itself unto the world. The celebrity in its most extreme and radical sense—here perhaps the rock star (Rousseau himself started out as a self-taught musician and composer) rather than the movie star or the TV star is most exemplary—is the thronging of the throng: the appearance of the throng in its throng. It is precisely at this moment, when the throng becomes throng, that the nobody passes over into the somebody and the somebody into the nobody. Nietzsche's *Birth of Tragedy*—perhaps this is the touch of truth to

Camille Paglia's Dionysian reading of the rock star in *Sexual Personae*—concerns nothing else than this double passage. Celebricity, the celebrity of the celebrity, is this phenomenality that, at the very moment it appears as it is, can no longer take the form of phenomenology, of a sober gathering of appearance. Precisely because television allows the thronging of celebrity to assume the form of recurrence, the frequency of repetition, it solemnizes and subdues celebrity, giving it the form of the festival, the celebration: securing the constant repetition of originary surplus. Television, by virtue of the chasm opening between the life that is mine and not mine to live, allows for a phenomenality of celebrity to the very degree that it renders phenomenology itself impossible.

Television nevertheless only presents celebrity in its weakest but most insistent and insinuating form: the form of intimate strangeness—in which celebrity appears, and appears most possible.[9] But there are still other forms of celebrity that are more precarious, perhaps barely possible, yet even more potent. *Beavis and Butt-head*, as a vehicle for music videos, itself stands at the threshold of these. It is not that the music video would actually conjure forth a celebrity beyond the appearance of celebrity. Yet even before *YouTube* made it impossible for any video to appear without being surrounded, almost from inception, with a host of paravideos, even before *"Weird Al" Yankovic* and *Beavis and Butt-head*, the music video would have the tragedy of celebrity, which perhaps never actually happened even once, repeat itself as parody, as farce—to celebrate what, in its celebricity, could never have been celebrated; the thronging that could have never frequented itself.[10]

The very concept of phenomenology, as conceived by Heidegger, depends on the grammatical properties of the middle voice. The "phenomenon," derived from the Greek *phainesthai*, in turn coming from *phainō* (to bring to light, *an den Tag bringen*) and *phōs* (light), is "that which shows itself," the manifest, *das Sichzeigende, das Offenbare*—and, indeed, what shows itself *in itself*.[11] Phenomenology accordingly involves *saying* (*legein*) and showing forth (*apophainesthai*) the phenomena: "to let that which shows itself be seen from itself in the very way in which it shows itself from itself."[12] Yet this definition of phenomenology still remains merely formal, and must be deformalized if it is to be properly distinguished from the vulgar concept of phenomenology. This deformalization is achieved by specifying what, in an exemplary sense, constitutes the phenomena that must be shown forth as they show themselves in themselves. Precisely, Heidegger answers, that which "proximally and for the most part" does not show itself—being hidden, concealed, covered over, distorted—but which, at the same time, belongs essentially to that which proximally and for the most part shows itself, and so much so that it indeed "constitutes its meaning [*Sinn*] and foundation [*Grund*]." This hidden yet foundational moment is the being of beings, and hence ontology is only possible as phenomenology.[13] This phenomenological fundamental ontology, moreover, must take its departure from the questioning and analysis of Dasein, as the being that, in its being, is concerned with its being; whose being is, in a fundamental and irreducible way, at issue for it. Dasein's being toward its own being becomes the starting point for showing forth that which, as the concealed ground of the self-showing of every being that shows itself, for the most part does not show itself. Thus phenomenological ontology must proceed as hermeneutics, interpreting the "authentic meaning of being" and the "basic structures of being which Dasein itself possesses," making these known to Dasein's own understanding of its being, and thus "working out the conditions on which the possibility of any ontological investigation depends."[14]

While Heidegger conceives of this passage from the formal concept of phenomenology to fundamental ontology and hermeneutics as a deformalization, this does not mean that the general concept of the phenomenon had been "filled in" with a certain specific content. Rather, the deformalization of the concept of phenomenology is nothing else than the unfolding and radicalization of the formal indication already contained in the merely formal concept. The merely formal concept of the phenomenon already contains, implicitly, the claim that the phenomenon shows itself in itself *to itself*: that the phenomena are precisely not to be conceived as the totality of beings that show themselves to a consciousness, mind, or subjectivity outside of themselves and separate from themselves. The vulgar concept of the phenomenon objectifies, and in a certain sense materializes, the phenomenon by turning it into the correlative of the epistemological subject. In contrast, by understanding phenomenology in terms of both fundamental ontology and the hermeneutics of Dasein, Heidegger is able to insist that the "to itself" implicit in the "self-showing of the phenomenon" remains held within the concept of the phenomenon in such a way that the very presupposition of subjectivity must appear as the culmination of the tendency, inherent to the phenomenon, to hide its own ground from itself by understanding its being in terms of beings out there in the world. What shows itself in itself to itself is, as it were, the very medial structure of this showing, which is only possible insofar as the giver and the recipient of the showing (that which is shown and the "to whom" of the showing) can show themselves in both the difference that opens up between them and the cobelonging that holds them together in the unity of showing.

By sundering Dasein into the nobody and the celebrity, television shatters this differential unity between the *giver* and the *recipient* of the showing. Inverting the disciplinary, still authoritarian logic of the panopticon, "a machine for dissociating the see/being seen dyad," celebrity is the one who is shown and the nobody is the one to whom is shown.[15] And here too we might recall Rousseau's *Dialogues*, with its conjuration of a conspiracy formed with the sole object of observing J.J.[16] As if inverting this paranoid vision, the nobody sees in the celebrity nobody but himself, and yet he sees him as the one who is seen—and thus nothing like himself, since he himself, as nobody, is nothing if not the one who is never seen. The celebrity and the nobody are bound to each other in the same event of showing, and yet all sense of mediality—of showing itself to itself—has been lost. This must not be understood, though, as a mere retreat from phenomenological depths; a return to a vulgar metaphysics of the subject. Metaphysics, with its hypostases of subject and object, must itself be understood as nothing more than a detour on the path that brings Dasein from a preontological self-interpretation to fundamental ontology. The vulgar concepts of space and time, as Heidegger goes to great lengths to show, are founded in and derivative of more original, properly ontological notions. The event and advent of television, in contrast, shatters Dasein in such a way that it cannot find its way back to itself. That this might be the mere accident of a technological innovation—though we are far from advocating any sort of technological determinism—does not contest the significance we attach to it. Rather: what is at stake is the ontological potency of the contingent and accidental, which presents itself not as the occasion for Dasein either to succeed or to fail in appropriating its historical context but as the very impossibility of existing either authentically or inauthentically, either as oneself or not as oneself. The "teletechnological" event, by posing and imposing a fundamental-ontological contingency, discloses—or indeed poses and imposes—a fallenness without prospect of recovery.

The phenomenological exigency of television—its contexigency, as it were—interrupts the solitary voice listening to itself, the voice given over to itself in absolute self-presence, listening to itself in absolute proximity, that Derrida would identify as the metaphysical telos still at work in Husserl's phenomenology, and indeed as the constitutive trait of metaphysics, which, in its desire for presence, has never ceased to subordinate the *grammē*, the written mark, to the *phonē*.[17] Or rather: the televisionary contexigency repeats and doubles—forcing upon us the paradoxical experience of the impossibility of experience—the operation of the trace, of arch-writing, of différance, that Derrida has already discovered within the onanistic autoaffectivity of metaphysical desire. Yet it is not merely the metaphysics of presence and the voice that the event of television will call into question. Even when, in his later thought, he abandons the phenomenological method and turns to the history of being, he still insists all the more vehemently that being is given over to itself, belonging to itself.[18] The medial structure of the phenomenon thus repeats itself in the simultaneously "subjective" and "objective" genitive of the thinking of being. As he explains in the "Letter on Humanism":

> The genitive says something double. Thinking is *of being*, insofar as thinking, propriated by being [*vom Sein ereignet*], belongs to being. Thinking is at the same time thinking *of* being, insofar as thinking, belonging to being, hearkens upon being [*auf das Sein hört*]. As that which, hearkening, belongs to being, thinking is what it is according to the provenance of its essence. Thinking is—this is to say: being has, in each case as its historical destination [*je geschicklich*], assumed for itself its essence.[19]

Thinking belongs to being as the *Ereignis* (the event, or enowning—as in Emad and Maly's English translation of *The Contributions to Philosophy*) of being, but thinking also, belonging to being, hearkens on being. Thinking is thus that by which being is dispatched to itself. Indeed, in this passage's final formulation, thinking itself disappears and only being remains.

It would not be difficult to show that, after the Second World War, the destiny of the phenomenological tradition and of continental philosophy will consist in so many different responses to the unsettling, uncanny event of television, to this televisionary contexigency. This explains the unrelenting preoccupation with becoming open to the encounter with, and the thinking of, the Other, beyond being or prior to being. Perhaps *différance* inscribes the gap between the life that is ours to live and that other life. Perhaps what appears as the ethical moment par excellence is the radically asymmetrical encounter with the celebrity. Perhaps with television, schizophrenia has become the normal state of affairs. Perhaps messianism is nothing else than waiting for the arrival of the world that has already arrived, and yet, like Kafka's hope, is not *for us*. Such claims are not to be taken lightly. For now they are little more than provocations. And it is certainly not a question of closing off, in the name of some sort of materialism or technological determinism, veins of inquiry that have yet to exhaust their riches. Even if we grant that the event of television is contingent in the most radical sense, that it has an ontological potency that cannot be brought back into the fold of a prior history of being, this does not mean that the sense of this event can be reduced to some more or less empirically verifiable change in technologies, relations of production, and social organization. The sense and truth of the event—it is in precisely this way that we must speak of a radical contingency—consists in its ontological ramifications. Whereas ordinary contingency operates within an a priori, transcendental dimension that (as Kant's critical philosophy will show) it serves only to confirm and reveal, radical contingency (contexigency) announces itself quite paradoxically in the unprecedented transformation of the a priori horizon—or in other words in the change after the fact of what must be prior to every change, every movement, every fact, every experience. *The radically contingent event, as it were, creates its own truth—its own a priori, its own sense.* To think the televisionary exigency in its radical contingency is not to deny the primacy and autonomy of ontological inquiry but rather to refuse to allow it to become resettled into the history of being and philosophy. It is to hold on to what is most unprecedented, most unsettling, by referring it to a contingency that is more radical the more it undoes its own contingency through the configuration of a new a priori, a new transcendental plane. Everything hinges on a reversal of the hermeneutic method: instead of seeking to lead the errors of metaphysics back to a more originary and radical perspective, one must demonstrate that this very "salvatory" operation, through which the unicity of being is preserved, is itself responding, in a problematic and indeed "reactive" fashion, to the ontological potency of radical contingency.

The Carousel achieves its haunting power by creating a threshold of indistinction between the images of celebrities—of those who exist in and as image—and the images of the rest of us, which remain, like the traces of Don Draper's past life, hidden away under lock and key, confined to purely private existence, not because they had some secret to reveal, but because they have nothing to reveal, nothing to show; because our very existence, as true and heartfelt as it is for us, has no meaning whatsoever to anyone beyond the sphere of our intimates. For since the *studium*, the realm of public knowledge, has been reduced to the most generic, all that remains is a *punctum* that pricks us with the abstract shame, manifest in each and every picture, of the fact of being mortal, at once living and given over to death. Yet with the slide projector, the image of the celebrity (perhaps actual childhood photos of a precelebrity self), projected onto the movie screen, assumes exactly the same form and appearance as the slide shows that we force upon sometimes less than eager audiences. Yet if this moment, in which the image of the celebrity and the rest of us can no longer be distinguished, represents the breakdown of the constitutive oppositions of celebrity culture, it is no more radically subversive, no more genuinely destructive of the given order, than the transgressive festivals of ancient times. For indeed the Carousel, this Saturnalia of celebrity, borrowing its very form from a cyclical theory of time, imposes a qualification on the moment of the collapse of distinction that is of the very greatest significance for upholding the logic of "televisionary celebrity": the moment of indistinction—the *Augenblick* when the supposed life of the character, the real life of the celebrity, and the pseudocelebrated, home-projected, self-published life of everyone else coincide—must belong to the realm of memory. The life that now appears the same must be past life. It can never be present. Nostalgia, in the age of television, has this sense above all: it is the ache to return to the time when we were not so different, not different at all; it imagines and shows the time before the image that divides us. Yet this remembrance of childhood is not merely the momentary release from the hold of celebrity— one should even hesitate to think of it as an actual experience, as some sort of Dionysian rite. Rather, this realm of memory, of precelebrity, is the factory in which the charisma of celebrity is brought forth. It generates the ongoing proof that they, who are nothing like us, are . . . just like us. A peculiar, seemingly aporetic ontology underlies this claim: celebrities are *not like us* since their images belong to the present, live in the present; they are suffused with potentiality. Yet celebrities are just like us since we were also—in the past, as children—like them. Every child indeed is like a miniature celebrity, and the child celebrity a monster—a little monster, to use Lady Gaga's sobriquet for her fans and followers, to be shepherded by a big monster. We are shamed before the celebrity as before a nature that, possessing the potential we can never appropriate or actualize, has become monstrous. When we existed as pure potentiality, we also had the potential to be celebrities, but now only celebrities can still be celebrities. And must be celebrities, since the image will always claim them: they can never escape from the paparazzi. The celebrity must exist as pure potentiality while we can no longer exist as potentiality but must become something else.

It is a telling indication of the end of the epoch of televisionary celebrity that the slide projector, having lost its original function, is now the object of nostalgia. More telling yet is what has taken its place: the mug shot. Whereas before the celebrity and the rest of us were brought together through the experience of the pure potentiality of childhood and innocence, now the only point of communion and "common ground" can be found in the sullen, glazed (if often still somehow charismatic) eyes of those who have been arrested, and, now in the system, will be submitted to judgment. The imprisoned celebrity, which should not be confused with the notorious or infamous criminal, cannot but unsettle us. Nothing could seem less natural than to put the celebrity in the one place in which, deprived of access to the Internet and no longer even hounded by paparazzi, he or she would experience an extreme form of social death, and can only communicate to the world through proxies. Before we shared the dream of potentiality with the celebrity. Now we share only shame. And prison is also the only place where we might still hope to meet the celebrity, to speak face-to-face.

4
BEING(S)

The advent of the televisionary Other constitutes a radically contingent event, a transformation of the transcendental horizon. There is no other evidence for this advent and event beyond its ontological effects, and yet these are themselves nothing that can be proven to exist, let alone empirically verified. The only possible proof of the ontological effects—or better, the ontological potency—of the radically contingent event emerges from the attempt to "make sense" of the event in its radical contingency. Yet the only possible evidence for radical contingency is the ontological effects that it provokes. We seem to find ourselves in a circle, and just as in Heidegger's *Being and Time*, the response to the charge of a "vicious circle" is to challenge the presupposition about the nature of reasoning that underlies this accusation. Circularity can only appear as a decisive charge against a philosophical argument if we believe that philosophy proceeds *more geometrico*, starting out from self-evident axioms and drawing out a chain of conclusions through established principles of deduction. Yet such a method is only possible once we have abandoned the task of coming to an understanding of the axioms—the foundations—and are satisfied with a complacent opposition between the intuition that grants access to first principles and the deductive sequences that follow from these.[1] To the extent that we enter into a fundamental inquiry and open ourselves up to the fundamental question, the question of ground and grounding, we cannot *avoid* what must appear, at least from an exterior and superficial perspective, as a dangerous circularity. The event by which being becomes open to its own truth, ex-isting in the clearing (*Lichtung*) of its truth, can never be understood in terms of the pseudoprecision of a "linear" mathematical reasoning. Yet the circularity of radical contingency is also different from the "hermeneutic" circularity by which being is given over to its own truth. The hermeneutic circularity of being allows for a narrative of the "history of being," in which the history of metaphysics is conceived as a "falling" away from an original rigor of questioning, an original experience of and openness to being. History—for it is really only the history of being (*Seynsgeschichte*) that matters—is thus deprived of the potency of contingency, of the possibility of anything happening other than the playing out of what is already contained in the beginning. And perhaps history itself is nothing but this deprivation. In Heidegger, a thinking that is open to the radically new can only be thought as a *new beginning*, and indeed a more originary repetition of the *first beginning*. The underlying presupposition, which is certainly not naive and un-thought-out, is that there is One history of being (with the history of *Sein* folded into the history of *Seyn*) and that this One history involves decisions that determine the path that it will take, since indeed it is as the history of decisions that the history of being (the *One* being) is held together in a unity.[2] The circularity of radical contingency, in contrast, rather than drawing the One being back to itself in the unity of its history, involves becoming open to experiences by way of registering ontological effects that cannot be anticipated by an original ontological horizon. To think radical contingency is to enter into the movement between the event (the experience) and its ontological effects—to respond to the event, and attend to it as event, by registering the ontological, transcendental horizon that cannot be anticipated prior to the event, which is without precedent, and yet is demanded by the event for the event to be possible as event. It is a matter of what we might call transcendental shock.

By insisting on a multiplicity of possible ontologies, rejecting the unicity of being, we are not denying that something like fundamental ontology, so far as this would seek to refer the multitude of beings back to a single sense of being, is possible. We are not trying to claim that *one* (and who is this *one*?) should no longer speak of being, or self-identity, or the like. Nor would we deny, conversely, that talk of fundamental ontology and ontological difference is itself necessarily transitional, and is only justified by the particular demands of thinking at and beyond the limit of metaphysics—or indeed forcing metaphysics beyond its limit. The point, rather, is that ontology, as the gathering of beings back to being as its transcendental horizon, is not only possible, but possible in a multitude of irreducible ways. To *ex-ist* is to be open to this multitude, and even indeed to modes of ontology that call into question the selfhood of Dasein.

Heidegger's 1933 lecture, "The Fundamental Question of Philosophy," shows how in the modern period the principle of noncontradiction, while assuming the role of the highest principle of philosophical thought, the principle of a possibility even beyond being itself and from which being itself can be derived, is at the same time turned into an almost untouchable, unquestionable, self-evidence. As a result of this ossification, which is at work from the merely apparent "new beginning" of Western metaphysics with Descartes to its culmination in Hegel, it is no longer possible to recognize in the principle of noncontradiction, as Aristotle would, a *decision for the human* that is also a decision for the danger of being human, the exposure to nothingness. For what is decided is nothing less than "whether human beings will to exist as human or not; this means, whether they elevate logos to the rank of the dominant *power* of their Dasein or not, whether they stand up to this essential possibility or not!" Yet precisely the possibility, indeed the necessity, of making this decision is what, by exposing us to the risk of falling to the level of a mere plant, distinguishes us from both plant and animal.[3]

The principle of noncontradiction, this suggests, should not be complacently and thoughtlessly rejected. At stake in this principle is our very humanity—that which distinguishes us from animals and plants. But just as one must draw a distinction between, on the one hand, the merely "formal," technical, unquestioning, thoughtless ascription to the principle of noncontradiction as a logical axiom that one can use, without further ado, to generate propositions and, on the other hand, a genuinely thinking, thoughtful comportment to the principle as "*a fundamental element of the existential structure of our Dasein in general*," we may also distinguish between the merely formal and vacuous rejection of the principle, made all too easy by the very fact that the principle has been emptied out as a result of its formalization, and a sober, thoughtful, rejection that reckons fully with its implications, and that does not make us blind to the danger of the Nothing but exposes us to an even greater danger. Heidegger alludes to this when he remarks, "If the principle and the way of treating it have been moving for a long time within a nearly unassailable self-evidence, this may not be taken as a definitive unquestionability pure and simple; rather, we must consider that this fundamentally thin veneer of the self-evident will one day *break apart* and that *we* will then *break through* into the *groundless* [*Bodenlose*], at least at first."[4]

It might be tempting to distinguish between vulgar and rigorous deconstruction. Rather than blindly rejecting the principles of logic and all seemingly metaphysical language, pluralizing every noun and using scare quotes when the plural is too unseemly, the latter seeks to enter into a thoughtful relation to the possibility of a decision against noncontradiction, accepting the radical implication of this for our sense of human dignity, and also recognizing the paradoxes that attend every attempt to think beyond this principle. But the very possibility of such a distinction, while not without a practical usefulness in distinguishing good and bad thinking even in the absence of traditional concepts of argumentative validity, depends on having decided for decision, and yet the decision for decision cannot but be the decision for noncontradiction, since there can only be a decision if there is a clear difference, and hence a selfsameness, to that between which is to be decided. What would it mean to decide against decision, or not decide for decision, or be in-decided for and against decision and indecision? Perhaps it would mean no longer being able to decide between vulgar and genuine deconstruction, yet without ever being exempt from having to make a decision.

Thinking the event of television as radical contingency means, above all else, entering into a thoughtful relation to this event as it breaks thought, making it "break apart." Yet here one can hardly help noticing a seemingly even more vicious circularity than that to which I have already called attention. The thought of radical contingency presupposes the multiplicity of ontologies, but it also makes this possible, indeed demands that it be possible, as ontological effect. It would seem then that there is, again, only one ontology, an ontology of multiplicity, and that this has already been presupposed in advance of the contingent event.[5]

This is, however, in no way an objection to such a notion of radical contingency but rather suggests precisely what is at stake in thinking it through. Multiplicity itself becomes a kind of closure, indeed a foreclosure. This movement of foreclosing, which puts the possibility unambiguously before the event that it makes possible and thus also makes this possibility itself possible, can never be banished from the contingent. It is the danger that is constantly present, and to which thinking must constantly answer. There is no method that can guarantee us a way out; no founding principle would suffice to avoid it.

Rather than trying to evade this danger, we will enter into it as fully as possible by demonstrating how the ontological horizon that develops around, answers to, and makes sense of the event of television becomes closed in upon itself such that *only this event can take place*, and the sense of this event becomes the only possible sense, even if seldom understood as such. For as I hope to show, the televisionary event, with its ontology, *constitutes a world of beings into which it is possible to fall, such that the multitude of ontologies—what we might call plural being—the horizontal openness that is itself a possibility and not a given, can only be grasped as the possibility given through and with these beings, these entities.* For indeed, just as the event of television does not allow for the simple opposition of authenticity and inauthenticity—does not allow for the simplicity of Dasein in its relation to itself—but forces a split (a split that can never be bridged by a decision) between the life that is ours to live (authentically or inauthentically) and the life that is not ours to live, it also calls into question the very possibility of the foundational distinction between being and beings. Plural being is also beings. If it were ultimately possible to discover, amid the multitude of beings, the being that, in its difference from beings, rages through all of them and gathers them together into One human world with One history, then we could no longer meaningfully speak of more than one ontology. There could be no plural being. The multitude of ontologies implies the collapsing of ontological difference, and vice versa. The world of television is a world of beings that are also being; of beings that, to the very extent that they appear as beings, in their being, also appear *as* being itself—or indeed, what we might call, to use Agamben's pregnant phrase, *a threshold of indistinction* between being and beings. We will call this and these, using a rather odd and ugly neologism, being(s). The mark of this indistinction is the fact that these beings only exist (are given) *in theory*, or better, *phenomenologically*—that they exist only in and through the phenomenological horizon that they themselves call into existence. Their phenomenality is phenomenological. Each being(s) has its own world, its own horizon. Seen from enough ontological distance, these being(s) would seem to belong to the same world, but as we approach them their horizon of intelligibility becomes ever more singular and discontinuous, until finally they have each one of them become their own world.

This being(s), ex-isting *in theory*, will, as it were, take the privilege of Dasein (to exist ontically insofar as it is ontological) upon itself. Yet whereas Dasein, as being-in-the-world, has a world that it can fall into and become captivated by, being(s) is *as* its world, deforming the world into the singularity of its own being, such that its world becomes indiscernible from its ontological horizon. One can no longer speak of fallenness but only *exposure*: being(s) is exposed to its truth, put out into its truth, such that ontic proximity is always also ontological proximity. This is obscenity in a radical sense.

There is another name for being(s): *the commodity*. It was indeed with a certain imprecision—or rather with precision, but from the side of everyday life—that we spoke of the obscene commodity and the dream-commodity. The commodity occupies the threshold between this life (everyday life with authenticity as a possible modification) and the other, televisionary life. From the perspective of everyday life, a perspective that is exterior to the commodity even if the commodity is also—as threshold—the possibility of this exteriority, certain commodities will present themselves as *obscene* and *dreamlike*, allowing for a kind of ontological experience (a *petite mort*, as one is wont to say) in the midst of everyday life. The obscene commodity, as it were, produces a schematism of the pleasures that, giving sense to everyday life, stand at the limit of ordinary enjoyment—not because they can't be enjoyed, but because they mustn't. In everyday life, the obscene commodity is subject to a taboo precisely because it remains a thing that can be possessed and experienced. Yet approached from the other side, the commodity is the site of a more radical kind of obscenity: the exposure consisting in the collapse of ontological difference. Ultimately, however, the commodity is not simply one kind of obscenity or the other but rather exists as the impossibility of distinguishing between the obscenity of desire and ontological obscenity.

This suggests the limits of Lukács's brilliant and influential analysis of the commodity in *History and Class Consciousness*. While commodity exchange itself, Lukács notes, existed even in very primitive societies, the problem of commodity fetishism is specific to modern capitalism. It is not merely that commodity exchange, originating at the fringes of society, has worked backward toward the interior, restructuring relations of production according to its logic, but that, for the commodity form to become constitutive of society itself, it must "penetrate society in all its aspects and . . . remould it in its own image."[6] The essence of the commodity, which becomes visible only when its dominion approaches realization, is reification: "man's own activity, his own labour becomes something objective and independent of him, something that controls him by virtue of an autonomy alien to man."[7] In the extraordinary analysis that follows, Lukács, going beyond the analysis of commodity fetishism in *Capital*, demonstrates how this structure of reification comes to sink ever "more deeply, more fatefully and more definitively into the consciousness of man."[8] The forms of ideology derived from the commodity fetish do not merely involve abstract philosophical or theological beliefs, but consist in the very way in which we relate to the world and to our own selves and to others. We come to see our qualities and abilities as things that we can "own" and "dispose of" just like external goods, and social relations such as marriage reduce themselves to a kind of reciprocal exchange of sexual organs and faculties.[9] Although such an understanding of ideology still involves illusion and falsehood, this is not merely a cognitive illusion emanating from the substructure without in any way determining it, but a functional consciousness intimately bound up with the capitalist mode of production and indeed necessary for its reproduction.

Lukács's analysis of commodity fetishism, as compelling as it is, depends not only on a humanistic concept of alienation, but conceives of reification fundamentally in terms of the relation of subject and object. While Lukács critiques the way in which the commodity fetish institutes an alienated relation between subject and object, and proposes the concept of totality as an overcoming of this alienation, he never calls into question the theoretical primacy of this opposition itself or the metaphysical distinctions on which it rests. The problem with such an approach, however, is not that it makes it impossible to actually overcome the alienated relation of subject and object—that such alienation is a problem presupposes the theoretical primacy of the subject/object distinction, and only makes sense in this context—but rather that it misconstrues the nature of commodity exchange as the metabolic structure organizing social relations. Yet the commodity is not first of all a means of bringing the human subject into a relation with objective reality, as if both already somehow existed, but what we might call, following Bruno Latour, a kind of hybridity, though even this term misleadingly suggests an original distinction between that which has subsequently been joined together. Lukács, as it were, starts out from within the philosophical framework of the "modern Constitution," which "invents a separation between the scientific power charged with representing things and the political power charged with representing subjects," insisting in effect on maintaining a separation of powers between science and politics while at the same time canceling out the separation that it insists upon.[10] The philosophical project of modernity operates within this separation of powers, even as it seeks to overcome it. And in so doing, it can only end up reinforcing this separation, and hence it begins with the subject/object opposition—itself merely one aspect of the more fundamental constitutional split—in order to fuse subject and object together.[11] Yet while the modern constitution says one thing, modern praxis does something quite different: modern practices involve constantly creating the very hybrids that the modern constitution refuses. And this has led to the crisis of the present moment: "*the proliferation of hybrids has saturated the constitutional framework of the moderns.*"[12] The practices of modernity have overwhelmed the "official constitution" with hybrid entities that exceed its powers of coping.

Latour himself dispatches rather hastily with Marxism in *We Have Never Been Modern*. Yet one could argue that Marx's analysis of the commodity is fundamentally an attempt, applying the theoretically inadequate conceptual resources of the modern philosophical and scientific tradition, to come to terms with precisely the hybrid nature of practice. The commodity fetish is what we might call an *organizer* of hybrid praxes: it not only conjoins human beings with things, things with things, and human beings with human beings, but allows them to link up into complex networks, organizing prodigiously complicated interactions between all the elements that it has brought into relation. Yet even if he could accept such a claim, Latour would no doubt hesitate to grant the commodity any special privilege among a vast array of hybrid practices. And we too might follow him in regarding any kind of economic or materialist determinism, however subtle and nonreductive—even if only a determination "in the last instance"—as a dangerous holdover from the "official constitution." Yet we might nevertheless also hesitate to go too far in the opposite direction by refusing to recognize the primary importance of certain hybrid structures, such as the commodity fetish, in coordinating diverse and seemingly disparate functions of human life. It is not a matter of vertical determinism, whether mediate or immediate, direct or analogical, but of the constitution, through certain dominant structures of interrelation, of the "environment" in which forms of life can thrive and reproduce themselves.

Perhaps, moreover, it is only in conjunction with Heidegger, to whom Latour dedicates several pages in *We Have Never Been Modern,* that we could begin to find the resources to carry through this tendency of Marx's thought. Latour will claim that Heidegger, by deconstructing metaphysics and recalling philosophy to the question of being, seeks to get at precisely those hybrid "quasi-objects" that have been banished by the "official constitution" of modernity. Yet the moment he discovers being, this potential wellspring of hybridity, he vacates it of all "substance": "Being cannot reside in ordinary beings. Everywhere, there is desert. The gods cannot reside in technology.... They are not to be sought in science, either, since science has no other essence but that of technology. They are absent from politics, sociology, psychology, anthropology, history," and even economics, even philosophy, even ontology. For Latour, in other words, the insistence on *ontological difference,* the difference of being and beings, serves to reproduce the fatal flaw of the modern constitution at the very moment when it should have been possible to overcome it. Needed, as it were, is not a return to the question of being but the posing of the question of being(s). Moreover, perhaps it is in Marx's account of the commodity fetish that we will begin to find the resources to undo the evacuation of being. And perhaps—if one more "perhaps" may be allowed—it will also be necessary to restore a dimension of the Heideggerian path that is neglected by both Latour and the Marxist tradition: the question of truth.

5

THE LIFE OF THINGS

One has to think that Marx didn't have the Young-Girl in mind when he wrote that "commodities cannot go to market and make exchanges of their own account."

    Tiqqun, *Preliminary Materials for a Theory of the Young-Girl*

Since Marx's *Capital*, the commodity, with its metaphysical subtleties and theological tricks, has played a vital role in the critique of capitalism, and above all when this critique, through some adventure or misadventure of thought, has fallen from the grasp of more sober-minded and empirical readers of Marx and into the hands of literary theorists. Yet if the commodity seems so familiar, both as an everyday reality and as a theoretical motif, it is precisely as the site of those uncanny processes through which everyday reality becomes estranged from itself. And it is worth asking whether the commodity doesn't still have some tricks up its sleeve: whether its strangeness exhausts itself in establishing a foundation for capitalism, as Marx's treatment of the commodity in the first chapter of *Capital* suggests, or whether it also remains at play in transformations of the system of production, and indeed in the very essence of production itself, that have yet to play themselves out.

    It will be useful to return to Marx's theorization of the commodity, not to restore it to its rightful place in an edifice of dogma, but rather to discover both its rich insight and its limits—limits that suggest not some lack of critical acumen but rather the transitional nature of the commodity itself. This will demand bringing Marx into dialogue with Heidegger: historical materialism into dialogue with phenomenology, fundamental ontology, and the history of be-ing (*Seynsgeschichte*). But perhaps "dialogue" is not quite the word. We cannot pretend to "speak for" either Heidegger or Marx, nor are we after some sort of gruesome synthesis. Perhaps we can't even claim to speak for ourselves anymore. Rather: repeating the gesture of Marx, we will seek to get the commodity, in all its strangeness and its mendacity, to speak for itself—or indeed, since it has always already been speaking, simply to hear what it is saying. It is the commodity itself, being(s) itself, that will demand that both Heidegger and Marx, brought into a sort of dialogue, speak for it. That the commodity *needs* theory and phenomenology, even *fundamental ontology*, even *Seynsgeschichte*, is no casual assertion but constitutes the horizon for understanding the commodity. The commodity is (the) being(s) that in (its) being(s) is concerned with (its) being(s). Yet it is preontologically a complete stranger to itself, and needs ontology—indeed needs Dasein's own relation to its being—to enter into a relation to (its) being(s). It is from this perspective, moreover, that the limits of the Marxian/Marxist concept of *ideology*, whose relation to the commodity fetish itself remains a matter of some dispute, will become evident.[1] Ideology is neither at base the veil of illusion that cloaks reality nor even the imaginary relation to the real but the theoretical detour by which the commodity—being(s)—comports itself toward its own being(s).

For Marx, the commodity is truly *mysterious, wunderlich*, and indeed monstrous, grotesque. The moment that the table, an ordinary sensible (*sinnlich*) thing, takes the stage as a commodity (*als Ware auftritt*), then "it not only stands with its feet on the ground, but it places itself, with respect to all other commodities, on its head, and develops out of its wooden brain fantastic ideas [*Grillen*], much more wonderful than if it began to dance of its own accord."[2] As commodities, things announce their independence from their producers, taking on a life of their own, indeed coming to govern the lives of human beings. Yet the commodity will never be completely free. It still needs us: it can turn everything on its head, but it can't quite stand on its own two feet. It can dance, but it still can't walk. For as the first lines of the second chapter declare, "Commodities cannot go to the market by themselves and exchange themselves on their own. Thus we must search around for their guardians, the possessors of commodities."[3] This suggests the limit of Marx's analysis. The commodity never achieves the full measure of its monstrosity. It remains a little monster in the stewardship of bigger monsters. Marx's thinking of the commodity—or is it the commodity itself?—shirks back from the limit at which it would no longer need guardians (*Hütern*) and (as Kant would say) *Vormünder*.

Marx seeks to capture the strangeness of the commodity in a single formulation: they are "sensual suprasensual things," *sinnlich übersinnliche Dinge*. While this exhibits the commodity in all its strangeness, it also returns the strangeness

THE LIFE OF THINGS

to a familiar place, the most familiar place: the metaphysical opposition between the sensual, natural, and the suprasensual, supernatural. The commodity is a mere thing, a sensually existent finite thing, that nevertheless transcends its own sensate nature without yet ceasing to be a mere thing. Its transcendence beyond its sensuality brings it back to its sensuality, while its "rescendence" to its sensuality allows it in turn to transcend its sensuality.[4] Marx's formulation thus folds the opposition of the sensual and the suprasensual—this most familiar place, the primal site of Western metaphysics—into the commodity's oddity, so far as the commodity, even as just a mere thing, itself becomes the site of the movement of transcendence and rescendence, the "oscillation" between the sensual and the suprasensual. Metaphysics will hence consist, first and foremost, in the way in which the thing shows itself, the mode of appearance of the thing: the mere thing showing itself as more than a thing, and what is more than a mere thing showing itself as a mere thing.

Yet the commodity is not just a thing, but a thing that is *produced*. The production of the commodity consists in producing, bringing forth into appearance, a mode of coming into appearance. Hence the production of the commodity is itself the origin of metaphysics. Yet it is not only the origin, the original production, of the horizon of metaphysics that is at stake here, but above all the possibility of the capitalist mode of production itself. It will not be possible, in the context of this book, to provide even a partial demonstration of this point, which is of the greatest importance for a reading of Marx, and show that the entire analysis of circulation, surplus-value production, and the critical opposition between labor and labor power depends on this interplay between transcendence and rescendence: a hybridizing operation that brings the sensual and the suprasensual, the real and the ideal, the concrete and the abstract, and even the private and the public into play. It is enough to indicate, as Michel Henry argues, that for Marx the entire system of capitalist exploitation depends on synthesizing the "objective" and "subjective" aspects of production: on the one side, the machinery of production, and on the other, the purely subjective individual praxis of labor itself.[5] The commodity form and its fetishism is not simply the illusory appearance of this imbroglio, but the very possibility of the intercalation of a pure subjectivity—Henry will understand it, existentially rather than epistemologically, as *life* in the sense of pure interiority, pure self-relation—and an equally pure objectivity. Or in other words: the commodity form is the simultaneous operation of disjunction and conjunction that brings together what it divides and divides what it brings together. Insisting on precisely this pure subjectivity as the ultimate ontological ground of Marx's thought while never challenging its conceptual coherence or its metaphysical presuppositions, Henry could never allow this last formulation. Yet his coherent and lucid interpretation of Marx nevertheless provides an important guide in my own investigation, even though I will part ways with it at a number of decisive points, and even collude with his antagonist: Althusser.

We must ask, however, whether this production belongs within the horizon of metaphysics or outside of it. Is the production of the commodity a function of the play of appearance that it itself implements, or is the production of metaphysics (reading the genitive as both objective and subjective) merely a certain mode of production in the more general sense? In a similar vein, we must also ask about the status of the one for whom appearance takes place, the recipient of appearance. Marx himself gets caught in a tangle of ambiguities when trying to grasp the "ideological" function of the commodity, its distorted presentation of the relations of production. He cannot decide whether this ideological function consists in the commodities "mirroring back" (*zurückspiegeln*) to human beings the social character of their own labors as objective characters of the products of labor or whether it is not rather a matter of the "brain of private producers" mirroring (*widerspiegeln*) the "doubled social character of their private labors . . . in the forms that appear in practical commerce, in the exchange of products."[6] In the first case, the appearance of objectivity, while originating in things, would nevertheless exist *for* human subjectivity, insofar as subjectivity presents itself as the condition of the possibility of things coming to appearance, and indeed all appearance is fundamentally appearance for a subject. But in the second case, the subject has been reduced to a mere "brain," and appearance, rather than involving an ultimately transcendental relation between subject and object, has become the mere, seemingly automatic if nevertheless practically efficacious, reflex of the relations of commodities. If Marx cannot decide between these two possibilities, it is because they remain undecidable. Because the coming to appearance of the metaphysical mode of appearance can appear only by way of metaphysics, then the nature of subjectivity, like the nature of production, precisely so far as it constitutes the limit of the horizon of metaphysics, cannot be adequately determined from within this horizon but must instead be left undecided, since, if it were determined to be itself metaphysical (thoroughly determined from within the horizon of metaphysics), then the metaphysical horizon would be inescapable, and if it were determined to be prior to or outside of metaphysics, then a metaphysical exposition of metaphysics must appear inadequate.

This suggests both the extraordinary power and the limit of Marx's conception of the commodity. By conceiving of the production of the commodity as itself the origin of metaphysics, Marx lays the rigorous foundation for a nondogmatic, nonreductive, nondeterministic historical materialism. The relation of superstructure to substructure, and ultimately of ideology to the material forces and relations of production, need not be reduced to causal categories (mere supervenance, a unidirectional or reciprocal efficient causality, resemblance). Rather: production produces metaphysics by inscribing the movement of transcendence and rescendence—self-transcendence and self-rescendence—into the *mere thing*. Production produces a being, indeed a plurality of beings (one could hardly speak of a solitary commodity) that do not merely transcend toward being, but are the very being that they pass over into, that are at once beings and being—in a word, being(s). Yet the commodity itself, even while staging the origin of metaphysics, is itself only able to appear metaphysically, which is to say, in terms of the movement (transcendence and rescendence) between the sensual and the suprasensual. This is indeed the central paradox of *ideology*. Conceived at its limit, ideology is nothing else than the metaphysical exposition of the origin and essence of metaphysics.

6

IDEOLOGY AND TRUTH

In his lecture course, "On the Essence of Truth," held in the 1933–34 winter semester, Heidegger, developing a reading of the "cave allegory" from Plato's *Republic*, will arrive at similar insights into the nature of ideology. Together with the rectorial address, the lecture courses of the surrounding semesters, and some "special education seminars," this lecture, reprising material covered in the winter semester of 1931–32, belongs among the central documents of Heidegger's philosophical engagement with National Socialism.[1] While Heidegger remains a dues-paying member of the Nazi party until the end of the war and never really backs away from the philosophical commitments (including a certain conception of the political) that motivated and underwrote his engagement with National Socialism, he will turn, after his failed rectorship, to a far more esoteric politics, appropriating Hölderlin, the poet of poets, as his guide.[2]

Though the ostensible aim of the lectures is to show the conflict in Plato between two different conceptions of truth, Plato's *mythos* of man's liberation from the cave itself becomes the occasion to "spiritualize" Nazism—the word *Geist*, which plays such a role in the rectorial address, appears throughout—staking the claim of the philosopher to a leading role within National Socialism. It is in this context that his passing references to Marx's doctrine of ideology (*Ideologienlehre*) assume the greatest weight, since the problem of ideology is central to any revolutionary movement, and especially to the extent that it conceives itself in terms of a truth to which some have privileged access. Moreover,

IDEOLOGY AND TRUTH

the question of ideology, understood in a sufficiently radical fashion, reaches into the very heart of the problem of the historicity of being, and thus points the way toward the "productive dialogue with Marxism" whose possibility Heidegger invokes in the "Letter on Humanism."[3]

Marx's doctrine of ideology, Heidegger maintains, must be understood in terms of a genealogy that traces backward through Hegel and the Christian concept of God to Plato's doctrine of the idea and forward to Kierkegaard and finally to Nietzsche's threefold struggle, using the weapons of his enemies, against humanism, a "baseless [*bodenlos*] Christianity," and the Enlightenment.[4] The implication is clear: while Marx's doctrine of ideology seeks to expose the Christian belief in God and indeed the entire conceptual apparatus of German Idealism, and hence of metaphysics as such, as a falsifying interpretation of material reality, it itself remains rooted in, and thus incapable of surmounting, the tradition that it seeks to overcome. The ultimate horizon for Marx's concept of ideology is Plato's doctrine of ideas and hence the interpretation of the being of beings as a "presence" (*Anwesenheit*) that offers itself through the *eidos*, conceived not simply as the "visual appearance" of a thing, but as the essence, not itself visible, by which a thing can be seen as the thing that it is.[5]

Because the doctrine of ideas determines "the entire spiritual existence of the West till today," and because indeed "if there were no doctrine of Ideas, then there would be no Marxism," Marxism itself can only be "defeated once and for all when we first confront the doctrine of ideas and its two-millennia-long history."[6] This reading of Marx anticipates Heidegger's approach to Nietzsche, of whom he is a more sympathetic if no less tendentious reader, in the lecture courses given in the years from 1936 to 1940 when his relation to the Nazi party had already soured. Whereas Marx reaches Plato by way of Hegel, and thus through the mediation of the Christianizing interpretation of Platonism that, with its synthesis of reason and faith, constitutes metaphysics in the strict sense, Nietzsche will reach back deeper into the Platonic origin of metaphysics, reversing Platonism and its valuations, yet without overturning its most foundational determinations.[7] Nietzsche's nihilism does not move us away from the Marxist problem of ideology but presents it in an even more radical form. Nietzsche's *will to power*, just like Marx's materialism, involves an attempt to overcome metaphysics within metaphysics.

Yet we shouldn't suppose from this that Heidegger's relation to the concept of ideology is merely negative. Rather, if we conceive of the problem of ideology in the broadest sense as the relation of politics to truth and untruth, then it becomes clear that he seeks not to do away with the question of ideology but rather to radicalize it and place it on its proper foundation. The allegory of the cave, Heidegger maintains, describes "human history."[8] This history, which is nothing else than the happening of truth (*Geschehen der Wahrheit*), consists not merely in man comporting himself to beings as manifest (*zum Seienden als einem Offenbaren*), not only in ex-istence as "that *creative* catching sight of the essence of things by *reaching forward* [*jenes vorgreifend schöpferische Erblicken des Wesens der Dinge*],"[9] but in the passage (*Übergang*) out of the cave into the light and back into the cave.[10] And this is precisely because "there is no pure unconcealment, but instead to this unconcealment there also belong semblance [*Schein*], disguise [*Verstellung*], and the covering-up [*Verdeckung*] of things, or, as we also say: *untruth*."[11] At stake in this liberation and return to the cave, moreover, is neither the godlike philosopher's pure contemplation nor the freedom of the individual from the constraints of dogma and superstition but the very possibility of the political. While it is true that for Plato the fundamental question concerns the essence of knowing, this is itself a political question, since "*knowing* constitutes the innermost content of the *being of the state* itself, inasmuch as the state is a *free*, which also means *binding* power of a people."[12]

Precisely here, moreover, Plato begins to speak for Heidegger, allowing him to say what, given the political circumstances, he cannot quite say directly: namely, that, as he puts it a bit earlier, "the people who bear within themselves the rule [*Herrschaft*] of the state must be philosophizing human beings."[13] Indeed, at the center of Heidegger's reading of the cave allegory, despite its seemingly abstruse focus on the problem of truth, stands the question of the relation of the philosopher—the "liberator" (*Befreier*)—to the community of human beings. While the cave allegory is the history of man as such, and thus would seem to suggest that all human beings should become philosophers if they are to actually (*eigentlich*, authentically) exist, this is true only so far as, among the many possibilities of existing, being a philosopher is the "fundamental way in which man takes a stance with respect to the *whole* of beings and toward the *history* of human beings."[14] Yet this does not do away with the problem of how the philosopher relates to a multitude who are not actually philosophers and who therefore do not actually, authentically ex-ist. The philosopher, Heidegger writes, is "the one who creates the preview [*Vorblick*] and purview [*Ausblick*] into which this happening presses and drives." He "is not the one who retrospectively applies philosophical concepts to his time; instead, he is the one who is cast out in advance of his time and anticipates its fate."[15] The philosopher ex-ists politically and historically, in relation to his historical age: he anticipates its fate, which is to say, takes over the factical way of being into which it is thrown as the free project of the future. Here Heidegger speaks with Plato and Nietzsche against Hegel—and also, perhaps, Aristotle. Marx, it would seem, is left in the middle . . .

For Heidegger, however, what is ultimately at stake in the cave allegory, though intimately bound up with this alethic politics, is the struggle between the two senses of truth: unconcealment (*Unverborgenheit*), which is the original Greek understanding, and correctness (*Richtigkeit*), which gains an iron grip on philosophy after Plato. This problematic seems almost to disappear from view in what follows, yet it returns suddenly in the third chapter of the first part of the lecture course as he concludes his discussion of the *Republic*, in part c of section 29 ("The disappearance of the fundamental experience of *alētheia* and the necessity of a transformed retrieval of the question of truth"). Plato, Heidegger argues, understands the *agathon*, the idea of the Good, as a *zugon*, a yoke that yokes together "being in the sense of the understanding of being as the seeing of the Idea" with "truth in the Greek sense as the unconcealment of beings."[16] Plato will nevertheless fail to interrogate the "specific character of the yoke in its being," and, due to this omission, the yoke will get reinterpreted as the relation between subject and object as two present-at-hand things. This sets in motion the decisive transformation in the character of truth. The "character of the idea" will recede in the face of that which steps forth as the individual thing that is seen (*einzelnes Gesehenes*).[17] What is "seen" in the ideas will be taken as present-at-hand things, in the sense that we see both the individual things and the ideas: "the individual perceptible mountain and the idea of the mountain."[18] And thus that which the ideas bring into relation—the understanding of being and the unconcealment of beings, the ontological and the ontic—will come to be regarded as an "objective stratification of different realms."[19] The unconcealment and patentness (*Offenbarkeit*), which originally belong not to the assertion or proposition but to the "being things" (*seienden Dinge*) themselves insofar as these show themselves as they are, recede from view. Philosophy now directs its view to that which "stands in unconcealment in each case." Unconcealment merely becomes the title for that which is unconcealed.[20] While Aristotle inquires after *alētheia* as the "unconcealed as such," he is fundamentally interested in the *unconcealed being*: the being in its being, *on, ousia, einai*. In this way, even though the Greeks experienced being, they were not able to "place" it in the location (*Ort*) where it could be interrogated.[21] They were not able to think the *yoke*: Dasein as the truth of being, the ecstatic openness to being. It is this failure that ultimately leads to the dominance of the second, derivate concept of truth.[22] The essences come to be regarded as present-at-hand prototypes, and sensible things in turn as images of these prototypes, and thus one arrives at the thought of a conformity—*homoiōsis, adaequatio*—between archetype and image.[23]

The entire subsequent history of Western thought stands under the ban of the determination of the essence of truth as correctness, which plays itself out not only in the ever more unquestioned dominance of a scientific model of knowledge, not only in a philosophical trajectory leading from Descartes through to Kant, Hegel, and Marx, but also in the prevailing "liberalistic" political culture, which, as Heidegger argues in his acerbic critique of the Nazi ideologue Erwin Guido Kolbenheyer, continues to hold sway even over the thought of National Socialism, and indeed precisely where it might imagine itself to be most modern, most advanced.[24] For this reason it will be necessary, at the eve of the National Socialist political revolution, to repeat, to take up again and take further, the question of the essence of truth that Plato approached in the *Republic*'s cave but that subsequently fell into oblivion. In order to think the essence of truth as unconcealment in a more radical, originary way, no longer conflating unconcealment itself with the unconcealed being, it will be necessary not only to recognize, following Plato, that the "*truth* is a *happening* that happens with humanity itself"—thus recalling the question of truth to the analysis of Dasein as the ec-static opening toward beings—but also to recognize that the truth as unconcealment is essentially related to concealment (*Verborgenheit*).[25] Precisely at this point, just as he recalls his reading of the *Republic* to these seemingly esoteric ontological questions, Heidegger also makes the most overtly and exoterically political claims of the lecture course: the history of human beings, as this happening of the truth, is not merely the history of theoretical thought and opinion, but the total history of a people (*Volk*).[26] In the 1930s, the concept of the *Volk*, which appeared only once in *Being and Time* (in the discussion of history in section 74), begins far more explicitly to assume the role in the history of being that, a careful reading of his earlier writings and lectures would suggest, had already been ordained for it.[27] This total history, which has "as a driving force within it the *liberation of man to the essence of his being*," is anticipated, for *us*, in the history of the Greeks, whose liberation begins with Homer and culminates in the formation of the Greek state in union with cult, tragedy, and architecture, as well as the awakening of philosophy.[28] This total happening (*Gesamtgeschehen*) accomplishes the *projection* of the world within which the Greek people existed, and precisely such a projection is the basis for what "we call today a worldview [*Weltanschauung*]." Far from being a "derivative superstructure [*nachträglicher Überbau*]," the *Weltanschauung* is "the projection of a world that a people carries out."[29] By identifying worldview (*Weltanschauung*)—

a concept that, in its overreaching vacuousness, exemplifies the idle chatter of the "one"—with world projection (*Weltentwurf*), Heidegger brings the esoteric and the exoteric, ontology and politics, into an unsettling and surprising proximity. It can hardly surprise then that in the next paragraph, his political rhetoric reaching its climax, Heidegger invokes the Führer, and will present himself, the philosopher and thinker—in a tactic that was perhaps too transparent to his contemporaries—as the one who can interpret the leader's own word, leading the leader.[30] The National Socialist revolution is nothing else than a *repetition* of the history of the Greek people—of the liberation, achieved through the formation of the state, that opens them up to the essence of being. But if this repetition is not to run aground, if the history of the German and European people is not to suffer the same fate as the Greeks and dissolve into bourgeois liberalism, then it will be necessary for the political repetition to be, at one and the same time, a repetition of the question of the essence of truth. As Heidegger puts it, "This beginning of a great history of a people, such as we see among the Greeks, extends to all the dimensions of human creativity. With this beginning, things come into openness and truth. But in the same moment, man also comes into *untruth*. Untruth begins only then."[31] The political and ontological must be returned to their unity. This will demand conceiving of *Weltanschauung* not as mere "superstructure" constituted in the wake of political praxis but as a projection of the possibility of a world into the future. The truth, it follows, cannot be conceived as the correctness of an assertion or proposition, or of thinking more generally, in its relation to reality, but as the "anticipation" of the world, the opening up of the world in its possibilities. This will in turn demand thinking of truth as unconcealment. But for this to be possible, it will be necessary to bring unconcealment into relation to concealment—to think the event of truth as the movement between concealment and unconcealment, as the movement in and out of the cave. Only by thus thinking this movement between concealment and unconcealment would it also be possible to inaugurate a more radical, more originary repetition of Greek politics.

If the question of ideology, as suggested earlier, is fundamentally the question of the relation of politics and truth, then it must now be clear that precisely this question is at the crux of Heidegger's 1933–34 lecture, "On the Essence of Truth." Needed, should the National Socialist revolution succeed, is a revolution in the understanding of ideology, a "repetition" of the thinking of ideology that radicalizes it by bringing it back to its origin. Whereas in Marx the concept of ideology remains rooted in metaphysics and its forgetting of unconcealment, leading him to conceive of it as mere "superstructure," a "reflection" of reality rendered after the fact, it will be necessary instead to think ideology as the movement between unconcealment and concealment, truth and untruth. What this demands, more concretely, is not only an unremitting critique of every aspect of National Socialistic thought that, like Kolbenheyer's noxious neo-Darwinian racialist musings, remains rooted in metaphysical conceptualities, but coming to terms with the very necessity of this untruth as the limit, the horizon, of the world-inaugurating truth of National Socialism.

7
THE TRUTH OF THE COMMODITY

The 1933–34 lecture course, "On the Essence of Truth," never explicitly addresses Marx's doctrine of the commodity, nor does it present any other aspect of his thought but in the vaguest terms. Heidegger never goes further than to suggest that Marxism, and Marx's concept of ideology, can only be understood from out of the history of Western metaphysics. On the surface this could hardly even count as an engagement with Marx, though it does recognize the momentousness of his thought and not only counters the crude racism of the prevailing Nazi discourse on Marxism, but even implies that precisely this racism, as an inheritance of English liberalism, stands far below Marx in philosophical rank. Yet it becomes clear, if we consider the radical rethinking of ideology implicitly at work, that nothing less is at stake than a transformative critique of Marx's analysis of the commodity as the metaphysical staging of the origin of metaphysics.[1] Whereas Marx will conceive of the commodity as a sensual thing inscribing within itself the movement of transcendence and rescendence that, passing back and forth between the sensual and the suprasensual, makes metaphysics itself possible as a mode of appearance (a mode of phenomenology, of self-showing), Heidegger will propose, at once with this and against this, that we try to think this movement not as a movement between beings (human beings and mere things) that present themselves, be it sensually or suprasensually, as present-at-hand—not, this is to say, as the passage between what is unconcealed and what is concealed—but as the movement between unconcealment and concealment as such. The problem with Marx's analysis of the commodity, from this perspective, is that it continues to understand truth as correctness even while thinking truth in its origination. Ideology is the *correct* account of the origination of correctness, of truth as correspondence, rather than the true revealing of the truth.[2]

Telling, in this regard, is the following passage from *Capital*, which motivates Marx's use of the term *fetish* to understand the commodity.

> Through this *quidproquo* the products of labor become commodities, sensual suprasensual or social things. In the same way, the impression of light of a thing on the optical nerve does not represent itself as the subjective excitation of the visual nerve itself, but rather as the objective form of a thing outside of the eye. Yet in the case of vision, light from one thing, the external object, is actually projected onto another thing, the eye. It is a physical relation [*Verhältnis*] between physical things. The commodity form and the value-relation [*Wertverhältnis*] of the products of labor in which the commodity form represents itself, in contrast, has absolutely nothing to do with its physical nature and the *thinglike* relationships [*Beziehungen*] that arise from it. It is nothing else than the determinate social relation [*Verhältnis*] of men themselves that here assumes for them the phantasmagoric form of a relation [*Verhältnis*] of things. In order therefore to find an analogy, we must flee into the nebulous region of the world of religion.[3]

That the impression of light on the optic nerve exhibits itself *as* the objective existence of the thing outside of the eye, in the outside world—that the subject transcends itself and enters into a relation to an objective realm exterior to itself—appears analogous to the operation of the commodity. The commodity, it follows, is the very genesis of the self-transcendence through which the relation between subject and object is constituted, and hence the condition of the possibility of truth as correspondence. While it might sound strange if not perverse to argue that a seemingly fundamental epistemological a priori is itself grounded in the production of the commodity, this makes perfect sense the moment we consider the subject-object relationship, and the constitution of subjectivity in its transcendence into the world, not as a real natural given, but as itself ideological, belonging to the horizon of a certain, historically emergent interpretation of beingness (*Seiendheit*) as the being of beings. To claim this is not to anachronistically impose a "Heideggerian" or "deconstructive" perspective on Marx but to recognize a possibility that his own thinking, with its intense critique of bourgeois ideology, is itself on the way toward. Here we follow an interpretive impulse already at work in Karl Korsch's rethinking of ideology and Lukács's analysis of the commodity fetish as reification, yet which could be taken

THE TRUTH OF THE COMMODITY

much further—beyond the "idealist" and, as Althusser will have it, "ideological" terms in which it is posed by them, and perhaps even (as will become more clear) beyond the presumption of a unitary and linear account of changing historical horizons. Marx nevertheless seems to shirk away from this insight, and indeed by denying the very Kantian perspective that he had just invoked. The commodity form, rather than having everything to do with the transcendence of the subject, has nothing to do with it, and precisely because the latter consists merely in a physical relation between physical things—as if (we can almost hear Heidegger say) the relation between physical things were itself something physical! The relation between mind (as physical brain) and world (outside nature), this is to say, cannot provide a correct picture of the commodity form, since the commodity form no longer involves a natural relation between natural things but rather another kind of relation in which the social relation of people takes the form of the phantasmagorical relation between things. It is as if, starting out from the assumption that the natural relation between natural things is a "correct" relation—indeed a relation whose correctness is somehow itself beyond doubt—Marx has no choice but to conceive of the inherently distorting, essentially "incorrect" relation as simply unnatural, and thus himself "take flight," if only for the sake of an interpretive metaphor, to the mysterious cloudy region of primitive religion. Starting out from the assumption that truth is correctness—indeed with the occlusion of the original truth of unconcealment reaching the extreme point where this correctness itself could only be conceived in terms of the natural sensate relation of natural sensate things—Marx must shroud the commodity form in mystery even while revealing its truth. This is because the commodity form, disclosing social relations in the distorted form of relations between things, distorts the reality of social relations to the very degree it represents them through the seemingly natural relations of natural things. Because Marx still remains somehow bound to the concept of correctness in its most reductive naturalistic variant, he cannot quite recognize that the untruth of the commodity consists not so much in its incorrectness as its correctness: in the very fact that it presents social relations in the same form as those relations between natural things to which the concept of correctness—of a correct description, a correct assertion or proposition—can apply. The fetish is what, in the last instance, preserves truth as correctness, as correspondence, even at the price of turning the world upside down.

Because Marx does not own up to his own Platonic legacy, failing to see how his analysis of the commodity fetish derives from the occlusion of concealment and the unchallenged dominance of correctness, he cannot carry through his most powerful insight into how the commodity, by establishing transcendence as the self-transcendence of the subject toward the object, opens up the ontological horizon for the determination of truth as correctness. Yet this does not mean that nothing will be left to learn from Marx's analysis of the commodity fetish once, following Heidegger into Plato's cave, we become open to a more originary conception of ideology. If Plato's cave stages the battle between concealment and correctness, it does so by way of a literary simile. The *Republic* is itself the literary staging, through a text that stands at the threshold separating tragic poetry from philosophy, of the tragic conflict between a poetic and a scientific concept of truth. There can be little doubt, moreover, that the 1933–34 lecture course offers what, from the perspective of historical materialism, could only appear as a one-sidedly "idealist," and indeed thoroughly reactionary, view of history. Not only is history the history of a "people," but this history begins not with its migrations and settlements, not with its archaic institutions, not with political pacts and class conflict, and certainly not with forces and relations of production, but with the work of the great poet. The history of the Greeks began with Homer, and perhaps the history of the Germans—and the Europeans—will find its new beginning in Hölderlin. Heidegger, of course, will hardly accept the Marxist objection to his purported idealism: great poetry and philosophy are not a mere "derivate superstructure," brought in after the fact, but a world-projection, projecting the opening—the horizon of truth bordered by untruth—in which beings can appear in their being. This projection, moreover, is neither the work of the poet as isolated individual nor of some group of humans: it is not merely a "human accomplishment" in even the broadest sense. Nor is it the achievement of the will to power. It is rather *being itself* that is at play, and plays itself out, in these historical formations.[4] This answer will hardly relieve the qualms of the historical materialist, for whom Heidegger's radicalization of the question of ideology must fall on deaf ears. But even if we grant the truth of Heidegger's challenge to the transparent self-evidence of scientific naturalism with all its metaphysical presuppositions, and above all the interpretation of truth as correctness; even if we grant that concepts such as "material," "historical," "dialectical" cannot be exempt from critique; even if we grant that "language is the house of being"—that nothing presents itself immediately, apart from textual mediation, since immediacy itself is a textual construct—even granting all this, we might still ask whether there is not also a truth in Marx's analysis of the commodity that eludes Heidegger's grasp and to which he cannot but fail to do justice. This is, namely, the truth of the commodity: that the opening of truth, the originary disclosure of the horizon in which disclosure can take place, itself takes place with the production of the commodity—is, as it were, inscribed into the thing, such that this thing, the commodity, is the very inscription of a certain mode of truth in its movement.[5]

It is telling in this regard that after the 1933–34 lecture course Heidegger will turn, even as he develops and consolidates his thinking of be-ing in its historicality, to the thing as the site of truth. This is most evident in his 1935–36 "Origin of the Work of Art," his lecture courses on Nietzsche, and postwar texts such as the Bremen lectures, "The Thing," and "The Question concerning Technology," as also in the *Contributions to Philosophy*, which thinks sheltering (*Bergung*) as belonging to the essence of truth.[6] This hardly brings Heidegger closer to some sort of materialism—such would be a grotesque misreading. But it does suggest an implicit engagement with the problem of the commodity that takes its departure from the radicalization of ideology in the lecture course "On the Essence of Truth" and yet does not end with this. It suggests that Marx remains Heidegger's worthy enemy and perhaps his only worthy enemy, since almost every other thinker is either made to serve Heidegger's narrative of the history of be-ing or simply ignored altogether. That Heidegger could not engage more openly with his enemy might nevertheless seem to suggest another kind of limit to his own thinking, and even the lack of a certain philosophical courage or, for want of a better word, nobility of spirit. Perhaps it is yet another instance of his silence. Or perhaps the true enemy for Heidegger would not be the one that you engage with, precisely because all engagement must already take place within a certain horizon that one has already decided for, but the one that you decide against. Perhaps, in the midst of the greatest danger of the forgetting of being, Marx discloses a different possibility of salvation.

Let us then decide, with Heidegger, against Heidegger, for Marx, toward Marx: returning to the question of the commodity and the truth of the commodity—repeating the question of the commodity and its fetish, trying to get past the mystery in which it comes to be shrouded in the very attempt at its demystification. Yet it will not fail to dawn on us, and this is the most critical point, that to decide, with and against Heidegger, for Marx is also to decide against decision. It is not a decision, but an un-decision, an in-decision: an *Ent-scheidung*. It is to decide for encountering the commodity as the *impossibility of deciding between being, or even be-ing, and beings*—the impossibility of thinking and upholding the difference, the *Unterschied*.

8

VALUE, PUBLICITY, POLITICS

For Marx the commodity is *a sensual suprasensual thing*. We have, up to this point, focused on this characterization, which attempts to interpret the strangeness of the commodity—to present the commodity in all the uncanniness of its operation—through a language that, borrowed from metaphysics, *seems* familiar. We barely touched on the commodity itself and what it does. This might lead us to think that the interpretation of the commodity is one thing and the commodity itself something else—or that Marx would need only to find a better language to speak of what the commodity is. There is some truth in this. We will seek to gain a sense for the commodity beyond its metaphysical interpretation. Yet we also must not forget that the commodity *is* nothing else than the interpretation that it gives of itself. The commodity is a power of bringing to appearance, making appear. It is of essence phenomenological, a phenomenological thing—a thing endowed with the power of making appear: a thing that is not merely able to appear, in a passive sense, through conditions of possibility that exist somehow beyond it—in the subject (for Kant), the Good (for Plato), or even perhaps being itself—but a thing that bears within it, and brings into being by bringing into appearance, the condition of possibility of being and appearance. By designating the commodity as a sensual suprasensual thing, Marx does not provide an incorrect account of what the commodity really is. Rather, he does not yet go far enough in exposing that the commodity is its appearance, and nothing else than this. The commodity that shows itself metaphysically, this is to say, is metaphysics in its origin.

The question cannot be what the commodity really is but rather what the metaphysical commodity also shows us—what it shows us beyond metaphysics. The long passage from Marx cited in chapter 7 hints toward this. For it would seem we have neglected, up to this point, a decisive turn in the argument hidden within an "or": commodities are *sensual suprasensual or social (sinnlich übersinnliche oder gesellschaftliche)*. It is not immediately clear if the social stands in apposition to suprasensual or to both sensual and suprasensual. Yet since it would be odd for Marx to argue that the social was not also somehow natural and sensual, we must suppose the latter—that the social consists in the very movement between the sensual and the suprasensual, substructure and superstructure, material reality and ideology, that is at play in the commodity. This is a point of great significance. Were the social simply identified with the suprasensual, then it would fall completely under the ban of the metaphysical opposition between nature and culture, *phusis* and *nomos*. This would force us into the rather conventional if no doubt "correct" claim that the ideological function of the commodity consists above all in presenting "social" relations as natural relations—naturalizing historical relations, and ultimately regarding them as unchanging facts of an eternally well-ordered cosmos. Marx is certainly saying this, but the tendency of the commodity goes much further. Even if it is true, as Michel Henry claims, that for Marx "social labor is precisely equal labor, that which, having lost all of its real, and, as such, particular properties is henceforth the same for all," it is nevertheless not possible to think of the social in this sense as merely the same as the nonreal, ideal, suprasensual, or abstract.[1] Rather: it is what we might call the "becoming ideal" of the real—the transitioning from real to ideal. To the extent that "social" gives a single name to the uncanny, impossible juxtaposition of the sensual and suprasensual, it suggests a new way of thinking metaphysics *as* transcendence. It shows the way toward a more radical interpretation of transcendence—an interpretation that will free it from its mystery and bring it into the open. The "social" will show another way of showing, of coming to appearance, of being open to and standing in the truth.

Keeping this in mind, let us now turn at last to Marx's description of the commodity itself, quoting at length from his account of the origin of the "metaphysical character of the commodity," up to the previously cited passage introducing the concept of the fetish.

> The mystical [*mystische*] character of the commodity does not arise from its use value. Just as little does it arise from the content of the determinations of value. For, firstly,

as different as the useful labors or productive activities may be, it is a physiological truth that they are functions of the human organism, and that every such function, regardless of its content and its form, is of essence the exertion of the human brain, nerves, muscles, sense organs, and so forth. Secondly: as for what lies at the basis of the determination of the quantity of value, the duration of that exertion or the quantity of labor, this quantity is differentiable from the quality of the labor, and indeed palpably [*sinnfällig*] so. Under all circumstances, the labor time that the production of the means of sustenance costs [*kostet*] would have interested human beings, though not in equal measure at every stage of development. Finally, as soon as human beings are in some way engaging in labor for one another, then their labor also receives a social form.

From whence does the enigmatic character of the product of labor arise as soon as it assumes commodity form? Manifestly [*Offenbar*] from this form itself. The equality of human labors receives the objective form [*sachliche Form*] of the equal value-objectivity of the products of labor, the measure of the expenditure of human labor power through its duration receives the form of the value-quantity of the products of labor, and finally the relations of the producers, in which those social determinations of their labors are activated, receive the form of a social relation of the products of labor.

The mysteriousness [*Geheimnisvolle*] of the commodity form consists simply in the fact that it mirrors back to human beings the social character of their own labor as the objective character of the products of labor themselves, as social natural properties of these things, hence the social relation [*Verhältnis*] of the producers to the totality of labor as a social relation, existing external to them [i.e., the producers], of objects.[2]

Marx begins with a negative determination: the mysterious character of the commodity consists neither in use value nor in the content of the determination of value. This is first of all because there is nothing mysterious about useful labor or productive work in itself: however many different forms these may assume, it is a *physiological truth* that they are all functions of the human organism, and can thus be reduced, regardless of their form and content, to the exertion of the human brain, nerves, muscles, sensory organisms. This formulation eliminates the mystery of use value only by way of a tautology: it is a physiological truth that productive labor can appear, from the perspective of physiology, as purely physiological. It is already evident that truth here can no longer simply mean a correct proposition, a description that corresponds to reality, but suggests the horizon of understanding and interpretation that opens up from the perspective of the physiological—which is to say, with the fundamental interpretation of human existence in physiological, naturalistic terms. Did this escape Marx? It might be tempting to believe that, having turned from the Hegelian folly of his youth, he accepted this sort of naturalism as self-evident. Yet might we not rather suppose, though it cannot ultimately be a question just of Marx's intentions, that this formulation must, as it were, call its own bluff. What is at issue is not the actual nature of useful labor and productive activity but the way they come into appearance through the commodity such that they appear absolutely without mystery or strangeness—as if thinking of the human being as a mere aggregation of functions, dissolved and dissected into a grotesque ensemble of pieces no longer even capable of belonging together as parts of a whole, were the most natural thing in the world. To say that this is not mysterious is not to affirm and appropriate the scientific worldview of modernity but to acknowledge precisely the aspect of the commodity that, without allowing itself to appear with the slightest trace of mystery, provides the impenetrable basis of ideology, perhaps even explaining the very fact that the commodity keeps its hold on us even when we peer through its mystery. The functionalist reduction of human existence—of Dasein as being-in-the-world—to use value is the "open secret" of the commodity: the secret that cannot be recognized as such since it appears as the very *openness* through which things show up to us.

The second justification Marx gives for his negative claim subtly confirms this reading. As for "the duration of that expenditure [*Vorausgabung*] or the quantity of work," Marx continues, the quantity of labor is differentiable from the quality, and is indeed even palpably (*sogar sinnfällig*) differentiable. We can hardly imagine that Marx, with his subtle understanding of the changing nature of work, could have believed that this "differentiability" was simply a natural, self-evident fact about work, and did not rather involve the way in which labor has come to present itself. For there is clearly nothing self-evident, nothing palpable, about the distinction between the quantity and quality of work. This is clearly not a natural and absolute fact about work but the result of its quantification. One need only consider those forms of labor that do not conform to the factory model of production—from domestic labor and childcare to various forms of intellectual or creative labor—to see that in many cases the quality of labor stands in direct proportion to the impossibility of quantifying its duration. Once again: the quantifiability of work, the abstraction of quantity from quality, is not a natural fact in any simple sense but is that by which the commodity shows itself as without mystery: the self-evidence that inhabits the mode in which the commodity *makes appear*. It would seem to contradict this, however, that neither use value nor labor time—the content of the determinations of value—*appear* essentially bound up with the commodity form *per se* but rather take on a completely independent existence as natural factors of production and indeed natural "facts of life." But this is precisely the point: the appearance that the commodity brings forth, the mode of appearance that it puts into play, appears without mystery to the very extent that it projects this appearance beyond the commodity, into a reality that appears completely independent from the commodity. In much the same way, the Kantian subject constitutes spatiotemporal reality as independent of itself, such that Kant can claim to be at once a transcendental idealist and an empirical realist.

The next two sentences will nevertheless seem to render this reading implausible. The time of labor needed for the production of the means of life must interest man under all conditions, though not in equal measure (*gleichmäßig*) at different stages of development. For "as soon as men in some way labor for one another, their labor obtains a social form." Here, Marx seems to maintain that the quantification of labor is somehow a universal truth of human life, manifesting itself in different ways at all stages of human economic development. While certainly assuming a far greater significance under industrial capitalism, it is always to some extent at play. Yet a closer look suggests that Marx is not maintaining the universality of the quantification of work but only the universality of an interest in the time that labor takes, and, perhaps even more important, of the implicit rather than explicit awareness that the time of one human being can somehow be brought into relation to the time of another. If we nevertheless maintain that *time* is of essence quantifiable, and that the social relation between my time and your time could only consist in the exchange of quantities of labor time, this would seem to be a mere sophistic subtlety. Yet such is clearly an absurd presupposition, and even if the problem of the nature of temporality did not yet assume the same urgency for Marx as it will for Heidegger, one cannot imagine that he would have failed to realize that there is a historical aspect to the social experience of time, and that the precise quantifiability of time, even if it may have a ground in the nature of things or the constitutive structure of subjectivity, is not itself a cultural universal. Moreover: regardless of what Marx did or did not think, we, reading *Capital* in the wake of *Being and Time*, cannot fail to sense the extraordinary implications for the critique of capitalism of Heidegger's de-struction (*Destruktion*) of the metaphysical understanding of spatiality and temporality and the Cartesian mathematical, quantifiable space-time in which it culminates. Indeed, Lukács's *History and Class Consciousness*, published four years before *Being and Time*, already observed that, as a result of the subordination to the machine in industrial labor, "time sheds its qualitative, variable, flowing nature; it freezes into an exactly delimited, quantifiable continuum filled with quantifiable 'things' . . . : in short, it becomes space."[3] Capitalism cannot simply be understood as a way of organizing the forces of production through relations of production and superstructure (law, the state, ideology), but as the social organization of the space and time of labor.

But what is it that *does* explain the mysterious character of the product of labor once it assumes the commodity form? From whence does it originate? Manifestly (*offenbar*) from this form itself. Once again, we find ourselves in the realm of tautology and circular reasoning. The *offenbar* (manifestly), which might first seem merely rhetorical, has not only more than a hint of irony, but is rich in philosophical implications. Whereas what is unmysterious about the commodity, what can only appear as absolutely natural, is palpable (*sinnfällig*)—it literally falls into the senses—the mystery of the commodity is *offenbar*: it becomes manifest, public, open, patent. It reveals itself—it is a matter of revelation—from the form. The mystery of the product of labor, as soon as it assumes commodity form, manifestly originates from out of the form itself. The mystery that comes to attach to the product of labor with the production of the commodity is nothing else than the becoming manifest of the form of the commodity *as* form. Whereas the use value and the content of exchange value (labor time) appear without mystery in a sensuous immediacy, the appearance of the form is the root and origin of all mystery precisely because the form appears without ever becoming immediately palpable as such. We cannot help but notice, recalling Heidegger's hint regarding Marx's concept of ideology, that the problem of form so conceived is nothing else than the problem of the *eidos*—of what is most eminently manifest as the ground of a sensate appearance that itself hides from the senses.

We must read what follows in this sense. Marx goes on to explain that "the equality of human labors receives the objective form [*sachliche Form*] of the equal value-objectivity of the products of labor, the measure of the expenditure of human labor power through its duration receives the form of the value-quantity of the products of labor, and finally the relations of the producers, in which those social determinations of their labors are activated, receive the form of a social relation of the products of labor." Should we fail to see that the problem of the *eidos* is at play in Marx's analysis of the mystery of the commodity, it might seem that the form received in each of these three instances is a mere property or determination of an object—in other words, something simply present-at-hand; *etwas Vorhandenes*, in Heidegger's German. Against this, we must maintain that the form that is in each instance received is nothing else than the ground of the appearance of the equality, measure, and relations in question, and that, to this extent, *the receiving of the form is the coming into appearance of these,* since equality, measure, and relation, so far as they are never given adequately through the mere sensually immediate presence of individual sensate things, are precisely what can only appear in the mode of transcendence. This would suggest moreover that, prior to the reception of these three forms through the production of the commodity, one could not even really speak, at least not in a full sense, of the equality, measure, and relations of labor. Yet such an interpretation would turn the problem of ideology into a structuralist paradox, according to which ideology must be eternal, standing out from history, since beyond ideology nothing is thinkable. Failing to take seriously Heidegger's admonition to think Marx through Plato leads us into the cul-de-sac that some, though without full justice, will find in Althusser. For indeed, precisely by leading Marx back to Plato, recognizing the deep kinship between Marx's form and Plato's *eidos*, we gain a sense for the difference: Marx's form is a *sachliche Form*—it is "objective," "material," it is bound up with the *Sache*. This is not to say that his form is merely something immediately present-at-hand as a thing out there in the world but rather that the form, as the ground of the appearance of equality, measure, and relation that appears in and as transcendence, nevertheless also appears *in and as* the thing itself, in its sensual finitude. Moreover, if it is possible and necessary for equality, measure, and relation to appear bound up in this way with things, it is precisely because the equality, measure, and relation in question is not equality, measure, and relation as such but only with regard to human labor: the equality of labor, the measurability of labor, and the relations of labor. What is at stake in the commodity form, this is to say, is neither the abstract presentation of the abstractly mathematical nor the mere replication through the commodity form of mathematical forms that are already concretely instantiated in the concrete existence of human beings but rather the production as objective form (*sachliche Form*) of both the transcendental ground of appearance and its appearance (its revelation, its self-presentation) as transcendental ground; of an equality, measure, and relationality that, as the equality, measure, and relationality of human labor, cannot be given to us or exist abstractly but only in and through the concreteness and objectivity of the thing. Kant, in the preface to the second edition of the *Critique of Pure Reason*, had observed that the more deeply bound up the a priori form is with materiality, the more difficult it is to liberate it and bring it into the open such that it can assume a scientific form.[4] Kant, one could say, sought to combine an Aristotelian insight into the concrete givenness of forms with Plato's epistemological radicalism. But Marx goes a step further, recognizing at once that the forms of labor are inextricably bound up with a concreteness that is neither a natural given nor a function of a constituting subjectivity but socially, historically produced through the production of the commodity form itself. This suggests the significance of the strange term *Wertgegenständlichkeit*—not "objective value," but, literally, "value-objectivity." What is at stake is the production of value as objectivity, as presence-at-hand.[5]

In the next paragraph, Marx finally reveals the essence of the commodity's mystery: the commodity "mirrors back to human beings the social character of their own labor as the objective character of the products of labor themselves, as social natural properties of these things, hence the social relation [*Verhältnis*] of the producers to the totality of labor as a social relation, existing external to them, of objects." He adds: "Through this *quidproquo* the products of labor become commodities, sensual suprasensual or social things." Having now pursued the itinerary that brings us to our earlier point of departure, we get a better sense for the stakes of this metaphysical characterization of the commodity. The basic structure of the commodity involves the appearance of A as B—of one kind of thing (the social characteristics of labor; social relations of production) as another kind of thing (objective characteristics of the products of labor; social relations of objects).[6] If we conceive this relation in terms of truth as correctness, we find ourselves in the realm of the symbolic. The commodity would be a kind of symbol, as indeed a symbol is nothing else than a sensual suprasensual thing; a sensual thing that makes appear to the senses something that cannot ordinarily be grasped by them. The symbol thus involves a correspondence that is not simple and direct but altogether mysterious, since an abyss seems to divide the signifier and the signified. It might indeed be tempting to say that such a perspective arises as the inevitable consequence of the metaphysical understanding of truth as correspondence, that language and other expressive acts can only be "literally" true or false of a reality that is itself given through the senses, and that everything else, even if dignified with the word *truth*, is true in a merely symbolic or figural sense—mere "poetry." The metaphysical understanding of truth as correctness thus leads to the dismissal of metaphysical language itself as mere poetic rambling. *La révolution dévore ses enfants.* The mystery of the commodity would hence involve the mysteriousness of a symbolic mode of representation, itself a kind of limit case of truth as correspondence. With the commodity, what is actually the case, the suprasensual reality of the actual relations of production, presents itself through the sensually given relation of things. The latter at once corresponds and does not correspond to the former. It corresponds, because the former appears through the latter, and can only appear through the latter. It does not correspond, since an ontological abyss separates the two: there is an essential and irreducible noncorrespondence between them. Whereas each particular commodity is a specific symbol for specific social relations of production, the commodity as such would name the symbolic mode of appearance that characterizes the capitalist system of production as a whole, and which, as such, exhaustively determines both theory and praxis. Ideology, in this more radical sense, would refer to nothing else than a constitutive symbolic mode whose mystery can be exposed, though only with great difficulty, but that continues to remain in play, and indeed cannot be rendered inoperative from within. We might even tentatively and provisionally draw a distinction between superstructure-ideology—ideology in the more conventional Marxist sense articulated in the *German Ideology*—and commodity-ideology or indeed fetish-ideology. Commodity-ideology is the ideology that, rather than supervening on the substructure or emanating from it (if not without a backward or reciprocal causality), is at work in the substructure as such, organizing and enabling the relations of production. For the theory of ideology to be complete, it must relate superstructure-ideology back to commodity-ideology. Or indeed, it must show that the surface ideological forms of late capitalism make manifest, if in an illusionary manner, the ideality actually at work in the relations of production as an ideal tendency within materiality, in its historical expression, that cannot itself be banished as mere illusion.

Yet precisely this metaphysical, symbolic understanding of ideology and the commodity form leads us into a dead end. If ordinary bourgeois ideology is a kind of positive theology, basking in the confidence that the secrets of social existence are immediately accessible since it has not yet even begun to comprehend that there is a reality beyond the symbols (the commodities) in which it trades, the symbolic-metaphysical understanding of the commodity would be a negative theology, which, far from putting the commodity out of work, makes the hold of its mystery on our lives even more absolute, even more ineluctable, since we will have ceased to ask of things that they make sense. Precisely this "negative theology of the commodity" has now become the everyday consciousness of capitalism: we see through it, at every moment, and stay with it.

It is for precisely this reason that—with Heidegger, against Heidegger, for Marx, toward Marx, beyond Marx—we must rethink the commodity and ideology in terms of truth as unconcealment rather than correctness. What this demands now becomes clearer: the essence of the commodity form must be shown to consist not in the symbolic relation of the sensual and the suprasensual but in the *as*-structure itself, in the very interpretation of this *as* that—indeed the appearance of this *as* that. The commodity is nothing else than a mode of interpretation by which beings *show themselves*. Before there can be truth in the sense of correspondence, things (beings) must show themselves in their being, and in this sense, there is absolutely nothing inherently *false* or *incorrect* about the commodity, nor is there something mysterious. Nevertheless, the *as*-structure of the commodity form involves concealment as well as disguise, distortion, and obstruction, and hence not only truth (unconcealment) but also untruth (concealment).[7] For on the one hand, the *mere thing* appears as a commodity, a ware for exchange. A shoe can be just a shoe, but it can also be a shoe as a commodity. On the other hand, the shoe, having shown itself as a commodity, through its relation to other commodities, allows for the social relations to appear *as* relations between things, as exchange value. It is worth noting that whereas when the shoe appears as commodity it never entirely ceases to also appear as a mere shoe, the relations of production have not yet appeared as what they are before they appear as something else.

What is the shoe before it is a commodity? What might it mean for the relations of production to appear *as* they are in themselves? If we think of the ideology of the commodity form in terms of a symbolic function, these questions will lead us nowhere. For it will become immediately clear that whereas *we* already know what the shoe is—namely, use value as a physiological function—we can know absolutely nothing about the relations of production as such. We can only get beyond this impasse by realizing that both the palpability of use value and labor time and the mystery of the relations of production are themselves interpretations that are produced through the commodity, or indeed brought forth as the production of the commodity. The metaphysical-symbolic function of the commodity follows from its interpretive labor. The commodity is a way in which Dasein *is* its there—is given over to the openness of the truth. Yet the commodity is not the *original* way that Dasein is its there. Rather, the truth of the commodity, which itself founds truth as correctness, is constituted in a different kind of truth. This more original truth, covered over by the commodity, involves what the shoe is in itself and what the relations of production are in themselves.

Heidegger's analysis in *Being and Time* of Dasein as being-in-the-world provides provisional answers to both these questions. It is in each case a matter of getting past the metaphysical interpretations that have imposed themselves on the phenomena, forcing them to show themselves in terms of a manner of conceptualization that is fundamentally inadequate and cannot but fail to show them as they are in themselves. What is the shoe in itself? It is first of all a *Zeug*—a tool, equipment. The *Zeug* is itself a translation of the Greek term for thing, *pragmata*, "that which one has to do with in one's concernful dealings (*praxis*)."[8] Yet Heidegger will seek to make explicit precisely the "pragmatic" character of the things that the Greeks, choosing to conceive of things as mere "things," left in the dark. To speak of the item of equipment *in itself* is nevertheless fundamentally misleading, since the "being of the tool" always belongs to an equipmental totality (*Zeugganze*). It is "essentially" "something in-order-to"— *etwas, um zu*. There are different manners of the "in order to"—serviceability (*Dienlichkeit*), conduciveness (*Beiträglichkeit*), usability or applicability (*Verwendbarkeit*), manipulability (*Handlichkeit*)—but in each case the "in order to" involves the "*assignment* or *reference* of something to something," and together these referential assignments constitute a whole.[9] The mode of being of the tool is readiness-to-hand (*Zuhandenheit*), and precisely this readiness-to-hand, he further explains, is what we can never discover in the mere "outward appearance" of the thing.[10] The tool, being in the manner of readiness-to-hand, thus necessarily escapes the theoretical gaze that, grasping the thing in terms of its *eidos* ("the outward appearance in whatever form it takes"), ultimately conceives of the thing as a substance, existing within space and time, with certain essential and accidental properties. Heidegger's invocation of the Kantian "thing in itself" is nevertheless rich in irony. If metaphysics, in its most radical critical tendency, was forced to the ultimately nihilistic recognition of the impossibility of knowing anything about the thing in itself, it is because it started out from the premise that the thing in itself is the thing that has been arrested by the theoretical gaze, uprooted from its relations to other things, and apprehended in this isolation. The tool, that which we encounter in our concernful praxis, is *itself* precisely insofar as it is not just and simply itself but belongs, rather, to a totality of other tools, bound up with these through a web of referential assignments. Or, in other words, the tool is what it is in itself in its belonging to the world. For the tool to show up as tool, for it to be accessible to circumspective concern, our world must already be disclosed in advance. Dasein, in its concernful praxis, is already in the world.

The being of the thing as it shows itself to the theoretical gaze, in contrast, is not readiness-to-hand but presence-at-hand (*Vorhandenheit*).[11] Even though presence-at-hand is in some sense ontically prior to readiness-to-hand, readiness-to-hand is ontologically prior. The presence-at-hand of the tool is founded in readiness-to-hand, announcing itself precisely when something goes wrong, when there is a disturbance in the referential assignments, and the tool becomes suddenly apparent to us in a certain un-readiness-to-hand. The unusable tool is now just lying there: "it shows itself as an equipmental Thing which looks so and so, and which, in its readiness-to-hand as looking that way, has constantly been present-at-hand too."[12] A certain "pure presence-at-hand" announces itself, but this does not dispense entirely with readiness-to-hand, since even if it is now just present-at-hand, it is so as a tool that is no longer usable, that is deficient in its readiness-to-hand. "Equipment which is present-at-hand *in this way* is still not just a Thing which occurs somewhere."[13]

We have only grazed the surface of Heidegger's analysis of the tool. And yet it must already be clear that use value stands in an intimate and complex relation to readiness-to-hand. They speak of exactly the same phenomenon, and yet in diametrically opposed ways. Use value, as it were, attempts to present readiness-to-hand, the tool in its tool-being, in the manner of presence-at-hand—as a property that belongs to the thing in its solitary, isolated existence. Even though use value is itself necessarily relational—something is useful not in itself but to someone and for some end—this relationality becomes wrapped up into the substantial being of the thing: the essence of the thing is its use.[14] Yet this substantialized relationality itself represents a rather unstable, contradictory formation, and hence must be immediately reformulated in terms of a physiological functionalism. Use value is not really even a property of the thing, but its "truth"—the ground of its comprehension—rests in the physiological-functional life of the human organism, which exerts its forces in various ways in order to satisfy its needs. Tool-being thus comes to be conceived purely in terms of presence-at-hand, and indeed a physiological, naturalistic reductionism.[15]

A conventional reading of Marx would maintain that use value and physiological need, as what are really real, become, with the production of the commodity, supplanted through exchange value. What I have been arguing instead—not so much interpreting Marx's intentions as radicalizing the analysis of the commodity—is that use value, and indeed the naturalistic-functionalist understanding of human existence, is itself also founded on the commodity form.[16] The only difference is that the former shows itself as without mystery, whereas the latter remains somehow mysterious. Use value and human need would thus represent an even deeper, more impenetrable form of ideology. Nothing less is at work than the complete occlusion by presence-at-hand of readiness-to-hand, the original concernful praxis, and indeed of the world itself as that which we must already be familiar with when we "take care" of things. The lack of mystery corresponds to the very fact that presence-at-hand presents itself as what is *simply there*, given in an immediacy that is beyond question. This is not to deny, of course, that Marx's entire analysis of capitalism ultimately depends on the transformation of use value into exchange value, with the increase in exchange value rather than the production of use value serving as the goal of the activities of the capitalist, and thus becoming the axis around which the entire system of capitalism turns. The point, rather, is that the appearance of things in terms of use value, as a theoretical abstraction from the rich texture of human existence, is grounded in the very process of the self-valorization of value (*Selbstverwertung des Werts*), to use Marx's pregnant expression, by which the never-ending production of ever greater value emerges as the end of human activity.[17] Exchange value does not emerge from use value but rather use value is the shadow cast by exchange value.[18] In light of this last claim we also can begin to sense the internal, constitutive limit of Michel Henry's phenomenological reading of Marx. While recognizing with great clarity the significance of value for Marx's thought, he never comes to terms with the strangeness of the fact that, even while exchange value comes to be identified with value as such, the term *use value* continues to be deployed in opposition to *exchange value*. Far from acknowledging this critical ambiguity in the concept of value—its seemingly irreducible bivalence—Henry insists all the more rigidly on the ontological difference between use value and value as such, without seeing that it is only through the equation of the different kinds of value—the positing of a certain equivalency, an equal value *as* value—that the very difference between these two essentially opposed kinds of values, and indeed between value as such and its opposite, can articulate itself. To the extent that the pure praxis of the individual itself, which Henry will posit not only as the ontological foundation of Marx's analysis, but as the real *tout court*, is understood in terms of use value, we must wonder if it is not merely an effect of the emergence of value as such. Moreover, this seemingly abstruse theoretical oversight leads Henry to contest the need for political revolution, arguing instead that the transformation of capitalism into socialism is a necessary consequence of the objective factors of production developing to the point of complete automation, liberating the production of use value from the production of exchange value, since, in the absence of subjective labor, the latter can no longer take place, freeing the individual to labor for his own self-fulfillment and enter into social relations that satisfy and develop his individuality. Whether or not Henry's idiosyncratic interpretation remains faithful to Marx, all the signs suggest that exploitation will not disappear with the complete automatism of labor. It seems possible, indeed, that the relations of production, in the abstract form of property and the concrete reality of exploitation, will prove capable of surviving the obsolescence of the mode of production from which they arose and in which they are sustained. This is possible precisely because the valuational horizon of capitalism will not itself disappear with the elimination of exchange value, should this indeed ever happen, but, retreating into use value, will become all the more deeply entrenched.

VALUE, PUBLICITY, POLITICS 89

Life itself, as the biological functions merge with industrial automatism, must itself submit to an ever greater degree to a logic of valuation. If previously the worker's labor power, as the origin of value, was itself that which could never have a value, and was thus exempt from submitting to judgments of valorization, now the pure life and praxis of the individual is what must prove itself to be of value: to be life worthy of being lived. If the great truth of the critique of biopolitics consists in recognizing this prospect, it goes astray when it fails to realize that such a critique cannot replace the analysis of capitalism, let alone seek to encompass Marxism (as Hannah Arendt and Agamben will attempt) in its fold.[19] And can we even hope, let alone expect, that exchange value will die a natural death? There is no reason to suppose that the commodity will loosen its grip, even if—or indeed precisely because—this grip has never been and will never be absolute. Capitalism is perhaps not first of all and in its essence a historical phenomenon with a historical telos but a self-reproducing structure that transforms itself, for the sake of its continuing reproduction, in response to both internal and external vicissitudes. Whereas Henry seeks to ontologize life and restrict it to the praxis of the laboring individual in his opposition to the deathly abstraction of capital, we must recognize that life itself is not a being with a discrete origin and locality and destination. At stake in surplus production is not simply the excrescence by life of a deathly excess, but the proliferation of new forms of life. Indeed, life is never really an origin but always already an afterlife, a survival. The ontology of life is a hauntology, if not an oncology. Far from supposing that exchange value, or value as such, will disappear with the automatism of production, we should rather anticipate that the very meaning of production, and all its ontological prerequisites, will be transformed so as to allow capitalism to continue. Capitalist production produces its own ontology.

This brings us to the second question: what are the relations of production in themselves? In a certain sense this question is easier, since the very mysteriousness of the commodity indicates an answer that can to some degree be recognized from within the horizon of metaphysics. It will not be necessary to stray so far from Marx's text. Marx is indeed very clear: the mystery of the commodity form consists in presenting the social relations between human beings as relations between things. We hardly need any help in making sense of this. Indeed, the mystery of the commodity seems in the end rather unmysterious. What could be plainer, after all, than the opposition between a thing and a human being. Yet what makes the commodity form mysterious is the very fact that this opposition, even while remaining as clear as the morning sun, has at the same time become infinitely obscured. If we look at a worker and look at a watch or a bushel of grain, it is still immediately clear what is what and who is who. Every aspect of our political, juridical, social, and economic existence presumes the self-evidence of this distinction, and it is only in certain extreme instances, such as a brain-dead patient, that this self-evidence is called into question. And even the brain-dead patient, even the corpse has a special juridical, social, economic status. Yet when we exchange a bushel of grain for a watch, we bring human labor into relation to human labor. The social relation between the watchmaker and the farmer *appears as, shows itself as*, the relation of one thing to another thing. This mode of appearance, moreover, comes to determine the actual relations between human beings. With capitalism, society, as the totality of human relations, comes to exist through the essential mediation of the commodity.

It was previously suggested that, so far as we conceive of the ideological function of the commodity in terms of the metaphysical interpretation of truth as correctness, then the commodity can only appear as the paradoxical conjunction of correspondence and noncorrespondence. Relations between people appear to us as relations of things, and thus the two kinds of relation must appear somehow analogous, and indeed, with the further development of capitalism, they will coincide more and more. Yet nevertheless things and human beings also continue to appear as completely different. The commodity shows us things at once as they are and in a completely false light—just as the Kantian subject presents us reality as it *objectively* is and yet also as it isn't, since it presents it to us as if things were things in themselves. And just as the distinction between presence-at-hand and readiness-to-hand helps us get past the impasse of Kant's critique of the thing in itself, so too in this case. So long as human beings and things appear as present-at-hand—as objects having a certain nature—then the difference between them shows itself with the utmost clarity. Yet to the extent that they show themselves in their "relationality," everything becomes confused. The problem seems to be that the relations between human beings, as they are shown to us through the commodity, can only appear to us as presence-at-hand, and indeed as a property—namely, exchange value—of things that are present-at-hand as commodities. The commodity thus announces a chasm between two ways in which beings show themselves as presence-at-hand: as this being, every being is different from every other being, and human beings are quite different from things. But in their relations to each other, everything becomes equivalent to everything else: relations between human beings appear as relations between things, and relations between things appear as exchange value.[20]

What the commodity fails to show us, in this way, is precisely that aspect of things and human beings that can only be understood in terms of what we might, in a still too metaphysical terminology, call their original relationality, or, better, difference: they are in themselves what they are only through their relations, which hence cannot be conceived of as mere properties but as ontologically prior—indeed a kind of original hybridity. This suggests, moreover, that to get beyond the impasse of the metaphysical-ideological understanding of the commodity, we must recognize that the difference between human beings and mere things cannot be adequately conceived as the difference between present-at-hand beings. Human being is not something present-at-hand. It *is* in a fundamentally different way from things that are present-at-hand, but it is also not a ready-to-hand tool. Human being is Dasein, the being that has its own being to be, that is consigned to itself in a responsibility and understanding and care for its own being. *"The 'Essence' of Dasein lies in its existence."* The being of Dasein, which is itself a being (*Seiende*), is neither presence-at-hand nor readiness-to-hand but existentiality. What this means is simply that the "characteristics" that are to be said of Dasein are "not 'properties' present-at-hand of some entity which 'looks' so and so and is itself present-at-hand, but are ways to be that are in each case possible for it, and only this."[21] The essence of Dasein is not "what it is," as if it had a certain essential nature—the *eidos* or *ousia*—that makes it what it is, and that is and must be preserved even as it undergoes changes with respect to merely accidental properties, but rather the possible ways for it to be, and indeed possible ways of being that are not merely indifferent properties of a thing, but that are its own—or indeed *my own*—ways of being.[22] Dasein can never be understood in terms of the characteristics that apply to beings that are not of the character of Dasein (*nicht daseinsmäßigen Seienden*). Thus Heidegger distinguishes between the *existentialia*, which articulate the existence-structure of Dasein, and the categories, "characteristics of being for beings whose character is not that of Dasein."[23] The significance of this distinction rests in the etymology of *category*, and the meaning that it had within the horizon of Greek ontology. As Heidegger explains, the Greek *katēgoreisthai* is the "always already preliminary address [*Ansprechen*] to being in the discussion (*logos*) of beings."[24] From the everyday juridical meaning ("making a public accusation, taking someone to task for something in the presence of everyone [*öffentlich anklagen, einem vor allen etwas auf den Kopf zusagen*]"), it develops an ontological sense that must be understood in light of the former. Crucial here is above all that the categories allow for a "public display" of the being in its being: it brings it, as it were, into the open of the marketplace, the *agora*, making it accessible for the "open society" of the public (*Öffentlichkeit*).[25] Existence, by contrast, is precisely what recedes from public accessibility: the ways that are possible for me to be are for me in a radically different way than they are for others. No exchange is possible, as becomes clear above all in the case of my death. Someone can save my life, he can sacrifice himself for me, but he cannot take my death from me—he cannot take away from me my own responsibility for living my own life and dying my own death.

Yet Dasein does not exist in some sort of solipsistic isolation. Dasein is *being in the world*, and *with other Dasein*. This seems to suggest how we might begin to conceive relations between human beings prior to the mode that they assume through the commodity form. The more original essence of human relations, before being shown by the commodity as relations between things, is being-there-with-others, Mitdasein. The "ideological" distortion of the commodity form consists in presenting existence in the manner of a being that is not of the character of, and in accordance with, Dasein. Or in other words: it consists in bringing existence into the *agora*, making it "visible to everyone"—presenting it in terms of an *eidos*, its appearance (*Aussehen*).

We can hardly fail to observe a tension between the existential analysis of Dasein and the "relational" nature of Mitdasein that would seem to threaten our interpretation with incoherence. If the existence of Dasein is characterized by its "mineness," by the fact that it has its *own* possibilities to be, and thus can exist either authentically, "owning up" to its own possibilities, or "inauthentically," losing itself in the "one," then how can a relation between Dasein be conceived in purely existential terms; how can we avoid recourse to categories? Doesn't Mitdasein already belong to the agora? Would it be possible to think Mitdasein other than in terms of an original ideology, a moment of *interpellation*—an original accusation that, if only by naming me, brings me into relation to others by placing me within a space of public visibility? How can we think a form of political existence, or being with others, that is not already characterized by the juridical and liturgical forms to which Agamben calls attention? Heidegger will approach these questions by distinguishing between inauthentic everydayness, the mode of being with others in which the "one" unfolds its dictatorship—only allowing beings to show themselves in the form of the openness and publicness of the public (*Öffentlichkeit*)—and authentic being with others. This authentic being with others founds the historical existence (*Geschichtlichkeit*) of the community, of the *Volk*. This historicizing and "co-historicizing" being-with-others constitutes the people as a destiny (*Geschick*) that is not merely cobbled together from individual fates, but has "already been guided in advance, in our being with one another in the same world and in our resoluteness for definite possibilities"—possibilities, moreover, that are only accomplished, allowing the "power of destiny" to become free, through communication and struggle.[26] Heidegger thus argues that the ground of the historical existence of the community is nothing else than the authentic existence of the Dasein that I myself am in my being toward death. Authentic historicality is only possible as authentic temporality. As he explains in the following paragraph, italicized for emphasis, only an entity that "*is essentially futural so that it is free for its death and can let itself be thrown back upon its factical 'there' by shattering itself against death[,] . . . only authentic temporality which is at the same time finite, makes possible something like fate—that is to say, authentic historicality.*"[27] Authentic historical existence, for Heidegger, must thus be understood as *Wiederholung*, repetition. And, indeed, the repetition of what is unrepeatable. For as he says in the *Contributions*: *nur das Einmalige is wieder-holbar.*[28]

This takes us to the point of both the greatest distance and the greatest proximity between Heidegger and Marx. Heidegger's radicalization of Marx's critique of ideology leads to the concept of the people in its historical existence, and indeed to a certain embrace of National Socialism, and the attempt, as already seen, to assume the spiritual leadership of the movement by directing it toward the question of being. The problem of modern politics becomes, fundamentally, the repetition of the history of the Greek people—a repetition that must take the form, ultimately, of a repetition of the question of being, turning from "fundamental ontology," the form that the question took with the Greeks, to the history of be-ing. Yet while the existential analytic of Dasein will become even more subordinate to the problem of history, historical existence, by continuing to be conceived as the history of a people, remains understood through a certain, perhaps more implicit than explicit, analogy with the authentic relation of Dasein to its own being. Only thus can we understand the necessity of the *Volk*: it is as a people, as a community (even if, granted, a community that has nothing in common, that cannot be conceived in terms of its representation through the *idea* as what is *koinon*), that the original being of "social relations"—of Mitdasein—must be thought.[29] When we try to understand how a people becomes a people, Heidegger explains in the *Contributions*, "all Platonic ways of thinking"—every attempt to assign "an idea, a meaning and value" to the body of the people—fail. It is not some common idea or essence that makes a people into a people but rather "a people first becomes a people when its most unique members appear and when they begin to experience a presentiment." Only thus is it that "a people first becomes free for its law (to be achieved through struggle) as the last necessity of its highest moment," and becomes destined "to stewardship of the truth of be-ing."[30]

The dilemma that we now face is this: if we fail to gain a sense for the nature of "social reality" beyond the way it shows itself through the commodity, then the analysis of the commodity can only repeat the perspective of metaphysics. But if we do gain a sense for this, we must end up conceiving of politics as nothing but the repetition of an original authenticity. How can we radicalize the analysis of the commodity without abandoning the commodity itself? Is there a path *between* Marx and Heidegger? Heidegger's approach marks the point at which the radicalization of the question of ideology leads to its negation—or at least the negation of the possibility of bringing the thought of ideology into relation to any possible materialism.

Is there another way to think the relations of human beings to each other, prior to how they show themselves in the commodity, that does not bring us into this dangerous proximity to the most catastrophic forms of nationalism? Is it enough to replace the *Volk* with the cosmopolitan openness of "communicative action"? Or to think in terms of an original ethical relation to the Other—a Mitdasein that is prior to Dasein—a relationship that cannot be conceived in terms of the authentic relation of the self to itself but involves radical asymmetry? Or perhaps we could think being-with as *différance*, dissemination, writing?[31] Each of these three approaches has its necessity and its justification. But in every case the danger, which becomes most evident when any of them congeals into a dogma to the exclusion of the other two, is that, in trying to get past the seemingly dangerous vagueness of Heidegger's politics, they end up replacing the difficult thought of the people—a thought that is perhaps more open than might at first seem to be the case—with an enforced *openness* that, quickly collapsing into the barren thought of an openness as such, itself becomes a kind of trap. It will then not only seem that social relations are somehow given to us in a prior originary experience that we can gain access to outside the commodity form, but that our access to this original experience is immediate and unproblematic, demanding neither the rigor of thinking nor the patience of history.

Yet before approaching this question, let us bring into clearer view the results of our attempt to read Marx's analysis of the commodity fetish by way of Heidegger. The essence of the mystery of the commodity form would consist in a double concealment, a double untruth. On the one hand, it completely conceals readiness-to-hand behind use value as a property of the thing as something present-at-hand, and ultimately as a function of human life conceived in purely physiological terms. On the other hand, it shows Mitdasein (Dasein with others)—the relations between human beings—as exchange value, a property of present-at-hand beings in their reciprocal relations. The essence of the commodity form, this suggests, is to *show as value*. Through the mystery of the commodity form, readiness-to-hand and Mitdasein show themselves as values.

The concept of value, already a fundamental word for Nietzsche, had assumed the greatest significance in the academic philosophy that was current as Heidegger was working on *Being and Time*, being employed to fill out the Cartesian world of *res extensa*. Thus he imagines an objection to his own rejection of Descartes's interpretation of the world. Even if we grant that with Descartes "the problem of the world and the being of beings encountered environmentally as closest to us remain concealed," perhaps we could treat the Cartesian account of material nature as the basis on which to build up a world by proceeding from the quantitative determinations of *res extensa* to qualitative determinations, including not only those which are reducible to extension but also a further order of nonreducible qualities. In this fashion, it would be possible to superimpose "non-quantifiable value-predicates"—e.g. *beautiful, ugly, useful, useless*—on the material thing, and thus reach, by way of this detour, "those beings which we have characterized ontologically as equipment ready-to-hand": "The Cartesian analysis of the 'world' would thus enable us for the first time to build up securely the structure of what is proximally ready-to-hand; all it takes is to round out the Thing of Nature until it becomes a full-fledged Thing of use, and this is easily done."[32]

Here, the concept of value serves as a supplement to Cartesian reductionism, allowing it, or at least seeming to allow it, to "save the phenomena" of readiness-to-hand. Through value it becomes possible for what is not immediately commensurate with the presence-at-hand of things (*Dingvorhandenheit*) to show itself as the latter. This attempt, as Heidegger observes, cannot be successful: readiness-to-hand cannot be reached in this way. The value-characteristics remain merely the ontic determinations of a being that has the mode of being of a present-at-hand thing: "Adding on value-predicates cannot tell us anything at all new about the being of goods, *but would merely presuppose again that goods have pure presence-at-hand as their kind of being.*"[33]

A similar attempt could be made to express human relations and human existence in terms of value. Kant's practical philosophy might itself be understood in this way. To act morally is to treat human beings as ends in themselves, possessing value (dignity) in themselves, rather than as mere instruments. The moral order rests with the opposition of absolute and relative value. And the same critique must also apply: the ethical dignity of man does not take us beyond the Cartesian horizon of the presence-at-hand of things, even if perhaps it does bring us to the threshold of its comprehensibility, insofar as the human being as an ethical agent, in its absolute value as end in itself, becomes a kind of un-thing (*Unding*) devoid of any content.

Value, in a word, is that through which *what is not originally and fundamentally present-at-hand shows itself as presence-at-hand*. Moreover, insofar as presence-at-hand is not itself originary but constituted, founded in Dasein and readiness-to-hand, then we must conclude that, while *value* is merely a supplement of presence-at-hand, filling it up and making up for what it lacks, it itself, as this supplement, constitutes presence-at-hand. The concept of value is in this way the very essence of ideology: it is what allows and forces every mode of being, and even perhaps being itself, to show itself in its *idea*, its *eidos*; in the *Aussehen* that is visible to all.[34] It brings all things into the *agora*, and submits them to the categories. Value is the original *accusation* that makes all being, and being itself, appear under accusation—and indeed, in a certain, extra-moral sense, guilty.

It is now possible to juxtapose Heidegger and Marx, gaining a sense for the stakes of the *polemos* between them. Heidegger brings into view the possible sense of being *beyond* value, and hence beyond the horizon of metaphysics and the concept of truth as correctness (ultimately: as the *truth value of a proposition*), but he forsakes the commodity as the site of the production of value. Marx thinks the commodity as the site of value production, but he remains within the horizon of metaphysics—so much so that "production" is itself only thinkable as the production of value, and not yet as the bringing forth into truth. How would it then be possible to think with the commodity beyond the commodity, to think the commodity as the site and origination of truth, without only thinking the truth of the commodity?

One could argue that, in his later thought, Heidegger will himself come closer to the thought of the commodity. He will seek to think the thing (*Ding*) as a *Versammlung*, a gathering, that allows for the world, as the coming together of earth and heaven, gods and mortals, to be.[35] *Das Ding dingt Welt. Jedes Ding verweilt das Geviert in ein je Weiliges von Einfalt der Welt*.[36] And at the same time, in thinking the essence of technology as *Ge-Stell*, he will give an even more radical turn to the problem of value. The subtle relation between the *Ge-Stell* and value appears with clarity in the second Bremen lecture. For if, as Heidegger explains, "the essence of technology is the Ge-Stell," which orders "what is present [*das Anwesende*] into standing reserve [*Bestand*]," the very constancy of the standing reserve "consists in the orderable replaceability of the constantly equivalent, which is in place and at the ready."[37] While "the orderable replaceability of the constantly equivalent" seems to refer first to the substitutability of mass-produced parts, it becomes clear that the notion of equivalency, and hence of value, belongs to the very essence of technology, which makes everything become *gleich-giltig*, equi-valent and indifferent. Moreover, as Heidegger argues, nature itself has come to show itself only as *Ge-Stell*, from which it follows that the Cartesian conception of the world as mathematical space-time is itself not the origin of technology but the application of the essence of technology to nature.[38]

These two initiatives divide the commodity into two separate moments: the original assembly (the *agoreuein*, we might say) of the world around the thing and the unworlding of the *Ge-Stell*. For indeed: *"In the essence of the Ge-Stell, the unguarding of the thing as thing occurs as event [Im Wesen des Ge-Stells ereignet sich die Verwahrlosung des Dinges als Ding]."*[39] The thing is left without *die Wahr*, left *wahrlos*, without guard—and thus the world itself is refused. As Heidegger writes, "In thinging, the thing brings the world near and lets the world abide. If the thing, unguarded as it is, does not thing, then the world as world remains denied. In the unguarding of the thing there takes place the refusal of the world."[40] Yet these two moments, precisely in their most radical juxtaposition, enter into a proximity, or indeed become *the same*. As he remarks, what is the same (*das Selbe*) is itself neither equivalent (*das Gleiche*) nor a "merely undifferentiated confluence of the identical" but rather a "relation of differentiation": "World and *Ge-Stell* are the same and thus, to the very extremes of their essence, set against one another."[41]

The same, but not equal, not equivalent. Everything will indeed depend on this distinction between the same and the equal. If we can no longer heed the difference, if we can only think of the same as the equal, then the original worlding assembly and the unworlding of the *Ge-Stell* could not help but appear identical. Yet the collapse of the same into the equal itself follows from the essence of the *Ge-Stell*, insofar as with the *Ge-Stell* everything comes to stand in indifferent equivalency—becomes *gleich-giltig*. By reducing everything to the indifference of equivalency, the *Ge-stell* would also reduce itself to the commodity, collapsing the difference between worlding and unworlding, and thus bring the commodity into view as that which originally gathers together into value, allowing beings to show themselves in their being as value. The commodity, we might say, is the unworld: the world that worlds only in its unworldliness. In this sense, the commodity, *Die Ware*, presents an even more radical unguarding (*Verwahrlosung*) than that achieved by the *Ge-Stell* as such. Indeed, the commodity is the thought of the most extreme, irreparable, *Verwahrlosung*. The guard (*die Wahr*) and the true (*Wahre*) appear simply as commodity, *Ware*. The commodity (*Ware*) is nothing but the truth (*Wahrheit*) that it shows, which is at one and the same time, in their perfect identity, truth and its destitution. To think the *Ge-Stell* as *Ge-Stell* and not as commodity is, above all, to insist on the difference between the same and the equal, and thus between the world and its unworlding: the guarding of the true—*Die Wahr(e)*—and its unguarding dilapidation (*Verwahrlosung*). The history of be-ing is the possibility of holding open this difference.

The equi-valency of the *Ge-Stell* yanks everything together into the homogeneous absence of distance (*gleichförmige Abstandlose*).[42] Nearness and distance of what is present remain lacking (*Nähe und Ferne des Anwesenden bleiben aus*).[43] The loss of distance, invoked in the introductory hint, is now understood in terms of the *Ge-Stell*. The *Ge-Stell* collapses proximity and distance together into the distance-less (*abstandlos*). Proximity and distance, brought into the equivalency of quantifiable values, come to appear fundamentally identical. Yet the *Ge-Stell* is not just the highest danger, the complete forgetting of the essence of being, but also the possibility of salvation. For "insofar as world refuses its worlding, what happens with world is not nothing, but rather from refusal there radiates the lofty nearness of the most distant distance of the world."[44] To the extent that the *Ge-Stell* is experienced as *Ge-Stell*—which is to say, in terms of the history of be-ing as the forgetting of the essence of being and the refusal (*Verweigerung*) of world—then the very collapse of the difference between proximity and distance, the very fact of their being posited as equals, shines a light on the world to come. This positing-as-equal, experienced as such, opens the way to an experience of the opposition (*Entgegensetzung*). What is most far appears in a lofty—not merely leveling, trivializing—proximity. For the *Ge-Stell* to show itself as commodity, however, would mean above all that distance and proximity are neither simply identical nor opposed but always both at once insofar as the opposition is at once posited and set aside. The commodity is hence *entsetzlich*, unsettling, outrageous: the *Ge-Stell* in its unsettling outrageousness—its *Entsetzlichkeit*. Precisely this will suggest the secret affinity of the commodity and television.

To hold the *Ge-Stell* back from the commodity means, more than anything, rooting it in the history of be-ing. This is achieved by situating "placing" (*Stellen*) and "putting" (*Setzen*) within the original destiny of be-ing. If positioning (*das Stellen*), as the essence of the *Ge-Stell*, determines the contemporary epoch of be-ing, it is because it belongs to be-ing from the beginning, resting in its "inceptual destiny." Yet while the *thesis* is "concealed in the essence of *phusis* at the dawn of the destiny of be-ing," it is only in the "later epochs of the modern dispensation of being," and above all with Kant's definition of being as "absolute position"—the "positedness and positionhood of the object"—that it is revealed as such through the language of philosophy.[45] The history of be-ing would thus be nothing else than thinking the *thesis* that is originally at play in *phusis*, since indeed the "initial destiny" of be-ing, responsible for the very fact that it exists historically, involves the radical (dis)jointure of *phusis* and *thesis*. The *thesis* concealed in *phusis* is, as it were, the original production, the original productivity, that dis-poses and un-settles (*ent-setzt*) nature from the beginning, bringing it outside the simplicity of its essence.[46] It is, as it were, *différance*. But, in just this sense, it would also be the impossibility of thinking *phusis-thesis* as a beginning, of claiming be-ing as a ground. To think the *Ge-Stell as* commodity would be to posit this originary productivity, the production of value as the positing of equivalency, as the impossibility of returning to the origin by *repeating* the unique beginning.

To think the commodity, to allow the *Ge-Stell* to show itself as commodity, is thus to decide against decision. The commodity is the *Ent-scheidung* that in-differentiates distance and proximity, *phusis* and *thesis*, world and unworld, truth and untruth, and even truth as correctness and truth as disconcealment-concealment. It is thus a kind of radical, always already disarticulated and disarticulating, hybridity: precisely that which the decision, be it the "official decision" of the modern constitution or its Heideggerian remedy and response, would seek to draw apart, sundering into two separate, if complementary or structurally united, realms.

9

REPRODUCTION

> The externality of the superstructure with respect to the base . . . is an externality exercised, in large measure, in the form of *interiority*.
>
> Louis Althusser, *On the Reproduction of Capital*

Precisely because the commodity shows itself as *de-decisioning*—as the destitution of decision—the "theorization" of the commodity does not demand choosing Marx over Heidegger, or Heidegger over Marx, but bringing both to a point of undecidability. This undecidability takes the form of two formulations that are in a sense equivalent. On the one hand, the commodity will show itself as the collapse of ontological difference, and indeed of the very possibility of the history of be-ing: the commodity is being(s). This is the path from Heidegger to Marx: with Heidegger against Heidegger for Marx. On the other hand, the commodity will appear as the production and reproduction of the phenomenological conditions of production—of the very mode of showing through which and as which production can take place. This is the path from Marx to Heidegger: with Marx against Marx for Heidegger. Starting out from this first path, we followed it to the end, but, in so doing, we could not help also taking a few steps down the second path as well. Now we must go further, taking our departure from Louis Althusser's famous discussion of ideology, published in English in *Lenin and Philosophy* under the title "Ideology and Ideological State Apparatuses (Notes Towards an Investigation)," referred to in what follows as "ISA."

This text presents special challenges. Its canonization as *the* text by Althusser read in introductory theory courses has led its readers to ignore not only its complex systematic interrelation to his other work but also the way in which all of his writings, according to his own account of his authorial practice, serve as interventions, responding in complex fashion to a certain *conjunction*: the confluence of factors determining the particular nature of the historical situation.[1] Moreover, as Warren Montag notes, the published text of "Ideology and Ideological State Apparatuses" is itself merely a collection of fragments drawn from a far longer study, which itself, published in 1995 as "De la superstructure," has only just recently been made available in English translation.[2] The latter text, conceived as a sort of manual of Marxism-Leninism, seeks to develop its principles in a plain and accessible fashion, and indeed, when read as a whole, possesses a didactic aspect that is not always apparent from the extracts on ideology.[3] Indeed, as Montag explains, the ISA essay jarringly juxtaposes two quite different kinds of material, combining a crude rehearsal of a "'fundamental principles'-like mode of production, base, and superstructure" with "absolutely unprecedented notions like the interpellation of the subject, whose exposition in 'plain' language renders them more rather than less obscure, more rather than less open to misunderstanding."[4] Moreover, what is most extraordinary about the essay, as Étienne Balibar notes, is lost rather than gained when it is read in the context of the whole from which its component parts were drawn: it suspends its "argument in the vicinity of the decisive articulation—signposted and simultaneously spirited away—which is materialized by the dotted line."[5] Readers were thus forced to themselves search for the answer to the question that was posed—an answer that Althusser himself provides in the longer work that had been held back. For this reason I have chosen to focus on the ISA essay considered as an isolated fragment: it is the potentiality of the text, rather than its actuality, that concerns us here.

Given all the complexities surrounding the ISA essay, one can easily lose sight of its most radical aspect: the attempt to rethink ideology beyond the limits of the "ideological conception of ideology" that, continuing to haunt the Marxist tradition in all its various overtly and covertly humanist variants, ultimately represents a failure to achieve a truly "scientific" perspective. It is a matter, as Montag puts it, of "an irreversible break with all preceding theories of ideology, which, once noted, prevents any regression back to a notion of ideology as ideality in both senses of the term: a system made up of ideas that in turn possesses an ideal (i.e., immaterial) existence of the conviction-persuasion of the minds of individuals who then determine themselves (or more precisely, their bodies) to act in witting or unwitting obedience to this system."[6] It is a question not only of getting beyond a "representational" account of ideology, according to which ideology involves the errant, illusionary representation of some nonideological reality, but of recognizing that this representational concept of ideology, by supposing ideology to consist in essence in some sort of representation or idea, is itself of essence ideological.[7] Even though the question of ideology per se seems to make a rather limited appearance in Althusser's work as a whole, it nevertheless assumes a central importance, serving, as it were, as the shibboleth granting passage into a scientific Marxism.

The significance of Althusser's concept of ideology for this inquiry consists above all in this transitional aspect: it will serve as a thread leading into another dimension of theory, and indeed beyond not only an "ideological theory of ideology," but the problematic of ideology as such. Yet we also mustn't lose sight of the invocation of a more classical, dogmatically Marxist vocabulary of "production," "base," "superstructure," if we are to discern the most radical tendency of Althusser's theorization of ideology. It is, as I hope to show, precisely by taking the idea of the "reproduction of the conditions of production" seriously that Althusser leads us to the greatest insights into what we might call the subterranean conjuncture of Marx and Heidegger: a conjuncture that even now, at the beginning of the new century, remains in force. It is to the hidden lineaments of this conjuncture, tectonic collisions that are still playing themselves out, that my own attempt at a "symptomatic reading" of Althusser's ISA essay will attend.

Althusser begins with an economic truth so rudimentary, so basic that it could not escape even a child: "As Marx said, every child knows that a social formation which did not reproduce the conditions of production at the same time as it produced would not last a year. The ultimate condition of production is therefore the reproduction of the conditions of production."[8] By inquiring into the reproduction of the conditions of production, Althusser enters a "domain which is both very familiar . . . and uniquely ignored [*singulièrement méconnu*]."[9] What is so plain to the child, however, is not something that is merely empirically given, not mere sense certainly, but a certain global, radical, thorough—in a word, philosophical—perspective that in the actions and vision of the average adult falls ever farther from view. This is because the perspective of production has become so entrenched in its "tenacious obviousness"—"ideological obviousnesses of an empiricist type," Althusser glosses—that the perspective of reproduction remains abstract: not only one-sided, but distorted. The very tenacious obviousness of the perspective of production itself demands the exclusion from the horizon of visibility of the reproduction of the conditions of production. The perspective of production thus involves an essential blindness to that which it itself draws into view as the consequent extension of its own inherent reasoning. The thought of the reproduction of the conditions of production is elicited, at a more or less purely theoretical level, by the perspective of production and yet repressed at the level of praxis, since, even though it is ultimately and indeed above all necessary for the praxis of production, which comes into contradiction with itself when reproduction is not taken into account, it must always be kept from view for actions to take place, since action demands a kind of narrowing of the theoretical perspective, a blindness to that which stands beyond a certain limit. This is not because praxis is necessarily illusory, self-deceived, but because it involves an essential limiting of perspective, a perspectival reduction, as becomes clear if we consider the sensory apparatus of an animal, which, filtering out the vast majority of possible stimuli, brings it into perceptual, motorial, and cognitive relation to only a few aspects of its environment. The manager of the firm is of course fully cognizant of the need to maintain the supply of raw materials and the machinery of production, preserve cash flow, and retain a competent workforce. Such awareness is essential to his managerial activities. But he will most likely have only a dim awareness, or even an almost willful blindness, to those aspects of the reproduction of the conditions of production that fall beyond his functional competency. The haute bourgeois industrialist may have a keener awareness of these things, but the "perspective of the firm" still orients his or her understanding. The child, however, lacking a cultivated practical sense—having yet to regard itself and the world from a certain narrowly practical perspective—will tend to see the very things that adults cannot: it will ask questions with a restless curiosity, and with no sense for their utility.

Starting out from the perspective of production within capitalism, Althusser discovers ever more deeply hidden forms of the reproduction of the conditions of production. Yet his own perspective is obviously not limited to bourgeois ideology—the perspective that is immediately produced within the bourgeois mode of production as something self-evident—but, following Marx, is, as it were, production historical, presupposing an understanding of production that transcends particular historically articulated modes of production while at the same time allowing these to come into view. Assuming that "every social formation arises [*relève*] from a dominant mode of production," "the process of production sets to work the existing productive forces in and under definite relations of production."[10] If production is to continue to take place, if the social order is to exist, then it "must reproduce the conditions of its production at the same time as it produces, and in order to be able to produce."[11] This is of course nothing more than the standard perspective of historical materialism—for Althusser, the *science of history*.[12] As he explains in "Contradiction and Overdetermination," the great discovery that leads beyond the impasse of both

Hegel's idealism and the "economico-political Phenomenology" of economists like Turgot and Smith is an understanding of abstract economic reality as "the effect of a deeper, more concrete reality: *the mode of production* of a determinate social formation" such that, for the first time, "individual economic behavior . . . is measured according to its *conditions of existence*" rather than merely described as an immediate given.[13] The theoretical innovation that underwrites the ISA essay, and that is developed in detail in *On the Reproduction of Capital*, consists above all in stressing the importance of the relations of production over the forces of production for the conceptualization of the base while regarding superstructure in terms of the structures enabling the reproduction of the relations of production.[14] Although continuing to insist that the base, and hence production, is "determining in the last instance," he is nevertheless thereby able to avoid the pitfall of vulgar Marxism, which, inverting Hegel, merely reverses the relative status of the ideal and the real without challenging idealism's more fundamental conceit: namely, that the relation between the real and ideal is an expressive, representational, or even illusionary relation between essence and appearance. Indeed, the reference to phenomenology that I already invoked is anything but casual, nor is it just a matter of a polemical engagement with an eclectic phenomenological Marxism such as that of Sartre or Merleau-Ponty. Phenomenology inhabits Marxism as the ideological residue that will prove to be most difficult to root out, since it takes form as the very conception of Marxism—above all the Marxist theory of ideology—as a theory of how substructure can show itself as it is in itself. The ISA essay confronts the humanistic and phenomenological tradition of thinking ideology—the ideological theory of ideology, in other words—by means of an extraordinary methodological wager. Rather than allowing the theorization of ideology to constitute itself through the resources of ideology, he will take an abrupt turn into what might seem like a purely materialist mode of explanation. This could easily lead one to suppose that Althusser's scientific antihumanism involves a simple rejection of the insights of the phenomenological tradition, offering in its place a dogmatic materialism, in which the very problem of access, of how materiality comes to show itself, can no longer be raised. If this were so, it would hardly seem possible to bring Althusser's Marxism and Henry's Marx into conversation. Yet Althusser's production-historical account of ideology does not so much reject the phenomenological problematic as transform it. Against a phenomenology of self-showing, which will find its economic expression in more or less transparent and immediate descriptions of economic agency, Althusser proposes what we might call an a-phenomenology: an account of the manner of phenomenality that belongs to that which can *never* show itself as itself. Materiality is not a nonphenomenological principle—it is precisely not the dogmatic first principle, given in a kind of immediacy, for scientific inquiry. Rather: it is that which is essentially dark, essentially withdrawn and withdrawing; that which can only show itself through irreparable displacements of what it is in itself, since its "in itself" is nothing else than this capacity for and necessity of displacement. This brings us before the blind spot that conditions Althusser's thought: this a-phenomenology runs up against an internal limit to its theorization, and is forced to take flight before its own insights. It is as if there were a tension between the perspective of perspectivity as such, which first allows Althusser to enter into the perspective of production, and the particular insights to which the perspective of production and reproduction itself seems to lead him. What I hope to show in what follows is that by conceiving of production in terms of an a-phenomenological materialism, the perspective of production can be developed in such a way as to open up rather than foreclose the question of ideology. And at the same time: by developing the perspective of production to its furthest consequences, even beyond Althusser, a certain return to the phenomenological problematic in the more proper sense becomes at once necessary and possible.

But let us again pick up the thread of Althusser's argument. He starts off with what is so obvious that even "the average economist"—literally, the first economist to come along—knows it, though indeed in this he is "no different . . . than the average capitalist": namely, it is necessary to anticipate the loss of the capital (raw material, fixed installations, instruments of production) expended in production. This is the perspective of the firm, of the immediate producer of commodities. But the perspective of the firm can only make sense of the reproduction of the material means of production. It fails to bring into view what is no less, indeed perhaps far more important: the reproduction of the *forces* of production—which is to say "of labor power." For indeed: "the reproduction of labor power takes place essentially outside the firm."[15] This reproduction nevertheless seems at first glance to be straightforward enough. The wages paid to the workers represent nothing else than "that part of the value produced by the expenditure of labor power which is indispensable for its reproduction," though this reflects not a "biological" but a "historical" minimum.[16] This historical minimum, moreover, is historical in a double sense, reflecting not only the capitalist class's recognition of the workers' needs, but "the historical needs imposed by the proletarian class struggle."[17]

Yet the reproduction of the forces of production itself requires more than just the material conditions of their reproduction. Labor power must be "competent": "suitable to be set to work in the complex system of the process of production." Within capitalism, the reproduction of the manifold skills needed by labor power mostly takes place not on the factory floor but in schools. Schools, moreover, teach not only technical "know-how" (savoir faire), but the rules of good behavior—the specific attitude each agent must observe following the division of labor, and hence "rules of morality, civic and professional conscience, which actually means rules of respect for the socio-technical division of labor and ultimately the rules of the order established by class domination."[18] Put "more scientifically," this means that the reproduction of labor power is not only a reproduction of skills needed by various occupations, but "a reproduction of its submission to the rules of the established order."[19] What must thus be reproduced differs dramatically according to the social division of labor: in the case of the "agents of exploitation and repression" it is no longer a question, as it is with the workers, of mere submission to the ruling ideology but of an ability to "manipulate the ruling ideology correctly," such as to "provide for the domination of the ruling class 'in words.'"[20] Starting out from the seemingly simple problem of the reproduction of the conditions of production, conceived purely in terms of "substructure," we are thus brought before the "effective presence [*présence efficace*] of a new reality: *ideology*."[21] It is a matter of the reproduction of the particular set of beliefs, affective dispositions, desires, and self-understanding—an *ethos*, one could say, or as Althusser puts it, an "ability"—that allows a certain individual to fulfill a certain role within the total labor process, entering into the necessary relations both to other individuals and to the means of production.[22] "Each mass ejected *en route*," Althusser explains, is "practically provided with the ideology which suits the role it has to fulfill in class society." Those who are destined to be exploited are provided with "a 'highly-developed' 'professional,' 'ethical,' 'civic,' 'national,' and a-political consciousness"; the agents of exploitation are given the "ability to give the workers orders and speak to them: 'human relations'"; the agents of repression, the "ability to give orders and enforce obedience 'without discussion,' or [the] ability to manipulate the demagogy of a political leader's rhetoric"; and finally the professional ideologist, the "ability to treat consciousnesses with the respect, i.e. with the contempt, blackmail, and demagogy they deserve, adapted to the accents of Morality, of Virtue, of 'Transcendence,' of the Nation, of France's World Role, etc."[23]

In this way, the inquiry into the reproduction of the relations of production ultimately challenges the "topographical" presentation of the "social whole" in terms of a substructure that supports the superstructure as its base. For it indeed becomes apparent that the problem of the relation between the different instances comprising the social whole must be posed in terms of the question of reproduction. This will demand going beyond a merely "descriptive theory" to "theory as such [*théorie tout court*]."[24] Whereas descriptive theory merely describes different entities within the social whole (such as the state), and thus allows for their interrelations to be conceived through the uncritical application of forms of causality drawn from the naturalistic perspective of ordinary language, theory as such will alone make it possible to "understand further the mechanisms of the State in its functioning" as it actually functions.[25] What eludes "descriptive theory" is above all the operation of the ideological state apparatuses, and precisely since these function not according to violence, which necessarily involves an efficient causality, but ideology.[26]

Althusser opens his discussion of ideology with an "astonishing paradox": while Marx presents an explicit theory of ideology, he does not offer a Marxist theory of ideology. Whereas the theorization of ideology in *The German Ideology* remains positivist and historicist, conceiving of ideology simply as "a pure illusion, a pure dream, i.e. as nothingness," *Capital*, while containing "many hints towards a theory of ideologies (most visibly, the ideology of the vulgar economists) . . . does not contain that theory itself, which depends for the most part on a theory of ideology in general."[27] It is curious that, as if to emphasize the astonishingness of this claim to the point that it might seem not only astonishing, but tendentious, Althusser does not elaborate what these hints might be. This makes his account of ideology seem even further than it actually is from others before him, such as Lukács, who have sought through sophisticated strategies to discover in Marx's later writings the resources for a more radical, and radically "Marxist," theorization of the commodity. It is as if Althusser sought, by repressing these connections and suppressing these hints, to hold open the space in which to develop, based on a seemingly rigorous application of materialist principles, a novel account of ideology, forcing the appearance of an "epistemological break" even while at the same time locating the essence of this break within Marx himself, and thus continuing to maintain its ultimate orthodoxy. Nevertheless, in the first part of *Reading Capital*, Althusser offers a striking indication of what one of these hints, and indeed the most important, might be. Explaining the provenance of his concept of a symptomatic (*symptomale*) reading in Marx and ultimately Spinoza, he claims that Marx became the thinker that he is by rejecting a "religious myth of *reading*" and founding his thinking on the rigorous distinction between ideology and science. Whereas in the *1844 Manuscripts* Marx believes that the essence of the human is immediately legible "in the transparency of its alienation," *Capital*, in contrast, "exactly measures a distance and an internal dislocation [*décalage*] in the real, inscribed in its *structure*, a distance and a dislocation such as to make their own effects themselves illegible, and the illusion of an immediate reading of them the ultimate apex of their effects: *fetishism*."[28] Fetishism, as the illusion of an immediate legibility, is thus the ultimate effect of an internal distance and dislocation inscribed in the very structure of the real; irreducibly bound up with the real in its very reality. The real's very reality—effectivity, activity, *energeia*—involves the effacement of its legibility. Whereas the cause of the ideal becomes perfectly legible in its effect, the real is that whose effect is precisely what refuses to allow the cause, the real itself, to be read off from it. Every realism that insists on the legibility of the real—every dogmatic empiricism or materialism—is nothing else than a covert idealism. It follows from this that fetishism is of the essence of ideology. This does not mean that every ideology is a fetish, or a form of commodity fetishism, but that what is most ideological about ideology—the promise that it offers of its own immediate legibility—is itself a kind of fetishism. Fetishism is, as it were, not ideology as such but that aspect of every ideology that allows for the ideological interpretation of ideology. It is the promise of legibility that every ideology bears within it.

I previously argued that the commodity form is nothing else than the originary, constitutive ideology of capitalism, presenting things and their relations, the relations between human beings, and even human existence itself in terms of value. The concept of value in the context of ideology nevertheless involves a fundamental ambiguity. Value is both the ideology of ideology—the way that ideology is represented within ideology—and the truth of ideology. Relations of production take place as relations of value, rooted in the equivalency of exchange, but they are also represented as values. This representation at once represents them as they are and as they are not—to wit, in a completely distorted fashion. The representation of relations of production as value is at once true and false: correct and incorrect.

Nevertheless, for Althusser, the concept of value is not the key to reading *Capital* but to its misreading: for indeed, if it is, as Henry will contend, the central concept of *Capital*, it is only because the latter remains basically Hegelian in character, seeking to reduce capitalism's history to the development of the simple, primitive, and original concept of value.[29] Yet it would not be difficult to show that the concept of value we have sought to articulate is itself compatible with, and indeed analogous to, Althusser's understanding of fetishism. If it is idealistic to regard values as rooted in material reality in such a way that they make its essence manifest, it is no less idealistic to regard value as a subjective fiction. What is no longer idealistic, no longer ideological, is to understand values as the dislocating effect of the real. The real, one could even say, exists as the power of valency and equivalency by which what is irreducibly singular is originarily dislocated from its irreducible singularity, and indeed becomes identifiable as singular, as comparatively different from everything else, by way of this power of dislocation. The mathematical, teleological, and even theological concepts of nature all remain in this way equally ideological, since in each case the axiological—be it natural or divine purposes, qualitative or quantitative determinations—presents itself as a kind of immediacy rather than as a structurally inherent dislocation of the real. Yet it may be harder to concede that our concept of value, and Althusser's understanding of fetishism, can help illuminate the discussion of ideology that emerges in the ISA essay, since on the surface this seems to move in an entirely different direction: toward the question of the subject—and the Subject; toward Freud, Lacan, the unconscious, and structuralism. Yet here too, as I will now argue, we discover theoretical convergences.

Taking up again the thread of Althusser's argument, let us consider his first two theses on the nature of ideology. These are

I) Ideology represents the imaginary relationship of individuals to their real conditions of existence.[30]

II) Ideology has a material existence.[31]

Regarding the first thesis: ideology does not involve the merely false, dreamlike, nugatory representation of a reality that really exists but rather the representation of the "imaginary" way in which human beings relate to real conditions of existence. Yet we should not suppose that the "imaginary" relationship represented by ideology could be somehow excluded from the real. Rather, the nature of the real is such that it can itself only allow an imaginary relationship. Precisely because the real is such that it only shows itself, or even relates to itself, through a dislocation, only an imaginary relation to the real is possible: the imaginary relation is the only possible *practical* relation to the real since the relation itself, to the real and within the real, takes place by way of imagination—by way of a simplification and reduction of the real. What Althusser understands as the subject, which does not correspond to any given reality and hence escapes a merely empirical analysis, is, I would suggest, precisely such a dislocation and simplification of the real.[32] At the same time, we also must not confuse the representation of the imaginary relation with the imaginary relation itself. The difference between them is crucial, and it would be a grave mistake to suppose that the imaginariness of the relation to the real already constitutes the essence of ideology. The imaginary relation to the real conditions of existence is the basis of ideology, and already involves a dislocation of the real. This dislocation concerns how we conceive of our place within the social whole; the virtues according to which we live; the things we believe in; even the emotions and moods that we have (cynicism, resignation . . .); all of these are forms of the complex "reduction" through which praxis is possible. Yet ideology does not consist simply in this dislocation itself, but rather in a representation of the dislocation—of the "imaginaries" through which agency and action are possible—that allow these to manifest themselves in a kind of cognitive immediacy and to appear as something naturally given, self-given. The dislocation, as it were, is itself achieved through its representation, since representation is of the very essence of the dislocation that has occurred. Or, indeed, one can hardly draw a *real* distinction between the dislocation itself and its representation. Ideology, in this sense, is itself grounded in an ideology of ideology: it is this ideology of ideology that allows for the fictional relation to the real conditions of existence to be represented as ideas that have an "immediate legibility," to use the expression from *Reading Capital*. This ideology of ideology is, fundamentally, the belief that one's material practices are motivated by ideas that are *either* true or false; that correspond or fail to correspond to reality. Yet the ideology of ideology itself is not completely false but already involves the recognition, albeit in a completely distorted form, that "the 'ideas' of a human subject exist in his actions, or ought to exist in his actions, and if that is not the case, it lends him other ideas corresponding to the actions (however perverse) that he does perform."[33] The ideology of ideology, this is to say, consists not only in the belief that our beliefs may be reduced to the ideas that we have, but in the insistence that these ideas determine our actions; that there must be a correspondence between belief and action, theory and praxis—a belief and insistence that is true to the extent that we exist in ideology. To pass beyond the ideology of ideology is first of all to change the order of priority between praxis and belief. This alone could free us from the circle in which we find ourselves trapped, though from within ideology this escape must appear as an absurd wager, a leap into the untruth of materiality.

This brings us to the second thesis. By claiming that ideology has a material existence, Althusser introduces another perspective from which the same phenomena, the fictional relations to the real conditions of existence, can be understood. Whereas the first perspective, the ideological interpretation of ideology, draws the fictional relations up toward the ethereal heavens of the pure Platonic ideas, allowing them to appear as immediately comprehensible on their own, this other perspective draws them back down to the real. In the case of a single individual, ideas *"are his material actions inserted into material practices governed by material rituals which are themselves defined by the material ideological apparatus from which derive the ideas of that subject."*[34]

At this point we might recall my reading of Heidegger's lecture course "On the Essence of Truth" as a radicalization of the question of ideology. Althusser's characterization of the ideology of ideology comes very close to the insight that the essence of ideology is the determination of being in terms of the idea, and hence *Vorhandenheit* and truth as correspondence. Here, moreover, he seems on the verge of repeating the claim that emerged from his brief discussion of fetishism in the first part of *Reading Capital*, recognizing in ideology the concealment of the dislocating effects of materiality, the promise of an immediate legibility. Yet at just this point, it would seem, Althusser draws back from this insight. Materiality comes to offer itself as a new kind of legibility, a new immediacy. In seeking to understand ideology beyond the perspective of ideology itself—beyond ideology's own ideology of ideology—Althusser ends up merely privileging one kind of presence-at-hand over another: the presence-at-hand of the idea is rooted in the presence-at-hand of materiality. Materiality thus emerges as the reality to which ideology, properly conceived, corresponds. The term *materiality* forces precisely that which is furthest from immediately presenting itself as presence-at-hand—most resistant to the theoretical gaze—to take form as something present-at-hand.[35] Ideology represents this materiality as ideality, yet materiality, to be thus representable, must have already shown itself as presence-at-hand. The originary ideology, the originary "imaginary," this suggests, is the presentation as present-at-hand. Thus Althusser seems to renounce his most radical theoretical impulses: rather than understanding materiality as that which by essence shows itself other than it is, as if its essence were to be always dislocating its essence, he instead opposes to a merely ideological legibility of the idea the genuine, scientific legibility of materiality. If the idea, understood ontologically rather than merely ontically, consists not in a certain kind of being (spiritual rather than material) but in the promise of immediate legibility—if the idea, as it were, is that which allows the thing to be understood as it is in itself, or is indeed its very legibility and visibility in itself—then it could seem that Althusser's invocation of materiality amounts to the worst kind of idealism; and indeed an idealism secured in the last instance through a kind of wordplay, preserving the old horizon of questioning by juggling around its terminology.

Justifying his expansive use of the concept of materiality, Althusser, "at the risk of being taken for a Neo-Aristotelian," applies the formula that Aristotle often uses to untangle aporiae: "'matter is discussed in many senses,' or rather . . . it exists in different modalities, all rooted in the last instance in 'physical' matter [*matière 'physique'*]."[36] Precisely this Aristotelian formulation, by insisting on "physical matter" as the root sense, represses what the invocation of Aristotle cannot but call attention to: the concept of matter not only has its own history, even if it will also present itself as the key to historical critique—but is itself fundamentally metaphysical. In a passage from the *Contributions to Philosophy*, Heidegger notes the Aristotelian origins of precisely those foundational concepts of Marx's materialist concept of history that in Althusser often appear self-evident. The thought of becoming and motion, Heidegger claims, is itself technical, is itself rooted in *technē*, implying that the concepts of movement and revolution (*Umschlag, metabolē*), even when applied to history as a whole, remain rooted in the interpretation of the beingness (*Seiendheit*) of beings in terms of constancy and presence (*ousia* and *parousia*), which itself in turn presupposes the interpretation of beings as *eidos/idea*, and hence also the opposition *morphē/hulē* (form/shape, matter).[37] But what is ultimately at work in these Platonic and Aristotelian formulations, and this is perhaps the most crucial point—anticipating the analysis of the *Ge-Stell* in "The Question concerning Technology"—is the relation of *technē* and *phusis*. *Phusis*, for Heidegger, names the "original interpretation" of beings within Greek thought.[38] It is not "nature" in any modern sense but a "going forth" (*aufgehen*). Yet while *phusis* is prior to *technē*, and indeed the latter can only be experienced and known on the basis of the former, for just this reason

> the more [the question] brings itself before beings *as beings* [*das Seiende als solches*] and thus interrogates beingness and entrenches itself in the formula *ti to hon*, the more *technē* must then precisely come to count as what determines the viewpoint. *Phusis* is not *technē*, which now means that what pertains to *technē*, namely, the skilled gaze in advance at the *eidos* ['look'], the *representing* and bringing before oneself of the look—precisely all this occurs *of its own accord* in *phusis*, in *hon ē hon*. *Ousia* is the *eidos*, *idea*, as emergent (*phusis*), as stepping forth (*alētheia*), yet as *offering a view* [*Anblick bietend*].[39]

What Heidegger thinks as *technē*, this passage seems to suggest, is a kind of original *placement* and *displacement* that is placed both within and outside of *phusis*, such that *phusis* can never enter into relation to itself, can never become an opening for its truth, without getting beyond and outside of itself. *Technē*, as it were, makes itself equivalent to, and indeed takes the place of, *phusis*. *Technē* comes to occur *of its own accord* in *phusis*, as if it were the very nature of nature.

The Aristotelian concept of materiality, this suggests, is itself bound up with, and in a sense both the product and the production of, what we might call an original ideology consisting in *stellen, setzen, gleichsetzen*, or indeed the positing of original equivalency, the *katagoreuein* that gathers into the open market.[40] Yet perhaps this is also precisely Althusser's point—that the "materiality" of social life, through which relations of production are constituted, is itself nothing else than original ideology. The problem with the ideological view of ideology is not that it fails to establish a theoretical relation to the "material substructure" as the "truth" of reality but rather that it never gets how materiality must be always already invested with ideology since it is by this alone that it can achieve a relational structure. Materiality, this is to say, is always already dislocated away from pure materiality. The trick, as it were, is to come to understand both materiality and ideality as two theoretically tendentious expressions for this dislocation, this "always-already-hybridity." Material is only the dislocation of ideality, and ideality only the dislocation of materiality. The dream of pure materiality, like the dream of pure ideality, is nothing else than the attempt to conceive as a "thing in itself" what can only be known through its dislocating effects. The claim that "ideology has no history" and is indeed eternal, being "omni-present, trans-historical and therefore immutable in form throughout the extent of history" has, of course, scandalized Althusser's readers, since it would seem to call into question the very possibility of a radically emancipatory revolution. Yet this really just means that materiality will always be dislocated within itself; that it can never present itself with a pure immediacy. Praxis for Althusser, like truth for Heidegger, involves a kind of inherent latency, dislocation, *Entstellung*. What is *ideological*, regardless of whether it takes the form of idealism or materialism, is the forgetting of this latency.

Keeping this in mind, let us now turn to Althusser's third, central thesis on the nature of ideology, the famous claim that ideology interpellates individuals as subjects.[41] Beyond merely involving the application of Lacanian structuralism to Marxism, it could be said to articulate precisely this original *katagoreuein*, the original equivalency that is the radical foundation of ideology. At stake is nothing else than the original "accusation," the accusation that makes us guilty in the most radical sense in our relation to others—which is to say: first capable of being guilty, of being responsible. It is in this sense that, even before being born, the child, through the very family structures that anticipate its arrival, has already been constituted as a subject. For indeed, to be a subject is to be both a "free subjectivity, a center of initiatives, author of and responsible for its actions" and "a subjected being, who submits to a higher authority, and is therefore stripped of all freedom except that of freely accepting his submission."[42] This structure, which Althusser will understand in terms of the Lacanian opposition of Subject and subject, is analogous to what Kant, in the second *Critique*, conceives as the essence of moral personhood: the free submission to a law that one has freely created for oneself. Indeed, it is the structure of the law itself: precisely what Agamben will understand as the relation of the sovereign to bare life—the originary subjugation of "life" to "law." Only for Althusser, unlike Kant, the seemingly pure circular structure of self-jurisdiction is itself referred to an exterior materiality; the appearance of a pure, tautological, hermeneutic circularity—and perhaps ideology is in its foundation nothing but this *appearance* of circularity by which the self believes itself given over to itself—reveals itself not as an illusion, since every opposition between illusion and reality belongs within this circle, but as the convoluted maze that keeps us from an encounter.

The problem with this analysis is that rather than conceiving of this original equivalency as bound up with materiality—determined in the last instance, as it were, by materiality—Althusser regards it as the autonomous effect of ideology, which thus seems to have a completely abstract relation to materiality. A strange fissure rends his analysis: while the existence of ideology is material, while materiality is always already ideological—a hybrid complex, not altogether unlike the strife between world and earth in Heidegger—the subject is itself a pure effect of ideology. An unbridgeable abyss opens between the individual, who exists through material praxis, and the subject, who emerges in what must ultimately appear as a kind of groundless theological event. While it may be true that, as in Pascal, belief follows from our behavior, the relation between them assumes a thoroughly mysterious character. It is as if the very insistence on the legibility of materiality demands for its correlate the immediate legibility of the spiritual. Repeating one of the most typical and constitutive gestures of metaphysics, all mystery is relegated to the relation between the material and spiritual. Precisely here Althusser seems to shirk back from the thought of the reciprocal dislocation of materiality and ideality, the impossibility of either the one or the other presenting itself immediately as it is in itself. The always-already-hybridity again risks falling apart into the elements, each of which promises a specious legibility.

I suggested earlier that there is a tension between the Marxist "perspective of production" and the perspective of perspectivality and horizontality. What I mean is perhaps now clearer: the perspective of production, as presented in the ISA essay, tends to repress the perspective of perspectivalism. Production, rather than being itself conceived as a historically emergent perspective, posits itself as an absolute, resulting in the elevation of materiality to a new principle of legibility while simultaneously granting an absolute legibility to ideology as well. What results is not even a phenomenological Marxism, taking seriously the problem of how what appears comes to appearance, but a prephenomenological dogmatism in which both materiality and ideology revel in dogmatic self-evidence even as the relation between them—the movement of self-showing, of coming to truth—falls into obscurity. Precisely this demands the exclusion of the problem of fetishism, and its relation to ideology, from the ISA essay. Moreover, the very question of the reproduction of the relations of production, while seeming to operate within a conventional materialist framework, leads to its aporetic dissolution. For it would seem that whereas production itself, as the production of use value or exchange value, always also itself produces and reproduces the dichotomous relation between ideality and materiality—the very possibility of production depends on the inscription of this opposition into the thing that is produced—the relations of production exist as nothing else than their more original jointure, their "always-already hybridity." Theorizing the relations of production thus demands reconceptualizing the very nature of production. And to the extent that the reproduction of the relations of production can itself no longer be more or less taken for granted and becomes a critical problem for the praxis of capitalism, the result is a crisis of production. This presents a peculiar paradox. Whereas Althusser's theory of ideology might seem to lead to a fatalistic conclusion about the impossibility of escaping from capitalist exploitation, in fact he could just as much be said to have produced an argument for the impossibility of capitalism. The reproduction of the relations of production, it would seem, is simply not possible, because production, as it has been understood, breaks apart that which must be must held together. Perhaps this explains the emergence of the televisionary fracture: an everyday life that is always with and yet utterly cut off from a luminous world of interpellations that will never interpellate us until the miraculous and catastrophic moment that the viewer is revealed as the unknown suspect, and the police from behind the screen also stand at the door, just about to burst through the threshold. The palpable effect of this is something that seems to have little or no place in Althusser's argument, despite its importance for psychoanalysis: the "unhappiness" in all its various forms that results from the need, by way of internalized (rather than overtly political) repression, to compensate for the dissonances, the internal fractures, that result from the structural failure of the reproduction of the relations of production. And yet: the impossible is possible, and we are not so unhappy. In fact, the catastrophe of the world notwithstanding, we are becoming happier—things are getting better—all the time. The challenge must be to understand how capitalism is possible despite its impossibility.

Precisely here, it might be tempting to argue that Heidegger's more ontologically radical perspective simply trumps Althusser's Marxism, which could at best claim to be a specialized science based on a "regional ontology." Heidegger after all develops the resources to deconstruct the notion of production itself, and conceive of it in its historicity. Yet we would thus lose sight of the problem of reproduction rather than bringing it to clarity. Or indeed: such an approach will do nothing more than continue to make the impossible possible. For this reason, it is necessary, once more, to insist that there is also an aspect of Althusser's concept of production, and his "production-historical" perspective, that offers a more powerful, resonant challenge to Heidegger.

Althusser's theory of "symptomatic reading," as it is presented in the first part of *Reading Capital*, indeed offers a trenchant, if sparingly developed, critique of Heidegger's thought.[43] At the heart of this critique is a rethinking of the nature of horizontality. Whereas Heidegger's entire approach to the question of being in *Being and Time* depends on the claim that a given being can only be understood in terms of a certain horizon—the "interpretation" of the kind of being that it is and the being of this being—Althusser, without rejecting the concept of horizon per se, maintains the opposite: the object of knowledge is not "grounded" in a certain horizon, which must then be carefully excavated either by means of a philosophical genealogy or by the patient phenomenological disclosure of the ontically close yet ontologically distant, but anticipates an unprecedented horizon; a horizon of understanding that has not yet been made manifest either to explicit thematic understanding or to a preontological preconception. For Althusser indeed, the "line of demarcation" between ideology and science has everything to do with whether one returns to the old horizon or looks forward to the new. Crucial to this opposition is an understanding of knowledge and horizontality in terms of production. Contrasting classical political economy with Marx—he will develop the concept of symptomatic reading from Marx's own understanding of this contrast—Althusser explains that what political economy does not see is not some preexisting object that somehow escaped its notice but rather the object that it has itself produced in its own epistemological operation, or indeed "precisely the production itself, which is identical with the object."[44] Political economy *is* fundamentally blind to what it *does*: "the production of a new latent question contained by default in this new answer."[45] The fundamental failure of an ideological way of thinking, such as classical political economy, consists in not recognizing that its own operation of knowledge produces objects that, being without precedent, demand a complete change in the original problematic; an entirely new horizon of questioning, as it were. In this way, the "perspective of production," elsewhere regarded simply as the essence of the Marxist "science" of historical materialism, is conceived in far more ontologically and epistemologically radical terms. Production, in the sense of knowledge production, is what brings forth an entirely new object, and indeed an entirely new horizon of understanding. Scientific thinking has nothing to do with obeying existing canons of evidence or logical deduction but involves being truly responsible to the novelty of the objects that the act of knowing, the production of knowledge, itself brings forth. In a footnote found in *On the Reproduction of Capital* that attests to both his proximity to and distance from Heidegger, Althusser writes, "Living science exists, let us say, in scientific research alone. . . . [L]et us say that the essence of living science consists less in solving problems than in *posing* the problems to be solved."[46] Marx surpassed classical political economy not because he invented an entirely new field of inquiry, or because he returned to a more original mode of questioning, but because he recognized what was genuinely new in the theoretical objects that classical political economy had already brought forth, raising the questions that responded to this novelty. The scope of this critique, however, reaching far beyond pre-Marxist economics, extends to the entire modern philosophical tradition, from Descartes on up to Husserl and Heidegger. In an extraordinary passage, Althusser suggests the philosophical stakes of his critique of ideological ways of thinking.

> Here we meet our greatest difficulty. For, practically alone in this undertaking, we have to resist the age-old "obviousness" [*aux "évidences" séculaires*] which *repetition*, not only the repetition of a false answer, but above all that of a false question, has produced in people's minds. We must leave the ideological space defined by this ideological question, this *necessarily closed* space . . . in order to open a new space in an other place—the space required for a *correct posing [juste position] of the problem, one which does not prejudge the solution*. The whole history of the "theory of knowledge" in Western philosophy from the famous "Cartesian circle" to the circle of the Hegelian or Husserlian teleology of Reason *shows* us that this "problem of knowledge" is a closed space, i.e., a vicious circle (the vicious circle of the mirror relation of ideological recognition). Its high point of consciousness and honesty was reached precisely with the philosophy (Husserl) which was prepared to take theoretical responsibility for the necessary existence of this *circle*, i.e., to think it as essential to its ideological undertaking; however, this did not *make it leave the circle*, did not deliver it from its ideological captivity—nor could the philosopher who has tried to think in an "openness" [*ouverture*] (which seems to be only the ideological non-closure of the closure) the absolute condition of possibility of this "closure," i.e., of the closed history of the "repetition" of this closure in Western metaphysics—Heidegger—leave this circle. It is impossible to leave a closed space simply by installing oneself in its simple *outside*, either of its exterior or its profundity: so long as this outside or profundity remain *its*

outside or profundity, they still belong to *that* circle, to *that* closed space, as its "repetition" in *its* other-than-itself. Not the repetition but the non-repetition of this space is the way out of this circle: the sole theoretically sound flight—which is precisely [*justement*] *not a flight*, which is always committed to what it is fleeing from, but the radical foundation of a new space, a new problematic which allows the real *problem* to be posed, the problem misrecognized [*méconnu*] in the recognition structure in which it is ideologically posed.[47]

The "theory of knowledge" that has dominated modern philosophy, Althusser suggests, involves endlessly repeating not only false answers, but false questions—and perhaps above all, we may surmise, the question of grounding, of how knowledge is possible, of how we can be certain of what we know. Precisely these false questions keep us trapped within a closed space, a vicious circle: we can only ever really know what we can be sure of knowing—what is already known to us. While the phenomenological tradition, starting with Husserl, will seek to take responsibility for the circularity of knowledge, conceiving of it as the necessary basis for knowledge as it understands it (its ideological undertaking), and while Heidegger will not only think the essentially circular, hermeneutic structure of human existence and understanding, but will leave the circle of certain knowledge and transcendental justification by thinking precisely that which is unthought within the circle itself—the withdrawal and concealment that inhabits the truth—Heidegger will not succeed in leaving the circle, since the outside that he tries to think remains the outside of the circle, and can thus always appear again as a kind of origin and ground. For it is not possible to flee from the circle by merely thinking its limit, its outside, its lacunae, exceptions, or depths. The only flight that is possible, a flight that is no longer a flight since it has lost all relation to that from which it is fleeing, is to become open to what is entirely new, without precedent; what is no longer a repetition.

It is precisely a kind of theoretical clarity that imprisons us within the vicious circle of ideology. Indeed, ideology is nothing else than the clarity of a horizon that, precisely in its clarity, has become impossible to escape—impossible even if we begin also to think the obscurity that surrounds and conditions its clarity. If it had previously seemed that the relation between the material and the ideal was akin to the strife between earth and world at play in the truth, and that the trap of ideology was to forget this play, now ideology, with all the resourcefulness of a tumor, has retreated into the very place from which it has been banished: it is to be found nowhere else than in the very playing out of the play of truth, insofar as this play poses itself in its clarity as a kind of a priori whose transcendental efficacy must be sustained through its theoretical repetition. While this discussion of ideology resonates with the ISA essay in certain crucial respects, it also allows us to recognize in the concept of "interpellation" a decisive and troubling narrowing of the problematic of ideology, even if this narrowing, to be sure, is itself already prefigured in *Reading Capital*. By conceiving of ideology in terms of interpellation, Althusser suggests that the closure of ideology has a certain luminous, immediately legible structure; a certain recognizable shape—indeed the shape of a circle. This would certainly be the case were one to understand ideology purely in terms of its philosophical manifestations, which Althusser classifies in terms of the "theory of knowledge." In these cases, to be sure, the circular structure imposes itself of a certain necessity, since here the very essence of ideology does indeed consist in constantly repeating the same questions, returning again and again to the beginning, and indeed the particular self-reflexive lucidity of philosophical thinking leads it, by way of a kind of internal necessity, to recognize with ever greater clarity this circular structure as the structure of a trap that it sets for itself, and indeed to trap itself ever more deeply in its closed circular space through this act of recognition. The problem, however, is that when Althusser's ISA essay turns to a very different aspect of ideology, conceiving of ideology no longer in terms of the sophisticated articulate philosophical or quasi-scientific systems of thought but rather the material practices of everyday life, then the reduction of ideology to an ultimately circular structure of recognition attributes to these a kind of lucidity that they do not possess. It takes, and mistakes, the philosophical-ideological interpretation of knowledge as circular for a genuine theorization of praxis. Here the wager of his thought, the leap into materiality, comes up against its limit. If we can speak of the practices of everyday life as ideological, it is not because they lead in a simple circle, always remaining within the same preinterpretation of reality, but because they are caught up in a far subtler labyrinth—a labyrinth whose entanglements do not reduce to a single legible figure.

It should now become clearer why the question of ideology as posed by Althusser—the question of the reproduction of the ideological conditions of production—leads into a certain theoretical and practical cul-de-sac. Even though Althusser seeks, through an extraordinary theoretical wager, to move from an ideological understanding of ideology to a materialist conception of ideology by conceiving of ideology in terms of material practices, his attempt to apply the concept of interpellation to bring to light the structure of these material practices ends up replicating the viciously circular trap in which ideology has always already entrapped itself by imagining the structure of its own self-entrapment to be far simpler than it actually is. It is as if the reproduction of ideology, at this deepest level, took place simply as the reproduction of the figure of the fundamentally cyclic structure of reproduction itself. The perspective of production and reproduction, despite presenting itself from the outset as purely materialist, converges, at a certain point of the inquiry and from a certain perspective, with the innermost figure of ideology.[48]

It might be tempting, at precisely this point, to take distance from the question of production and reproduction, and seek to "deconstruct" production itself as a horizon of understanding, as both Heidegger and Agamben attempt. Yet to do so would be to deny the insinuating power of reproduction—a power that consists not least of all in always being more subtle, more labyrinthine than the figures through which it seems to take place, and whose seeming is always part of their operativity. Yet perhaps it is possible to carry through Althusser's thinking beyond this impasse without merely repeating Heidegger, or, rather, a certain Heideggerianism. Perhaps we should not seek to take distance from the perspective of production, but rather, taking seriously the concept of "symptomatic reading" articulated in *Reading Capital*, we should try to enter even more deeply into the nexus that binds together horizontality, production, and reproduction. Needed, as it were, is a new theoretical wager.

10
THE GADGET

If there were that commodity soul of which Marx occasionally speaks in jest, it would be the most empathetic that has ever been met with in the realm of souls. For in each person it would have to see the buyer whose hand and house it wishes to snuggle its way into.

> Walter Benjamin, *Das Paris des Second Empire bei Baudelaire* (my translation)

Miley Cyrus is either singing about drugs or herself.

> *The Marquee Blog,* CNN, June 5, 2013

Althusser's analysis of ideology departs from and returns to the question of the reproduction of the conditions of production. Thus he concludes the main body of the essay: "The reality in question in this mechanism, the reality which is necessarily *ignored* [*méconnue*] in the very forms of recognition (ideology = misrecognition/ignorance) is indeed, in the last resort, the reproduction of the relations of production and of the relations deriving from them."[1] Yet we might ask, is ideology itself the ultimate level of analysis possible for the problem of reproduction? Is there not perhaps a deeper, more radical level at which the reproduction of the conditions of production takes place, or even a perspective that is more primordial, more "originary" so far as it calls the origin itself into question, writing the origin "under erasure"? Heidegger's radicalization of Marx's concept of ideology consists in referring it back to the question of the essence of truth. Yet the essence of truth itself involves production—though, needless to say, not in a sense that could immediately be equated with Marx's or Althusser's use of the term. For as Heidegger will claim in "The Question concerning Technology," *phusis*, as "the arising of something from out of itself [*das von-sich-her Aufgehen*]," is a "bringing-forth [*Her-vor-bringen*], *poiēsis*," and indeed "*poiēsis* in the highest sense."[2] Nature is originally "productive," where productivity is itself the event of truth: "Bringing-forth propriates only [*es ereignet sich nur*] insofar as something concealed comes into unconcealment."[3] *Technē*, in its original sense, is itself poetic, productive, alethic. Modern technology in turn is characterized by a change in the mode of its alethic productivity. For while modern technology is also a manner of revealing, "the revealing that holds sway throughout modern technology does not unfold into a bringing-forth in the sense of *poiēsis*. The revealing that rules in modern technology is a challenging [*Herausfordern*], which puts to nature the unreasonable demand that it supply energy which can be extracted and stored as such."[4] This of course leads us to one of Heidegger's most daring terminological innovations: "We now name the challenging claim that gathers man with a view to ordering the self-revealing as standing-reserve: *Ge-stell*."[5]

The ground of ideology, the "condition of its possibility," this again suggests, is nothing else than the mode of production that will be named the *Ge-stell*, which, derived from the very ordinary German word *Gestell* (frame), is translated variously as "enframing" and "positionality," or even as *dispositif*. The reproduction of the relations of production would thus depend not only on ideology, not only on the reproduction of the various ideological apparatuses, but on the reproduction of the mode of production itself through which ideology is first possible. Beyond material and infrastructural conditions of production, beyond even ideology and the state apparatus as a whole, we discover what we might call the *alethic* conditions of production. This reaches into the very nature of productivity itself. It is immediately evident from Althusser's analysis of ideology that the problem of ideology comes more and more to the fore with the development of specifically capitalist relations of production. The reproduction of ideology is necessary at every stage of the development of relations of production, yet with capitalism it enters into an increasingly abstract relation to the economic relations sensu stricto. Whereas in the Middle Ages the dominant ideological state apparatus was the church, which presented itself explicitly as the organ of transcendental valuation, espousing an explicit ideology of economic relations that brought them in line with the principle of order governing the world as a whole, it has now been replaced by the School—precisely that which "bourgeois ideology" presents as a "neutral environment purged of ideology (because it is . . . lay), where teachers respectful of the 'conscience' and 'freedom' of the children who are entrusted to them (in complete confidence) by their 'parents' (who are free, too, i.e. the owners of their children) open up for them the path to the freedom, morality and responsibility of adults by their own example, by knowledge, literature and their 'liberating' virtues."[6] To the extent that ideology, as in the case of feudalism, is explicitly bound up with the relations of production, it can be taken for granted even if it remains vitally necessary. But with capitalism, since ideology conceals its own nature from itself, the reproduction of ideology becomes absolutely critical, becomes a problem in its own right, even if, granted, a problem that is continuously being solved and must be solved ever anew for things to continue.

This same logic repeats itself, in an even more extreme form, with the alethic, "phenomenological" conditions of production. It is indeed only at an extreme stage in the development of capitalism that ideology is no longer enough, and that capitalism must, as it were, take upon itself the production of the "manner" of production: of the essence of production, the event of production, insofar as it can no longer be taken for granted that production does in fact take place—that production does not itself have to be produced. If this is necessary, it is precisely because the dominant mode of production that has characterized the rise of capitalism—that which Heidegger, under the rubric of a critique of modern technology will call the *Ge-stell*—is no longer adequate to uphold the system of production itself. For Althusser as for Marx, the radicalization of the problem of ideology in capitalism takes the form of "Protestant" fundamentalism; the Catholic Church gives way to the purer ideology of the New Testament and early Christianity. Precisely because the church itself becomes dispensable and even indeed a hindrance to the operation of an ideology that must above all else conceal its existence as ideology, it is now possible and even necessary for ideology, while religious in its origin, to become instituted, in its most extreme form, in the "lay" institution of the School. Whereas the perspective of ideology remains caught up in the problematic of early Christianity, the alethic conditions of production bring us back to Plato's cave, and to what is for Heidegger the even more original Greek experience of truth. Whereas the *Ge-stell* happens as the forgetting of the poetic productivity of truth, involving a kind of productivity in which the truth in its essence holds itself back from showing itself, postideological capitalism involves nothing less than the production of the "truthing of truth," of lighting-opening concealment.

Precisely this suggests the extraordinary ambiguity of Heidegger's project: without in any way contesting the radical tendencies of his approach, without denying that it represents a momentous event in the history of thinking, we can nevertheless begin to sense that in a certain way his thought, precisely where it is least compromised and most radical, serves to reproduce the conditions of production of a stage of capitalism that is only just beginning to come into view.

Capitalism enters its postideological stage when the conception of productivity that has held sway since Aristotle proves insufficient with regard to the forces and relations of production—when the expansion of productive forces, the extension of the paradigm of production to an ever greater sphere of phenomena, and the transformation of relations of production, grates up against the limits of the existing theory and praxis of production. Production can no longer "understand" and "enact" itself as *energeia*, or, as this will come to be construed in the subsequent history of metaphysics, as actuality, effectivity, *Wirklichkeit*.[7] This is not to say that all of the sudden production in the traditional sense becomes impossible, or that at a conscious, explicit level a new "theory" of production is necessary. Production exists neither as theory nor as praxis but rather comes before this distinction, supporting it from beneath. What has begun to happen, though, is that the transformations that have taken place in production have made it necessary to produce and reproduce the very manner of production as that which this new production produces. If production could appear as base, as material, and hence serve as the starting point for historical materialism, it is only because production itself produced itself, and indeed produced the appearance and theory of itself, as that which was already given and could thus be taken for granted. Marx's materialism, his insistence on production as determinate in the last instance, was itself only possible because of the importance that production had assumed in the praxis of industrial capitalism. Yet he still was able to understand the perspective of production in a way that would isolate production "itself" from the product of production, and treat only the latter as produced while regarding the former as given. Production in this sense is the production of an ontological difference between that which is produced and the unproduced, grounding, event of production itself. The tendency of the development of production within capitalism is to move away from the possibility of such a distinction, which ultimately must appear as a kind of compromise formation. The theoretical crisis in Marxism issues from this tendency within production itself: its orthodoxies can no longer be maintained, even if they retain descriptive validity over a large terrain. Heidegger, by posing the question of production with ontological radicalness, anticipated this theoretical crisis, paving the way for various forms of postmodernist post-Marxism. Needed, however, is neither an abandonment of the primacy of production nor of the theoretical apparatus of Marxist critique but rather a transformative reconceptualization. The challenge is not to get beyond the question of production but to enter even more deeply into it.

Invoking the need for a theory and praxis of production would seem to hopelessly confuse the material and ideological, substructure and superstructure. Yet the horizon of production is precisely what calls this opposition into question. There can be no practice of production without a theory, no theory without a practice. The theory of production is not an interpretation after the fact of some real, material occurrence but that which enables production to take place by opening up the horizon of the very sense of production: of what it *is* to produce. But at the same time this theory does not exist first of all as mere theorization only then to be "realized" in practice. Rather: it can only be articulated, put into play in "practice." Such formulations, however, are not only awkward, but indeed provisional and fundamentally inadequate, since they remain caught up in the metaphysical terms, rooted in the dominant conception of production, that it will be necessary to get beyond.

In postideological capitalism, production can no longer sustain itself as *effectivity*: it must produce its own alethic horizontality; it must bring being into its Da; it must play out the play between hiddenness and concealment. But it must do all of this by way of the commodity: being(s). It would be possible to attempt a "materialist" if no doubt inadequate formulation of this necessity: at a certain stage of production, the putatively actual needs of actual human beings and other functional entities, while certainly not being "satisfied" in any actual sense, become inadequate to the expansion of productive forces. Production at this point must not only take on concretely new forms, but must abandon to some extent, at least at the margins, production as effectivity. Human need or even human desire can no longer sustain the growth of production. These needs and desires must appear as a limiting factor, because of an essential finitude and inertia but also because their own secret depths, the hiddenness that is the reserve of their truth, have themselves been destroyed to the very extent that, for the sake of increased production, they have been brought to the surface. The expansion of production thus demands that the commodity, which had always still somehow in the last analysis been there for the other, made for the other, must now, to an ever greater degree, be for itself: it must ex-ist. It must become the opening to its own truth. It must be the being that in its being is "concerned" with its being, and indeed the being that is also being, that at once opens up and collapses ontological difference. *The truth must happen, but not for us.* The commodity is that which forecloses on the difference between being and beings in the very moment that it allows this difference to appear. It is from this perspective, let us remark in passing, that we could begin to address that intellectual agitation that, itself arising at the margins of philosophical discourse and the academy, threatens to claim its heart: object-oriented ontology (OOO), speculative materialism, speculative realism. Object-oriented ontology, by endeavoring to think the object outside of its "correlation" with the subject, postulating that the object (without reducing itself to the indeterminacy of the Kantian thing in itself) not only withdraws from subjective comprehension, but in a fundamental way exceeds the subject, provides compelling if not entirely novel insight into the being of the commodity. Yet it confuses this insight into the commodity with an absolute, a-historically valid ontology, and thus, far from allowing a critical stance toward the commodity, merely reinforces its dominion. It could even be said to become the purest expression of commodity fetishism. What is needed, as it were, is a critical turn in OOO, and, more specifically, a renewed engagement with the question of truth as it emerges from Heidegger.

The shift in focus from production to consumption is a consequence of this transformation, as is the increasing turn away from the Fordist model of production with the emergence of immaterial, social, and affective labor and the collapse of the distinction between the "real" economy of production/consumption and the financial economy.[8] Consumption is indeed the principal mode in which the reproduction of the alethic conditions of production takes place. This, moreover, explains why in postideological capitalism, even though the School remains the principal apparatus of ideology, providing training in the various *ethoi* of production, it may seem increasingly irrelevant. The School is still necessary to reproduce the ideological conditions of production, but these, while themselves no less necessary than before, are no longer the most critical site for the future of capitalism: they are no longer where the most difficult and also subtlest battles are being waged. It is not surprising in this regard that in the United States the schools seem almost to have abandoned their ideological vocation: if students are not already sufficiently docile to accept everything the way it is, then prisons, which hardly serve any conceivable disciplinary or corrective function, await. What has taken the place of the School is the "culture industry," and above all television. But precisely this must be understood in terms of conditions of production that are no longer ideological but phenomenological, alethic—the showing forth of the life that is not ours to live. Nor is television the consummation of the society of the spectacle. But in just this sense, the television is also the harbinger of something else, brought into view through advertising: the *gadget*. The gadget is the commodity that has taken upon itself alethic production. That the gadget, which, through a strange ambivalence, names both the "novelty" item without use and the eminently useful item without name (it was originally sailors' slang for anonymous tools)—and thus, by a savage and strange irony, would also be the name bestowed on the first atom bomb, the first of the things to end all things—indicates that a momentous shift has taken place.[9] This is not to conjure up some kind of dystopian vision of a world of autonomous machines.[10] Nor is it a question of the subtler horror that Bernard Stiegler, while certainly acknowledging the pharmacological ambiguity of technology, conjures forth in *The Re-Enchantment of the World* through the image of an addictive "hyperconsumerism" that, by destroying sociality and affectivity, leads to a "proletarianization of the higher cognitive functions," resulting in the loss of "that which constitutes the life of spirit as a critical, that is, rational instance, capable of theoretical self-formalizing, and therefore of self-critique."[11] It is not that human beings will cease to exist, nor even that they will lose their dignity or become "reified" or submit to an externalized cybernetic automation, but that in a certain way they will be used, in their very existence and the truth of their existence, by the commodity, which thereby appropriates Dasein as its own, turning our own Dasein, the very being that we are, against us as the life that is not ours to live. Things thus come to make a perverse claim to authenticity at the very moment that human authenticity seems to have become impossible. It is not only, or not even, that things run *us*, but that—as in the perfectly prescient grammatical barbarism of a recent pop song showing off the obscene commodity in all its obscenity—*things run we*. And it is perhaps no accident that the life of the gadget, the commodity that has finally found its way to the soul that Marx promised to it in jest, should announce itself with such perfect clarity in the hit song or that the contemporary reign of the gadget should have begun with the personal cassette player, the *Walkman*, whose name alone already tells us almost everything. The hit song, the "musical commodity," the virally replicating musical parasite whose life Peter Szendy has explored in his masterful study of the "philosophy in the jukebox," could be said to anticipate the more general logic of the gadget, and moreover provide the first vehicle through which the gadget, which transforms the "repetition compulsion" of the "earworm" into the basis for making manifest the pluripotentiality of the commodity, can establish itself.[12] The living, pluripotent gadget-commodity becomes, at the same time, the paradigm for processes of subject formation that are just beginning to play themselves out.[13] It is not that, subjected to the anonymous violence of capitalism, our human dignity falls prey to the realm of instrumental reason. Rather: through a paradoxical gesture whose strangeness has yet to be comprehended, we, as having already chosen commodity-being, choose commodity-being as the way to be.[14] The commodity, as *we*, as our *radical freedom*, chooses itself.[15] It is this mode of subjectification, or perhaps rather a transitory phenomenon on the way toward it, that the Tiqqun collective, though too dependent on a certain concept of specularity, has sketched out in its *Preliminary Materials for a*

Theory of the Young-Girl. The Young-Girl, which is emphatically *not* merely a gendered concept, is subjectivity—or let us say rather: Dasein—as commodity-life (one could say self-commodification, but the self must be written under erasure): "With the Young-Girl, it is not only that commodities take hold of human subjectivity. It is human subjectivity that first reveals itself as the interiorization of commodities."[16] In a world of gadgets, the Young-Girl is sure to take the place of the celebrity: whereas the celebrity, in its classical form, is still somehow the appearance of what is common to us all, the categorial re-presentation of that which is of the nature of Dasein, the Young-Girl, which becomes celebrity-like to the very degree that it is deindividuated, presents the inhuman potentiality of the thing. Celebrity is merely the quantification of the rate of its incessantly repeated consumption. Indeed: "The Young-Girl is the commodity that insists on being consumed, at every instant, because at every instant she becomes more obsolete."[17] Yet this does not mean that the gadget-commodity is a pure "feminine" passivity. Taking up the scattered members and organs that televisionary celebrity, derailing the phenomenological machine, has left behind as grotesque relics of sexual difference—caricatures of difference cut off from every prospect of even the most transitory overcoming—the gadget-commodity puts these into play, plays these against themselves, acting out rituals of self-commodification and self-consumption. Consumption, which had once offered at least the fictive promise of pleasure or satisfaction, becomes what we might tentatively call a disaffected, affectless, moodless, autoaffectivity: truth-play without truth.

The gadget-commodity in this way becomes the site of a staging or screening of our life, our Dasein, as its life. It is not that it submits human life to a regime of thoroughgoing automation, not that it colonizes us and draws our affective and mental life into the machine of capitalist flows. The point is neither that we are becoming machines nor that machines are becoming human but rather that the gadget-commodity *plays us*: it puts *our* life, the very fact of our Dasein being our own, into play as its own. Or better, since we must not think of this as a mere reproduction or imitation—it will have little to do with Siri's clumsy sassy servitude—the gadget-commodity comes into its own, appropriates the possibility of being its own to be, the possibility of having possibilities, by playing our Dasein and putting it into play not just as its own, but as an indication of its own ownness. Slowly—indeed almost imperceptibly—the gadget-commodity gathers us around it to have us play out its truthless truth. The gadget-commodity is immanently a-phenomenological, and the only theoretical mode by which we can gain access to it is an a-phenomenology taking a televisionary leap beyond *our* Dasein, the life that is ours to live. If there is a certain *theatrum* in which we can catch a glimpse of gadget-commodity-life in the moment of its becoming, a kind of gadget-commodity-*Augenblick* that, in one and the same instant, looks into itself and stares back at us, it would be the music video, and above all those which have not only banished every trace of the Dionysian rock star with his train of hysterical screaming Maenads, but which, even while offering the most grotesquely hypersexualized, one-sided view of the female body—even while determining the feminine entirely through a commodifying, sexualizing male gaze—nevertheless manages either to banish every trace of the masculine or reduce it to a position of mere servitude and secondary objectification, putting it in service of the "pure" feminine sexuality that would seem to have been produced through it. Madonna's Material Girl may have pointed the way to this, by showing us the Young-Girl glitteringly, joyfully materialized through her desire for materiality, taking ownership of her desire as commodity-desire. But the climax of this tendency is only now being reached, and perhaps nowhere more so than in South Korea, where the girl group's Young-Girls, shaking their money makers, hold sway. An analysis of K-Pop girl groups would reveal the hidden schema of the possible manifestations of an "abstract" feminine sexuality that takes ownership as commodity of the very gaze that seems to have produced it, turning this gaze back against itself and into its own truth. Each of these abstracted, abject yet self-projecting femininities opens onto a different truthless truth-play: a play of concealment-unconcealment that the gadget-commodity will take upon itself. Each, as it were, schematizes a different mode of alethic self-play, a different dance of veils and secrets and revelations.

This suggests a different, even more dangerous danger than that which Heidegger saw. The danger is not that abandonment by being (*Seinsverlassenheit*) will become absolutely entrenched as it reaches the point where it can no longer even recognize itself but rather that the thinking of ontological difference, and even of event and being, will fall back into the commodity, that it will merely serve to reproduce the conditions of production of the commodity. The more that thinking thinks it has evaded the danger by becoming once again receptive to being, the greater the danger becomes, since it is precisely as a kind of commodity-forgetfulness, and indeed commodity-self-forgetfulness, rather than the forgetfulness of being, that the commodity will seek to take the play of the truth upon itself. There is, moreover, a more purely economic, "materialist" expression of the alethic dimension of commodity life: what Marx, in the third volume of *Capital*, will identify as the "autonomization of the form of surplus-value," the theorization of which, as Düzenli suggests, is intimately connected with the analysis of commodity fetishism.[18] Wagering a simple formulation for this relation, one might say that insofar as the commodity becomes alethically productive, taking the play of truth upon itself, then it allows for the autonomization of the form of surplus value, the automata of capital, to secure the condition not only for coming into appearance but also for becoming a sphere of life, of ex-istence. The truth-play of the commodity is the life interface for the hyperobject capital. One often hears how rich one would have become had one just invested the money that one had spent on an iPod, back when it came out, in Apple stocks. This comparison might at first seem to have a merely moralizing message: we, the consumer, chose the pleasure of the possession and use of the thing, a present gratification, over the true ownership of the means of production. But there is more to it: to consume is to allow the gadget-commodity to unfold the alethic play that brings into play the accumulation of surplus value. We, the consumer, have been called on to make this sacrifice: to sacrifice use value and exchange value alike for what we might call play value, the value of value, that is, value in its movement of origination. Capitalism will increasingly play itself out as the pas de deux of these three different modes of valuation, endlessly intertwining in the torturous arabesques of the commodity fetish. To consume, to *use* the gadget or rather to play with it, is to produce the alethic conditions of production.

Every formulation that is possible within "otherwise inceptual thinking" contains an extreme ambivalence. And perhaps we could go even further: perhaps even the discourse of postwar phenomenology, and deconstruction with its ethics of radical alterity, of keeping open an openness for the future event—"messianicity without messianism"—might also in the end serve the gadget-commodity as it dreams its dream of life into being. Perhaps the arrival of the Other is just what the thing is waiting for; the gadget-commodity is itself—one thinks of the film *A.I.*—an infinite longing for singularity, for death, for home and radical hospitality. It is waiting for us to come. The gadget-commodity is perhaps the harbinger of a new hybrid: a "superrace," in the words of A. Kiarina Kordela, whose immortal bodies will be able to redeem an infinite debt.[19]

We are not quite there yet. To confront these dangers will demand taking the problem of the commodity far more seriously, returning to and tarrying with the thought of the commodity as being(s). We must allow the truth of being(s) to come to a critical point of ambivalence at which the life of the thing, without being safely brought back to human needs or desires or even situated within an analytic of Dasein, can open up to what we might call, awkwardly and imprecisely, a third life: neither human nor inhuman and least of all divine . . . or natural. This third life is, like the life of "the Jews in the pores of the Polish society," intermundial, interstitial.[20] It is no longer the time for revolution but for the interstitial excrescence of truths that, seemingly insignificant and inconspicuous, are not unlike the anonymous transcendental numbers that outnumber, in their nondenumerable multitude, the algebraic numbers in whose gaps they are found.

Production brings forth new beings, and the great challenge that faces us is to become responsible for these. The danger is that we will interpret these new things in terms of the old questions, the old horizons of understanding; that we will fail to respond to what is most shockingly new about them. To ex-ist historically is to take up this responsibility. Production does not simply operate within a given horizon; it brings forth new horizons. But it does not bring these forth fully formed: indeed to suppose that the horizon could ever present itself in a sort of implicit, preontological preconception as already somehow present, accessible, comprehensible is to fall back into what has already been given, what is already there, and fail in the responsibility to the event of the new.

Yet *now* something has changed. It is no longer enough to draw a line of demarcation between science and ideology. The new being is no longer a being, anticipating an unprecedented horizon, but it is both a being and being, being(s), having taken upon itself the alethic, phenomenological reproduction of production itself as coming into appearance, as the play of truth. This play of truth itself, perhaps the great philosophical discovery of the past century, has now become thoroughly equivocal, ambivalent. It can be taken as the essence of the givenness of what is given, its very givenness; in this case what is most unprecedented is deprived of its novelty and becomes nothing more than the unseen basis of all visibility, the unapparent ground of all appearance. And in just this way, the essencing of truth, the infinite play of the signifier, becomes merely the luminous labyrinth of theory in which praxis gets itself lost: every legitimate, trenchant critique of "postmodernism" amounts to this. Or it can become the prospect, the possibility, perhaps only the glimpsing of an opening toward truth, new truth. This new truth will demand, above all else, commitment: what we must now come to understand as thinking is nothing else than drawing a distinction between truth and nontruth. And perhaps this is also what philosophy has always been doing. This is not to say that the truth is arbitrary, a human product of the imagination or even the will to power. A responsibility to the new being(s) is needed above all else. Perhaps the truth to which we must commit ourselves is nothing else than the play of truth inscribed in being(s). But we must commit to it as truth—as the opening of the political—and not as untruth. Praxis must itself come to be a praxis toward truth and not toward untruth. It must become truthful.[21]

11
TO THE THINGS THEMSELVES

I like gestures (they are so rare, probably even impossible, and in any case, nonprogrammable) which unite the hyperactual with the anachronistic.

        Jacques Derrida, interview (1993), in Derrida and Stiegler, *Echographies of Television*

The aim of deconstruction—indeed its ethical imperative—has been to become open to the event, the arrival of the Other, by undermining the tendency of thinking to foreclose upon its possibilities in the name of presence, self-certainty, the *logos*. Yet in what follows we will seek instead to *come before the thing*, to *approach the thing before it approaches us*. This is not deconstruction, not fabulation, not deconfabulation, but a kind of perverse prevarication in the literal sense: a collusion for and against these things and their truth, turning their own truth, the truth of these things, against them. We will repeat the path that we have already taken: from television to celebrity to the gadget, but our method in this repetition will also be completely different, starting out from the other side; from beyond the screen, from the side of the thing—not as if it could be grasped in isolation from us, in some kind of original purity, without relation, but in the thoughts, desires, dreams that these things, coming from the other side, will assemble around themselves; from a seemingly endless pluralization of objects, interests, theoretical motifs, affective investments. It is not a matter, moreover, of deconstructing the closure of metaphysics, of opening up another possibility at its limit, but of constructing the life of the thing; of constructing the play of truth, and evental openness, that the commodity-gadget takes upon itself. A certain moment of critique, irreducible to any utopian idea but also to the deconstruction of the metaphysics of presence and to the critique of capitalism in its given forms, must intercede if the future is to have a future.

If the future is to have a future, it cannot have just any future. Yes, we must be blunt, at the risk of sounding "reactionary," or even seeming to wish to return to a certain superannuated humanism. Hospitality must not be taken too far: we must be wary of the empathetic, gentle soul of the commodity, perhaps the most beautiful soul there has ever been. We must let it show itself, and perhaps show itself out, before it has arrived. For once it has truly arrived, we can be sure that it is all there will be. And it is already coming. This should not be confused with an immunological procedure, or with any other form of deterrence. The prevaricating construction of the life of the commodity-gadget, of its truth and event, is also a way of inhabiting this truth and event—dwelling in it without appropriating; without seeking to return the dwelling to the abode of the proper; dwelling in this strangeness, as strangeness; dwelling in it as out there. The truth of the thing must come before the thing in its truth, since it is by being in its truth, by reproducing itself as the reproduction of the truth, that the regime of the commodity-gadget itself recedes from visibility while at the same time enforcing itself all the more absolutely.

Walter Benjamin, in the epistemological preface to the *Origin of the German Mourning Play*, writes of the rhythm of contemplation:

> Representation as detour—this is the methodical [*methodische*] character of the treatise. The renunciation of the uninterrupted unfolding of its intension is what first of all characterizes it. It persists in constantly beginning to think anew; it returns roundaboutly to the matter at hand. Relentlessly catching its breath is the most proper form of the existence of contemplation. For by pursuing various levels of meaning in the contemplation of one and the same object, it receives the impetus for its constant renewal as well as the justification for its intermittent rhythm. Just as the mosaic remains majestic even when it has been broken apart into capricious particles, philosophical contemplation does not worry about losing its momentum.[1]

Can what follows claim, imitating the inimitable, to be a treatise in this sense? Yes and no. Precisely this rhythm of contemplation—precisely what has been sought after most intensely—is what the thing itself (television, the celebrity, the gadget-commodity) will thwart at every turn. Perhaps in the end it is nothing but this thwarting. To approach the thing before it approaches us is paradoxically to allow the thing to forbid us from finding our way around it. Theory, metaphysics, phenomenology have always amounted to allowing a contemplative detour. We must learn instead to run out of breath and catch our breath at the same time; to fall and keep from falling in the same instant. We must take up again, and precisely by dislocating thinking from the element in which it could be at home to itself, the strange task, adumbrated but abandoned in *Capital* (if only because the commodity was not yet ready), of allowing the commodity to speak and indeed to dance.

Who is this *we*, this *us*? Are you with me still? Were you ever with me? *We* is me and you and you and you. And where am I in all this? To approach this truth-play, the dance of the seven (or is it seventy, or seven thousand?) veils, we must allow ourselves to be seduced without losing our minds—or our heads. But being seduced is always in each case my own thing, even when I am with others. (This, in a word, is the secret of television.) Without exactly pretending to return to some moment of authenticity, without awkwardly banishing the imperious academic "we," I will nevertheless submit to seductions that will speak to me, and perhaps only to me: only to my obsessions, inversions and perversions, eccentricities. But, of course, none of these are just mine. Perhaps none of them are mine at all. The most secret is also the most common. Can you follow?

PART II

Rousseau, perhaps the first thinker of celebrity, even the first celebrity, turned in his late days of wandering and exile to botany. Here I am in my obscurity: I will become a botanist too, when the time comes, gathering up and describing (even taxonomizing, in a way) these strange monster-flowers we call celebrities. And I too promise: I will not extract poison, at least not only poison, from them.

12
METHODS

CONCEPTS OF CRITICISM

Heidegger warned against forgetting the original meaning of words. But let's not forget that the truest sense of a word often belongs not to the past but the future.

The poet invokes the muses; the philosopher, reason. Who then does the critic call upon in the act of criticism? Perhaps only a reader who does not yet exist.

Philosophy and poetry, if they speak to each other at all, speak as lovers, and as always with lovers, every conversation turns to love. Literature, however, is like a married couple. It looks upon its youthful effusions and enthusiasms with gentle bemusement, realizing they had served an unexpected end.

The critic must allow not only his reason and good sense, but even the tradition, to follow a few steps behind as he escapes from the catastrophes of the present. Filled with anxiety, he turns to look back—but they have disappeared. He retreats to find them again. In vain. Yet like Aeneas's wife, they return as ghosts to haunt him: and to show him the way into the future.

Often the hardest thing for a refined person to grasp is when tact demands vulgarity.

Of all forms of nostalgia, the nostalgia for revolution is perhaps the most insidious. But has there ever been a revolution that did not begin with the nostalgia for revolution? Is nostalgia itself revolutionary?

A thinker must be a partisan not only of certain thoughts, but of thought.

LANGUAGE IS THE . . . OF BEING

The trailer park is a privileged figure for late capitalism: a home for the homeless and rootless; a vehicle (the triumph of technology, dynamism, movement) brought to rest; the transport of commodities turned into a human dwelling. But if dwelling has a history that is material, cultural, economic, then the history of being can no longer be just its own. And the history of dwelling is also poetic, literary, linguistic, theological, philosophical, mystical, ecological. And perhaps we humans are animals that choose a dwelling, and must choose, though this choice is also never simply our own. The nomadic and the settled, the mundane and the heavenly, the soul and the body, the country and the city are only the crudest examples of such choices. But there are many others: some even without names.

There are many ways that being (and its truth) dwells in language. It wanders restlessly across the face. It becomes entrenched in a lonely fortress. It founds dynasties and builds palaces. It just passes through: sporadically, unexpectedly, just once and never again. It haunts. It transgresses. It is brought to a place that is no place and incinerated.

Language is always subject to the enormous gravitational pull not only of life (of utility, of the everyday, of every form of necessity that reduces language to a mere tool), but of the truth of the already true, of the momentous weight of everything that has been revealed, exposed, and awaits language as a means of conveyance. This pulls language into its orbit. Criticism is the clinamen: the slight twist and spin that sends it heading another way. Thus it finds in language the possibility of risk, chance, strangeness, wonder, shock—the shock in which language becomes open to the strangeness of things.

SATANIC LAUGHTER

There is a humor in the accidental meeting of two elements that seem to stand in no relationship to one another, and yet whose encounter reveals an affinity that, however groundless, transitory, incomprehensible, cannot be denied. But there is also a humor when things that never belonged together fall apart. Such humor is sinister, even satanic, and it holds an infinite attraction. Nuclear rather than chemical, it releases the accumulated tension of the world's disease, its lack of cohesion—a tension originating in the feeling that consciousness alone, the power of the mind, gives order to things, yet an order that is always, still, *of* things. With the tension of thought released, things return to the first strangeness with which they came into the world.

Did Adam, giving names to the strange beings he found before him, also laugh? Was there a knowledge, a satanic knowledge, in this laughter?

We, the critics, must do the same . . .

TECHNIQUES OF WRITING

The unnamable origin, the origin that is not an origin: not the production of pure difference through the trace, which at once gives and withdraws the Other, but the touching of singularities. Singularity is given to us as impossible nostalgia, anticipation, promise, hope without hope; given as a weak force of singularity that, without ever allowing its singularity to show itself as such, and without arresting the differential play of signifiers through a transcendental signified, brings us into relations.

The system of colors is instructive, so far as it is neither a purely differential system nor the absolute givenness of a sensual immediacy but the promise, sketched out in difference, of a singularity that passes infinitely beyond possible experience.

Philosophy cannot think the traced presence-absence of differential singularity save through a gesture of transcendental abstraction and reduction that, despite all rigor of method, despite all mistrust of the transcendental and abstract and general, can only efface singularity and difference by trying to think singularity and difference as such. But the answer cannot be to transform philosophy into a method of reading that repeats the play of signification. In either case: the rigor of method becomes the most austere testament to a compulsive drive toward truth as correspondence and correctness.

It sounds naive (the beginning always demands a certain naïveté), but it must be said, it has been decided: literature, literary theory, literary criticism—the three can no longer quite be kept apart—begin on the other side of philosophy; beyond the threshold toward which philosophy could only gesture. With singularity not as such but in a singularity that remains singular: in the development of this singularity (as the visual arts relentlessly approach the problem of color), its intensification and extensification.

VITA CONTEMPLATIVA

Metaphysics is unnecessary—a secret rejoicing in pointlessness; the frivolity of an excess flowing beyond the immanence of nature (the iron circle of necessity and determinate causality). Yet perhaps when the metaphysician insisted on presence, ground, truth—all these spectral repetitions of what *is*—this was only a sign of his coming down to earth, returning to the cave, making himself useful. The grounding of experience is a souvenir that the metaphysician brings back from his travels. Truth is his lie. His truths are otherwise: experiences, and not experience.

THE RACCOON TRAP

I remember the following description of a raccoon trap from a book I once read as a child. A narrow tube, just wide enough for the animal's clenched paw to pass through, opens out into a slightly larger cavity where a shiny piece of metal has been placed. The raccoon reaches inside, unclenches its paw to grasp the shiny metal, and remains stuck. It does not think to relax its grip, even though it then would have been able to free itself. For the dogmatist or the skeptic, every trap is like this. The only difference is that the dogmatist keeps on grasping, while the skeptic always just lets go. The critic, however, clenches his entire body, fits his way through the narrow hole, forces himself into the tiny cavity, and finds a way of escaping with the shining silver. His impossible entry allows an impossible exit.

13
CELEBRITY

EPIC FORM

Hegel said that a new epic could only come from a new land: America. Perhaps this is the thread that can guide us through the labyrinth of popular culture.

Kafka's first, unfinished novel bids farewell to the old country. Yet something essential has remained behind: it is impossible to disembark. It is almost as if the figure of the Jew still connects the new world to the old, just as it links the lands and peoples of the earth, with their rises and falls, into the continuity of history, and just as it gave Rome a dominion over time exceeding even its dominion over space.

The new epic is to the old as baseball is to football (rugby, soccer—every game played on a field of conquest: the essential topology of Homer's *Iliad*).

Crime rather than war: opposed to a heroic community is the solitude of the criminal and the anticriminal—both exist only in relation to a secret.

Of course: Achilles and Odysseus both already point the way toward the solitude of crime, but they are safely returned in the end to a community.

Star Wars is a false start: the epic motifs cannot be brought in from the past through comparative mythology. Lucas produced an *Aeneid* with all the propaganda but lacking its one virtue: literature. Yet there is also a sobering truth, which he realized in the end (an end that is, strangely but significantly, a beginning): America is also fated to repeat Rome. Radical democracy can only constitute itself through the destruction of Empire, but Empire will always return.

The new epic has the character of a pastoral: it exists outside of time.

Crime is the spirit of anachronism. Terrorism, by contrast, is historical and constitutive, and thus can in the end only produce empires.

The new epic is to the old as cats are to dogs. Every other epic hero is an expression of a certain modality of "doggedness." A wolf might understand the *Iliad* perfectly . . .

Star Trek: the modern office place, or the impossibly well-regulated military, at the center of epic experience. Bureaucracy as the denial of the very possibility of crime. Conquest as exploration.

Batman comes closest: its rigor consists in placing crime at the center of epic by identifying the criminal (antihero) and the crime fighter (anti-antihero), marginalizing the police, presenting wealth as the catastrophic substance of the social order, locating epic in the metropolis, and positing felinity (one thinks of Catwoman) as the most seductive, essential trait of the modern world. (Everything will belong to the order of cats and their rodentine or avian prey.) But perhaps the most probing and prescient moment of *Batman* is this: the dual nature of anti-antihero and antihero alike; the need that both sides (of the same coin, no less) will have for costumes and masks.

The new epic could only exist as farce and masquerade. For Bakhtin the epic became the novel through parody. Yet the new epic exists, from the beginning, as urbane parody, though this parody (better: parody of parody), this saturnalia finding its way into everyday life, has a sublime grandeur: the mask masks a life that has been emptied out and revealed in its substancelessness. The masks of the superheroes and supervillains, ridiculous as they are, expose far more than they conceal. For what they conceal is realism and the Socratic culture. Nietzsche, of course, understood this already, as did Arthur Schnitzler.

The duality of masks is the negative of the cult of celebrity: thus we can see the celebrity in America as the absolute symbol for ideology. But it also takes us beyond the symbol, beyond ideology.

Michael Jackson's face: the chiasmus of these two dualities.

Paris Hilton reveals the infinitely imperfect, even grotesque, identity of money and beauty. She is the living demolition of the cult of celebrity.

Scientology—psychosis-machine as religion—affords the most intimate glance into the labyrinth of the machinations and psychic contortions needed to produce a celebrity.

Paris Hilton has exploded celebrity. Celebrities can now only survive as scientologists, humiliating themselves again and again on Oprah's couch. The appearance of their truth (the truth of appearance) destroyed, they must painstakingly, and publicly, go through the motions of becoming what they were.

Kubrick's *Eyes Wide Shut*: revelatory in its terribleness.

The mendacious American epic spurns the city—and discovers the infinity of outer space. It spurns masks—and discovers space aliens. It spurns criminals; it discovers the terrorist with a pure heart. It is as if all roads led us back to Wagner's *Parsifal*, and from Wagner to Virgil.

What Heidegger could never understand is that Hölderlin is Virgilian. Virgil's *Aeneid*, which Hölderlin translated (granted at Schiller's condescending behest) while working on *Hyperion*, is the secret to understanding his Greekness. He did not so much wish simply to rewrite the Greeks in a modern idiom as somehow to repeat Virgil's repetition.

(*Dexter* is done. I just watched the last episode. He ends up neither dead nor imprisoned. He does not flee to start a new, almost normal life. He fakes his own death. He outlives himself. And so we find him at last in that bleak, massive landscape of the Pacific Northwest (or so I suppose); a logger, a tree among trees. *But you, you lordly ones, you stand like a race of titans in the tamer world and belong only to yourselves and to the heaven that nourished and raised you, and to the earth that bore you.* Alone . . . and, alone, with so many other solitary walkers and dark passengers: with Handke, with Bernhard, with Hamsun, with Hölderlin, with Rousseau. We had expected a tragedy or a comedy. We find something else. Just as Bernhard, after the theater—after Ibsen, whom Hamsun hated, after the Sophoclean, Oedipean Wild Duck (Tragedy: the old devour the young. Comedy: the young devour the old)—will dream of solitude, of cutting wood, as if forgetting that even the violence of the most acerbic language remains a form of sociality. Dexter is in the last instance an idyll. The serial killer who kills serial killers—like the writer who destroys language, like the proposition that turns against its own untruth—is the annihilation of that terrible duration during which justice takes place. One is still guilty, to be sure, but one is not condemned to one's guilt: the immediacy of a punishment, brought secretly and without trial, frees divine justice from the cruelty of time.)

CELEBRITY AND SINGULARITY

With celebrity, the singularity of the thing and the way it appears and becomes theorizable—its phenomenality—are twisted back into each other, threatening every attempt at tranquil divine contemplation. A multitude of beautiful smiles disappears in the celebrity's countenance; nothing remains but an oblique celluloid grin. We are forced back into history.

The celebrity is thus the one whose appearance consolidates and exemplifies a theory of appearance—whose very appearance makes appearance possible. Hence the celebrity must appear as the perversion of the romantic theory of the work of art. The celebrity comes into being at the very moment that the artwork fails to live up to the extraordinary theoretical and critical tasks with which it has become invested: the artwork fails, and its burden falls to the celebrity, conjured into existence at the very moment it is needed. The celebrity thus saves appearances—keeps them up, as we might say—but at the cost of falling outside of history and becoming mythic. Or in a word: the celebrity is the historicity of the a-historical. The smile of the celebrity banishes the luxurious flowing smiles of everyday life; even now celebrities always seem somehow iconic—and hence dated. But in taking up history, it destroys it: history itself becomes personal charisma.

It is no longer enough to aim critique, as Benjamin had done so valiantly, at the work. Criticism must take aim at the celebrity, this strange offspring of the work's miscarriage. The only criticism that matters is ad hominem, and cannot do without savage vulgarity. The celebrity, this monster of appearances, must appear in his or her celebricity.

INNOCENCE

There are two kinds of celebrities: some die a timely death, others outlive their life. The first make everything seem innocent again; with the second even innocence appears grotesque. But perhaps this grotesquerie of innocence is characteristic of the times. And in time it may even become a new innocence.

OF CELEBRICITY, OR: TOWARD A PHENOMENOLOGY OF MADONNA

1. The logic of truth, and even the logic of writing, is a special case of the logic of celebricity.

2. Truth is manifest appearance before it is correspondence, and the play of concealment and disclosure before it is manifest appearance. Uprooted from the modalities of celebricity that together constitute a constellation of differentia, the thinking of the play of concealment and disclosure collapses into an ultra-transcendental platitude.

3. Gods, human beings, animals, forms of language and forms of life, every single thing in, of, and beyond the world, comes about with and in a certain celebricity.

4. Each single world and the world of worlds are held together by a certain mode of celebricity. (Olympus is the celebricity of the gods.)

5. The sacred and the profane belong to the topology of celebricity; they are locations to which celebricity belongs.

6. Distance and proximity are aspects of celebricity.

7. Fame is an exemplary type of celebricity. The famous is extremely visible in its preeminence; distant, yet not too distant. Preeminence in virtue, beauty, strength, power make up for distance, but it still always keeps a certain distance—think of Achilles withdrawing into his tent. It can be seen sometimes, approached sometimes, and

touches much more than it is touched. The famous requires a political space. (Thus the significance of Thersites's words and Odysseus's blows.) The hero is famous, and thus even now, when our heroes seem so ordinary measured against Hercules and Achilles, this very ordinariness has become a trait of the heroic, and the hero is more often than not the everyday joe who performs a single act of tremendous courage or generosity. The hero is always a local hero, even if the locality is the world.

8. The common is visible in either a plainness that does not attract or an ugliness that repulses.

9. The everyday is the common that retreats from view, allowing itself to become distant and invisible.

10. The abject is the common that has been hidden away, or hides itself away, out of shame.

11. The base is the common that tries to become famous by making its ugliness visible.

12. The wretched is the common driven by need to expose itself.

13. Divinity is at once extremely invisible and extremely untouchable. It still touches: this is necessary to its celebrity, but can only happen rarely (the caresses of Thetis).

14. The universal is the simple plainness that the famous, the divine, the common, the abject, the everyday, and the wretched share: the visible invisibility and invisible visibility, distant proximity and proximate distance, profane sacredness and sacred profanity that conjoins these in a community with nothing in common. It is a zone of indistinction, specter and ghost.

15. Celebrity is a type of celebricity: it consists in the trinity of the divine (the Father), the famous (the Son), and the universal (the Holy Ghost) that joins the divine to the famous. Celebrity is the movement in which the divine (the ideal) becomes common (naive), the common becomes famous (heroic), and the heroic becomes ideal.

16. Celebrity is a type of celebricity but also the celebricity of celebricity. The One world is held together by celebrity: the celebricity of celebricity.

17. The celebrity of celebrities is the triune One holding the One world together by exposing celebrity.

18. Celebrities are the many who expose the One celebrity.

19. In the Common Era everyone who is anyone has appeared as a celebrity. (Vico spoke of modern history as a repetition of ancient history.)

20. There are two aspects of celebrity: celebrities who do not appear as celebrities but as something else and celebrities who appear as celebrities.

21. There are three kinds of celebrities: celebrities who play the famous; celebrities who play the universal; and celebrities who play the divine.

22. Of celebrities who do not appear as celebrities there are martyrs, who play the divine by imitating the divine sacrifice that is celebrity; there are warriors, who play the famous; and there are philosophers, who play the common.

23. Hegel in this sense was the last philosopher. Analytic philosophers in contrast are not post-Hegelian but pre-Hegelian: they know only the ordinary (the essence of which is prosaic language—what is unseen only because it is bland) or the scientific (the ordinary made exact).

24. After Hegel, perhaps already with Rousseau, the true philosopher could only appear as a celebrity. This is both because there was nothing left to say about the common and because they could only speak about the uncommon. The moment the philosopher speaks about the uncommon he becomes a celebrity-philosopher. Yet as soon as he becomes a celebrity-philosopher, he becomes impossible as philosopher, since the philosopher can only ever be the one who plays at the common. Whatever he says becomes common.

25. There are three kinds of celebrity-philosophers: those who speak of the divine; those who speak of the famous; and those who speak of the abject. (Rousseau and Plato already combined all three modes.)

26. Of these three, the third (Marx, Freud) are the greatest celebrities, since they speak of what is still common, indeed what is most common and uncommon to the common: the uncanny remainder, thrown off from the common,

that the common is at once exposed to within itself and of necessity excludes from itself.

27. Since all three try to speak of the uncommon to the common, all three must confront the danger to which philosophy is only ever exposed during those rare moments when it becomes important: vulgarization.

28. Philosophers were the first celebrities to appear as celebrities. But once philosophers could only appear as celebrities, once they became celebrities in this narrow sense, all other celebrities also had to appear as celebrities.

29. Thus the world of those who are somebody and yet not philosophers (we could speak of these quaintly as the ambitious, or with Plato, the spirited) split into two types: mere functionaries who gave up every trace of celebrity in return for effective power and wealth (the ordinary bourgeoisie) and those actual celebrities who have renounced every social function in return for the life of pure appearance.

30. Actual celebrities divide into the pure and the impure.

31. Impure actual celebrities are actual celebrities whose celebrity involves a functional skill that it at once includes and excludes, relies on and transcends.

32. Impure actual celebrities divide into managers and laborers: managers function through others, whereas laborers possess a tangible productive skill of their own.

33. Impure actual celebrity managers include military leaders, businesspeople, and politicians. Military leaders play at being famous; businesspeople play at being divine; politicians play at being common. The ideal type of the dictator combines all three.

34. Impure actual celebrity laborers include athletes, producing artists, and performing artists. These in turn correspond to the famous, divine, and common. (Hence the myths that surround each and mitigate our envy: athletes are set apart from us, yet not too far apart, by their physique and prowess; producing artists are either divine, if they are good, or nothing at all, if they aren't; performing artists do what we could do if we had only practiced enough and had a certain modicum of natural mechanical talent.)

35. The scholar is either an artist (theoretical physicists and mathematicians, Nobel Prize–winning chemists and biologists who make their greatest discoveries while dreaming or tripping) or a mere functionary. Or he is obscure.

36. Athletes are either superstars (who gravitate toward the divine: Michael Jordan), or great players (who gravitate toward the heroic: Scottie Pippen), or team players (Dickie Simpkins, the Thersites of the Chicago Bulls). Football tends toward the famous, basketball the divine, and baseball the common.

37. This explains why there can never be another Michael Jordan. And it also explains why Dennis Rodman had to be there, playing the Dionysus to Michael Jordan's Apollo—embodying that abject remnant (the rebound) that the divine tosses away from itself. If Michael Jordan had also been Dennis Rodman, this would have been too much.

38. Producing artists are either novelists and directors (the heroic), or poets and composers (the divine), or painters (the common). Hence the myths that surround these: everybody wants to be a novelist or filmmaker but they lack the time, money, resources, endurance, quiet . . . or perhaps even (but this is always an afterthought) the talent; almost no one wants to be a poet or a composer, and almost no one can be; everyone could be a painter, since all they do is scribble or drip paint on a canvas. And now the painter who everyone thinks they can be has assumed a very concrete form: the photographer.

39. Performing artists are either dancers (the heroic), or musicians (the divine), or actors (the common).

40. There is an obscurity to labor. This obscurity transgresses these boundaries in an essential way, and indeed the power of all forms of celebrity labor consists only in these transgressions. (With the rise of the ballerina *en pointe* the heroic dancer became divine, and with Nijinsky the divine dancer became common.)

41. Pure actual celebrities are celebrities whose functional skill appears as a magical aptitude.

42. The purely pure actual celebrity is the actor (the myth of acting is that it is a purely natural talent—thus the child actor) or the model. The impurely pure actual celebrity is the pop star.

43. The model is at once a pure celebrity and a noncelebrity. Her beauty represents celebrity, yet the celebrity that it represents cannot outlive the beauty that represents.

44. The model who is past her prime either disappears or, if she is a supermodel, reinvents herself as a commodity by taking possession of an image that has already become alien to her.

45. The actor plays either the famous or the common.

46. The purely pure actual celebrity who plays the divine is not possible, but the exposure of this impossibility is of the essence of celebrity.

47. This impossibility takes three forms. First: the actor (Mel Gibson) who plays the divine by playing a martyr. Though in this case the divine becomes common, and can only be represented as an odious fusion of the famous hero (Christ made buff as if he were in an action film) and the everyman (Christ as humble carpenter). Second, the actress who plays the divine by being beautiful. (But in this case her acting freezes into modeling: she seems cold, distant, unapproachable. The divine has again resumed a mythic form.) Third, the rock star, who must choose between growing old and thus becoming common and ridiculous or dying a martyr's death.

48. Madonna has tried to do it all. But this can only amount to nothing. The transformation between these forms offers no release from the entrapment of the spirit in the body of these forms.

49. Even if she were to adopt every orphan in the world, Madonna will never be a hero.

(The voice, the voice—where is the voice? Where is the singing celebrity? Why this silence? All the articulations of celebrity have something to do with the voice. Even the dancer, whose voice is silence. Yet the celebrity voice is not the solitary voice listening to itself but the voice of celebricity: of the phenomenality of truth-play, the play of concealment-unconcealment in its ever originary, originating singularity. The voice listening to itself never hears anything but its commonality, its ideality. But there is a trace of the singular voice that is there for others, and it is precisely this singularity that is also the kernel of the voice's publicness. Yet this is never *there for us*: it can never be made present. It is scattered into possibilities, and always ever exists, as it were, ecstatically, in the transition between these—or, better, in the impossible moment when one possibility touches another. The dancer, in silence, comes closest to exhibiting this touching.)

THE STRANGE CELEBRITY

Most celebrities are relatively simple. If the location of celebrity is the triune relationship between the divine, the heroic, and the universal, the ordinary celebrity connects up with only one of these moments. We in turn connect with the celebrity through this connection. The celebrity type involves a certain conflation of an archetype (a root form of celebricity) and its contingent historical permutation. Nothing is strange in this, and the entire connection could be reduced to a simple identification with a simple, manifestly exposed, intensely concentrated aspect of human being.

The strange celebrity is something entirely different. While more universally popular than any other celebrity, this popularity has almost nothing to do with a simple identification.

(A point of clarification: Marilyn Manson or Boy George, not to mention Psy or Miley Cyrus, is not the least bit strange in this sense. The strange has nothing to do with the identifiably grotesque, Goth, androgynous, or every other deflection of the normal into an extreme of fashionable coolness. Nor does the strange have anything to do with an intellectual sophistication. David Bowie, Lou Reed, Iggy Pop, Björk only seem strange, measured against other celebrities, to the degree that they verge away from their own celebrity by supplementing it with a discourse of self-representation.)

The strange celebrity is an infinite set of fragmentary qualities: the *disjecta membra* of the human. We connect with the celebrity only because we find an infinity of our own fragmentary qualities in him. We do not identify simply but infinitely.

The ordinary celebrity is either the singleton of the null set ($\emptyset$) (the universal), or ω (the divine), or a finite ordinal (the heroic). The strange celebrity is a real number as defined within the system of surreal numbers: ω is its matter, and its form and residue are both infinite. The infinite form "represents" the infinite system of fractional qualities. And hence the profound difference in how we relate to the ordinary versus the strange celebrity: with the former we connect through a single aspect, which nevertheless may be either void or the first order of infinity; with the latter through an infinite multitude of aspects that nevertheless remain as mere ordinals between 0 and ω, scattered across an infinity; merely finite fragments.

These fragments all have a heroic quality. The hero's qualities converge in simple gestures. The heroic fragment is a gesture that has been torn away from its "natural" belonging to the fluid, vital, active motions of the body: the body at war.

The infinite set of heroic fragmentary gestures constituting the strange celebrity corresponds to the fragmentary gestures of labor that industrialization released from the fluid, active, motions of the body. The strange celebrity is the negative real to the positive real of *homo laborans*.

The strange celebrity is strange because he is infinitely similar to everybody (in their real existence as laborers) and yet Ø, the simple expression of the everybody (the universal, that which is not only included, but belongs to everybody), does not belong to his form.

History obeys an economy of limitation: if the mathematical kingdom of numbers extends beyond our wildest imagination into an infinity of infinities contained within the untotalizable system of surreal numbers, historical becoming is constrained by a limited quantity of force. In the realm of thinking (the ideal) this limit loosens up. But in the real (the realm of becoming most strictly bound by this limitation) real numbers are produced only by way of approximation. Thus they are rare, indeed singular, events. The most closely approximate real number is the epoch itself: an infinite set of fragments. (Every epoch, as its becoming, is always infinitely fragmentary. There was never an epoch of simple totality. It is only the representation of an epoch that is simple.) The strange celebrity is an infinite approximation to this infinite approximation of the real in the real.

There can only ever be one strange celebrity at any time: this is Michael Jackson. And perhaps there is only one, ever. Perhaps there really will be only one King of Pop.

Any attempt to distinguish between Michael Jackson's talent and his strangeness must fail. Michael Jackson's dancing, more than anything—and certainly more than his personal life—exemplifies a strangeness that is also our own. This dancing consists in a continuous flow of odd, dissociated gestures. He pulls back his hair, pulls up his pants, touches his crotch, bows to the audience, walks backward and forward at the same time (as if on an assembly line), points off into nowhere, tips his hat. It is more modern than the most modern dancing, yet held together by the style of pure grace—tied to a voice that is at once soulful and rich, fragile, frenetic, and strained.

Grace is the principle of the continuum: it makes it possible to identify (with) the unidentifiable. The strange celebrity must be infinitely graceful. His is the grace of labor. Yet this grace must at the same time become style; it must assume commercial form. Pure grace does not sell, but style does. Style is the commodity form of grace.

Thus the ambiguity of the strange celebrity: as grace, he shows what we are as fragmentary labor, but as style, his grace and our labor decay into an auratic property that can be attached to almost anything, allowing for the general (a sugary brown liquid, for example) to join with the singular and become a brand.

(The ordinary celebrity can and will die of a drug overdose. But the strange celebrity, who seemed so intent on substituting growing strange for growing old, has found a death fitting his strangeness. Sixty days without sleep, without true sleep: or rather, with a sleep that had been artificially induced. Sleep has become commodity-sleep, gadget-sleep. We can only fall asleep, just as we can only fall in love. And for most of us, most of the time, it is so easy. If it has become impossible for the strange celebrity, it is because he has himself become a gadget: his potentialities—and we might regard sleep, not death, as the outermost of these—are commodity-potentialities. The IV drip becomes the input through which sleep is induced. And to a point we have all experienced this: the strange freedom of turning the body over to medicine, submitting it to grotesque and unimaginable interventions. But is this so different from falling asleep watching TV?)

THE UNCANDY

The celebrity seduces, and every seduction must be taken seriously. For it is never the known and familiar pleasure, but the promise of an unknown pleasure, that seduces; perhaps even the pleasure of the unknown. Happiness is the name for this promise of pleasure. Every age has its own happiness, its own seductions: these are felt everywhere in the suspension of their realization, and recognized, if at all, only at the peripheries. Thus the celebrity comes to us in dreams.

(Kim Yuna comes to me, and I awaken to the memory of a pleasure that bore possibility as if in its womb. Yet it was not another awakening of the body's desires—life has many of these awakenings—or the abstract, pure, possessionless pleasures of dream-sex, but something more intoxicating, unsettling, voluptuous. She showed nothing intimate; we did not touch. She needed me, but only to watch her and celebrate her—from amidst the multitude; just one of many, yet special to her, infinitely special. My own *vita nuova* could have begun here. Perhaps it did. I was struck by a terrifying question: is mankind God's celebrity?)

These dreams can be interpreted only in the sobriety of philosophical reflection. Hence the strange power of the music video, of music television (music-vision from afar—an unfathomed dialectical subtlety hides here): that odd companion to my adolescence. Dreams suddenly became visible, colliding with consciousness, as with the strifeful interplay of the Apollonian-Dionysian. Yet a different play was at work, for there was rarely tragic bitterness or tragic depth but something sickeningly, seductively sweet, like those candied apples that my mother forbade me to eat.

Brian Wilson composed "California Girls" while tripping for the first time. The most powerful utopian visions are always born of terror. Psychedelic drugs keep us dangling at the threshold between the divinatory and the childish—like *Alice in Wonderland, The Nutcracker,* or *Charlie and the Chocolate Factory*—bringing to its fulfillment a motif born in the furnaces of industrial capitalism. The ground beneath our feet, the walls of our house, become edible. Commodities begin to dance. And if the Christmas sweets hidden away in cardboard chambers and meted out with the days of the month is the only form of eschatology that could insinuate itself into a purely secular upbringing, then perhaps only this remains of the Christian God: a sugar daddy.

Uncanny, uncandy. A bad pun, no doubt: but it gives a name to the feeling that grips me as I watch this video for the nth time, trying to trace out the slight, strange, sinuous convulsions in that resonance machine of a soul that has already been infiltrated and left tender by world spirit.

Fine, fresh, fierce—the triune aspect not only of the commodity come to life, and the flesh turned into commodity, but a moment of revelation. The contradiction between these attributes is telling: what could be at once refined and savage, fresh yet processed, new to the world like a child yet already inducted into its ways. At once consumer and consumed. Hence the numbing repetition of a candied-over fellation: oral intercourse, in which the delectable becomes delector, is the iconic gesture of late capitalism.

CANDY CANDY

The genius of this video, by the Japanese pop star Kyary Pamyu Pamyu, is to have banished men, and almost even the phallus signifier, from the land of candy: only a lollipop remains, and perhaps a faceless onion (a certain bitterness: the clitoris?): but this is a customary symbol of femininity as well, and appears for only an instant. Key changes, almost always signifying an intensification leading to climax and release, have also been banished. There is almost nothing hard about love anymore: it has become chewy, sweet, girls' love. The spell of the commodity has been dispelled—and perhaps also the spell of love. The commodity no longer dreams beyond itself, no longer insists on its dream: it no longer dreams of others, lovers, fulfillment, success, money, wealth, cars. Not completely dispelled, the spell of the celebrity remains, beyond love: the girl-celebrity, the cute-celebrity in all her spotless purity—she who can almost, through the veil of obvious metaphors and with monstrous, Muppet-like feet, show herself masturbating.

(in counterpoint: *No No No* by the Korean girl group APink. Here we still remain in the realm of classical narratives, a rhetoric of modulation, the sacred/profane, negation, jilted lovers . . .)

WHAT PERCENTAGE OF THE AMERICAN POPULATION
ARE CELEBRITIES?

If information is the driving force of our economy, then celebrity is a class category. For the celebrity exists as a radiating center of information that draws all attention to itself, giving information a human shape and even a bit of old-world charisma. Yet even in our age, when the political has been reduced to statistics, this question still finds no answer in all of cyberspace. Perhaps no answer is possible. Celebrity—unlike wealth, intelligence, power—cannot be counted but at the price of its glamour. Is celebrity nondenumerable, transfinite? Or perhaps the celebrity is only counted in death: and what we think of as a celebrity is only an eerie bleeding over of the obituary into the front pages of the daily news. But then we would all be celebrities in death; and all dead . . . as celebrities. And does this not beckon us toward the vanishing point where the destinations of information technology and Christianity converge?

The bourgeoisie is, for Barthes, an "anonymous society"—a "joint-stock company"—a community to which one can belong only by no longer belonging in name. Yet the celebrity blurs this anonymity at both ends: if everything must appear general, universal, static, a-historical, these qualities cannot themselves appear in any immediacy without summoning their opposites. If the ideological function of mythology, to dehistoricize the historical, were to reach its end and produce the appearance of the a-historical as such—if it were actually to produce the signification that it always intends—then it would flip out into the very opposite (chaos, revolution, pure history). The celebrity thus must intervene to introduce infinite deferment, difference, distortion, delay into the semiological-ideological system. The celebrity allows everything nameless, everything denominated and profaned, to be given a name, though only the one name of celebrity: the everyman, the mass who passes like a ghost through history as the one who has always been there without being represented, becomes Forest Gump, becomes Tom Hanks—who governs like Zeus over an inverted, upward-turned pantheon of celebrities who can multiply their number only by becoming more freakish, more strange, more beautiful-grotesque; whose nymphs and satyrs reach into the heavens with glorious, naive-beautiful deaths.

SPECTERS OF SPECTOR

Thomas Bernhard's prince: from on high in his mountain palace, surrounded by forest, his schizophrenic gaze sees through everything. A vision of a model of vision (again we might speak of Old Europe, of a certain faded feudal order) that still perhaps speaks to us, and yet has less and less to say about who we are, about how our world is. And it is not only the bourgeois mole's cavernous, subterranean excavations that did it in. (*Verstörung*, after all, undermines Kafka's burrow from above and behind, and through a gesture that is of necessity epigonal, from an author who ostentatiously scorned the prizes that Kafka never had a chance to win, and even shared a death that by his time could only appear quaintly anachronistic.)

If the law is a visor, seeing everything without being seen, then the aristocrats, descendants of knights who once wore visors, were the uncanny, unsettling (Kleist might have said *entsetzlich*) coincidence and conjunction of the law and the body of a single man: uncanny, because these things could of course never coincide; the conjunction could only be a disjunction. The spirit of the law haunts the body, makes one become two, a ghost of itself, and precisely because it is more than itself: and this doubling of the body, whose law must come to nothing if it cannot settle on the question of its succession—if it cannot live beyond its proper, legitimate life long enough to settle on another legitimate successor—is the richest theme of Shakespeare's plays. And Bernhard knew that (in Austria at least) the Old Europe, exorcised from Realpolitik, could not but live on in a spirit that still claims its rights to everything. The bourgeois can gather his worms and grubs, he can call them capital, and imagine he rules the world: the weight of the world still oppresses him.

The celebrity has at once nothing and everything to do with aristocracy. (Vienna and Hollywood, Austria and California? A tension and affinity more fascinating than Athens and Jerusalem: here I think not only of Schwarzenegger but Schoenberg—we could almost fit everything between these two signatures.)

On the one hand: the existence of the aristocrat undoes the public sphere, and yet the public sphere could only ever exist as a community of aristocrats, arising not from the triumph of the masses over the few, but of the few over themselves. The few overcome themselves by becoming the many. They agree to multiply their gazes and their laws through an endless process of conjunctions and disjunctions. A true public is rare: perhaps there has never been such a thing, not even in Greece.

On the other hand: the existence of the people, of us, this travesty of the public, produces celebrity in a curious attempt to see itself. The people, this single invisible body of the law that sees without being seen, must see itself, and precisely also in order to be enforceable: capable of touching the other to which it must refer. (Here too we could speak of a certain logic of supplementarity: the law can only exist as pure law—belonging to anybody would contaminate it—and yet it also needs a body to supplement it, since this very purity, a purely formal purity, can grant it neither purpose nor efficacy.)

The aristocrat would see without being seen or touched (though even he cannot keep the physician from visiting). The celebrity would be seen without seeing, or rather (celebrities should not be confused with bards or with Oedipus—they have neither an eye too few or too many) seeing only what everyone else sees. (What do celebrities do in their mansions? Watch TV.) The true celebrity wishes to be exposed: if he does not bare all it is only out of coyness, or because he stupidly supposes he is a "real artist," or because he is a man and cannot expose everything without revealing something that would interrupt the logic of exhibitionism.

This celebrity-vision envisions the phantasmic body of the law of the people. Thus a certain almost dialectical necessity, oddly confirmed in real life: the celebrity who would have sought to escape absolutely from the gaze—who would build his own castle in a neverland outside the public sphere and beyond the people's gaze, or who would become a voyeur, or take the law into his own hands—must become the object of the "public spectacle" of a juridical process.

The process of justice, the violence of which is for the most part hidden away, must appear, as if to confirm that we, the public, exist; as if it could not exist unless it were capable of touching the one thing of whose existence we can be sure. Yet something still unsettles us: the culmination and realization of justice, punishment in its subtle brutality, remains strictly off-limits. The celebrity, sent to prison, cannot remain a celebrity. For if the prison is a panopticon, if the prison door turns the visor on its head, making the one inside the one who is seen without being able to see, the power of vision has nevertheless been restricted to a few, just as the execution, hidden away in a secret chamber and entrusted to the care of those whose trade can never become a profession, remains perhaps the last remnant of the mystery rites of the ancient world.

If the "culture of celebrity" depends to the last on the death of the imagination—the exclusion of the imagination as the schizo-productive power that would allow a true public sphere to emerge by granting a sovereign power to all—then here, at the very point where the power of the public has almost realized its most radical, if paradoxical, intention; just as the public is on the verge of passing beyond the limit of voyeurism; precisely now, when the celebrity, having already given away everything, whose private moments we have observed, has been remanded to custody, is being processed, and will be submitted to those humiliating inspections of the body; just at the moment when the celebrity has been reduced to pure passivity, with the law's long arm breaching his intimate places: just at this moment, we the people must forbid ourselves to see what we most desire to see.

At the very moment when a politics founded on the rejection of a multitudinous imagination in favor of the spectacular reality of commodity-dream-life—on the dreamworks of an industry that makes us imagine everything and allows us to imagine nothing—has envisioned its spectral fulfillment, we are left to imagine what has been forbidden us to imagine.

Some celebrities—young, pretty, female—will be sent to prison for a few days or a few hours. They remain celebrities even in prison, speaking through their lawyers as if from beyond the grave. This can satisfy us . . . for a time. Coming back to the world, they are perhaps a bit more ghastly and ghostly, but they are still with us, to amuse us—and if they have been touched by something terrible, it does not really touch us because we can still touch them. Oprah Winfrey awaits: to assure us that we know what they are going through.

But others will be sent away for life, and perhaps even someday a celebrity will be executed. (The serial killer, famous only by becoming infamous, does not count: they are not like us.) And thus someday the strain on the public imagination will become acute, and the public itself will reach its breaking point.

Castles and prison, the lifestyle of the rich and famous and the solitude of the cell, sexual gratification and body cavity searches: all will converge into a single explosive point—counterpoint to Josef Fritzl's (or was it Bernhard's) Austrian incest-dungeon.

EXCREMENT AND ENTERPRISE

The problem of consumption, the need to produce consumption, marks the limit not only of a neoliberal model of governance, but of governance as such. There is a certain shame before consumption: it cannot be taught in the schools even if it is learned in the schools. There is no governmental apparatus subtle enough not to make a mockery of it. The cult of individual consumption (as opposed to grand Keynesian gestures: the equivalent of a vulgar political theology of mass spectacles) must be kept at a distance from government if not from politics. Not because government must be forbidden such powers, but because such powers could not be realized, but only destroyed, by government. Nor could the government rely on the markets, with their putative rationality, to produce the a-rational, if not irrational, effects of infinite consumption.

Celebrities are first of all the masters of self-marketing. They turn the self (whether the mind, the spirit, or the body, or some combination thereof) not into a commodity but into an enterprise. Prostitutes sell their bodies; celebrities market the idea of their bodies. But the enterprise of the celebrity always combines production and consumption: it is nothing but this combination. What the celebrity produces and markets is above all the immanently realized dream of consumption as production and production as consumption. (The ideal of enterprise is of fulfilled activity.)

Every celebrity is the patron saint for a certain style of production-consumption, the exemplary form of a singular mode of self-marketing—a self produced through and as marketing. We might call this a lifestyle. The most extreme celebrity lifestyle is suicide. An early death is always good. But old age, in which the body is consumed without producing so much as a beautiful corpse, is the death of celebrity. The tabloid may still turn this to profit, yet it falls outside the celebrity's own enterprise.

This enterprise reaches deep into the body: pregnancy and sex are eminently marketable. Are there limits? Does the excrement of a celebrity also have value?

To imitate celebrities is to imitate at once their type and the originality of their type. Losers are those who are incapable of this dialectical trick: who either do not seem to imitate at all or seem to imitate too much. Popularity can only exist in a state of thoughtlessness. Self-reflection makes it impossible.

THE DISSOCIATING PLEASURE OF THINGS

Power produces a language of power, since the operation of power and the formation of language coincide and even (though this cooperation is diachronic rather than synchronic and structural) cooperate and collaborate. Power functions through operations of singularization, generalization, particularization, subordination, and superordination—the structure of power is logical. The operation of power is a logical operation, and thus every form of power assumes a logical form. Power produces the possibility of the logos, of discursive language, from within. And this logos in turn confirms the operation of power. Yet this does not mean that the articulated language of power (the language-apparatus of power) always names power literally and prosaically. When it does so, indeed, the specific modality of power is already nearing its end. Rather: power avails itself of a language that more or less obliquely reproduces its structure through a general organization of things.

Yet power depends not only on this logical language, which determines what we might call the normal operation. There is a mystique to power, a mystery: an aspect that recedes at once from presence and from the operations of logic. This mystique has at least two ends. Hölderlin called these heaven and earth, Agamben calls them sovereignty and bare life. But perhaps there are other ends, other limits to logic. Power recedes from logic at its height and its depths, and the normal operation of power, with its various modalities of operation, itself depends on this very obscurity.

Vico tried to think the relation between the formation of language and the formation of power, taking neither for granted. The rigor of his project (his romantic followers produce a hollow echo) remains to be grasped.

To speak of power is itself problematic. Power names the nexus of power-logics: and precisely insofar as these, for all their differentiated multitude of operations, nevertheless function in accord (the grand harmony of a global system of power, of Empire) through a logic of generalization. That we can and must speak of power as such: this is at once a demand that arises from within power so far as it seeks to solidify and extend its operations, but it also exposes power to a certain liability. At a certain point (Shakespeare's *King Lear* shows us just this point) power cannot draw on its mysteries as mysteries but must expose them.

To think this exposure is perilously difficult, even dangerous. If power articulates itself through language, then every discourse about power is also a discourse of power. We must avoid the rhetoric of coming communities, otherwise beginning beginnings, messianic expectations—every attempt to force an indiscernible difference. The moment that power is exposed in language, language itself exposes, or is exposed as, or is simply there as an immanent possibility that escapes power. Power, in all its modalities, could only appear as a certain special case of language.

This possibility of language, or rather this opening in language, might be called (if we need a name) its literariness, though this should not be thought of as an ultra-transcendental structure but rather as the nontranscendentalizable; that which can never be reduced to structure, however paradoxical in its articulation.

Writing this literariness is not a question of inscribing its paradoxical structure through a never-ending discourse of difference. This must always appear as a ruse: someone will always be waiting to show the emperor in the nakedness of a vestment that has become infinitely threadbare. It is a matter of showing the literariness that belongs to everything as the residue of an operation of power that cannot help but take place within a linguistic element beyond its command. But this residue is not the mystery of the thing; it is not earth and concealment.

Such a strategy might begin by exploring the dissociating pleasures of the commodity. These are pleasures that have become detached, and are capable of detaching us, from power. For example: wrapping and unwrapping, connecting and disconnecting, finishing and unfinishing, sending and receiving. These, to be sure, operate within a system of power, but they also elude it.

The computer (like the cell phone) suggests the ambiguity of these dissociating pleasures. On the one hand: the computer confirms a dream of power, and more specifically of power as enterprise. The computer gives us the power of self-marketing but makes us at the very same moment the target of a marketing tailored in ominous fashion to our individuality. This power operates through the operations of dissociating pleasure—pleasures that are without self, without subjectivity, even without pleasure in the neural-psychological sense. These dissociating, abstracting pleasures can be dislodged from all the dreams of power. They can exist on their own. The genius of Steve Jobs was to realize this. By giving the logical, hierarchical architecture of the computer a visual form, he opened up a world of pleasures taking place either at the transitory threshold of a logical operation (we are made to experience in time that which in the operations of the computer has no time) or in the surface without depth of the visual display.

ABSTRACT PLEASURES

The Internet grants an unusual insight into abstract pleasures: pleasures that are not physical and sensual, spiritual, or even intellectual—that are not related to the experience of a given faculty of the mind or the body; that have neither the duration of sensation nor the duration of contemplation, and yet also have no relation to the satisfaction of our needs or to the eventual fulfillment of a certain ideal we have of ourselves.

It is tempting to relate these back to the more substantial, "real" pleasures with which philosophers have long been familiar. But this would be a mistake. Let us rather say that abstract pleasures are the pure form of every real pleasure, and that a reduction, if necessary, should proceed in the opposite direction. For perhaps the pleasure of experience, of enjoying the very reality of our enjoyment, should itself be ranked among such abstract pleasures.

The concept of virtual reality misses what is at stake in these abstract pleasures. The joy of games of simulation is not that they allow us to mimic reality or live vicariously but rather that they free abstract pleasures from the pleasure of the real. The obsession with replicating the experience of reality reflects one of those numbing laws of culture—that the most absurd expenditures of energy and innovation are often devoted to recuperating antiquated forms of experience.

So much of history's melancholic barbarism has resulted from the attempt to add the pleasure of the real to abstract pleasures that have nothing to do with reality. Accumulation is an abstract pleasure, but when the pleasure of accumulation can only be achieved by way of an elaborate detour through the concreteness of material reality, it loses all its innocence. Granted: there can be no accumulation without finitude, and the pleasures of finitude. But we should not suppose that material reality is the only form that finitude can take.

Perhaps someday we will realize that everything that has been said by philosophers about the soul was only a groping attempt to translate back into the language of the real those forms of pleasure that have nothing intrinsically to do with the real. And that the body, like the soul, is nothing but the imprecise location of a certain nexus of abstract pleasures.

Writing has a way of producing a certain abstraction of pleasure. It is indeed in this way that we might avoid both psychologism and historicism. The effect of writing is clearest whenever Epicureans commit their thoughts to paper: the very attempt to communicate the real pleasures of the body graces them with an unreality that, without being exactly spiritual, exceeds every materialist postulate. The writings of Lucretius are exemplary in this regard. The pleasure of reading is at the limit of hedonism. Yet the effects of writing are no less evident in the writing of Platonists and mystics.

The critique of the metaphysics of presence belongs to the critique of pleasure, and is perhaps nothing more than a special case of the latter.

(There is something quite charming about more mundane, stupid pornography, portrayed by actors whose words are as clumsy as their bodies are carefree and graceful. In a world where everyone always knows where everything should be put, the adult films' stars betray, in their halfhearted attempts at acting, the philosophical embarrassment that all of us feel with our bodies. They seem like children, playing insouciantly with gifts that they did not ask for, never expected to receive, and have no idea how to use. Extravagant pleasure is the correlate not of expertise but of a certain ignorance.)

EXPERIENCES

The idea is not the ground or measure of experience but its illumination. Yet there is no simple correspondence between experience and the illumination of experience. The illumination of experience at once belongs to experience and transcends it. Every experience awaits illumination, and yet what it awaits is not absent but excessively, superfluously, *there*. The task of criticism is to reduce the excess to a single point.

The medium of illumination is language—a pure language of philosophy that has freed itself from the task of explaining or judging reality. It is not a question of rejecting metaphysics by returning either to physics or to the deceptive commonsense virtuosity with which language explains itself but of inventing in language figures of truth.

Philosophy can approach politics only when it has abandoned the pretenses of political philosophy. It is not for philosophy either to judge politics or to abandon it but to touch upon it, gently and yet with a transfiguring force. Politics is both a practice and a theory of experience. Philosophy in contrast is neither theory nor practice but the sense of theory and practice.

The transcendental grounding of experience is not the goal of philosophy but only a starting point. A transcendental deduction should do nothing more than allow experience to appear in its sufficiency—not as an end in itself, but so that it can become exposed to sense.

The distance of theory and practice is always the result of a philosophical violence—the violence of making experience subject to judgment. Experience becomes virtuosic—automatic, one might say—when this distance collapses, and it is only in this virtuosity that it becomes possible to lead experience back to, and beyond, its sufficiency.

THE THEORY OF SUFFERING

The most difficult thing is to find the point at which the impossibility of individual and historical existence converge. Most thinkers, failing this, retreat to a terrain where thinking is still easy or at least possible. But it is with this double impossibility—the impossible thinking of the impossibility of existence—that thinking begins. And even for those who have found this point, it mostly remains a mere feeling, the somber companion to their days. The words, the virtuosity of thinking, have escaped them.

True suffering is the index of an impossibility. And thus the entire theory of moods must be drawn back to a theory of suffering.

The heaviness of thinking finds its counterpoise in the levity of writing. Writing is playful, virtuosic, apathetic, infinitely forgetful and infinitely mindful—an act of pure creation; a play of chance. Thinking is like the afterburner of a rocket pulled back to earth.

When we are happy now we are like machines. Everything points this way. True suffering happens only when we lose our momentum; only when we become dislodged from our virtuosic systems. But to find the suffering of our age, we must refuse its happiness. To find words for its suffering, we must become like machines again.

Yet it is a mistake to suppose that thinking has a political task, even if it concerns itself intimately with the political. One should not think that any age fails to know what it means to be happy. An age is nothing but this knowledge: a knowledge that is only granted through a mode of existence transcending all individual reflection and irreducible to all philosophical insight. Political thinking is essentially mediocre and constrained in its vision. It sees only this one form of happiness and can seek nothing beyond it. But the thinker must not try to destroy the happiness (and let us not say: the illusions) of the others, or replace it with another happiness. He must only destroy it for himself. He cannot hope to share a suffering that, being shared, falls back into the orbit of the happiness of the age.

The suffering of the thinker must become purely imaginary. Real suffering is not only always too much—it immobilizes—but it always refers us back to the thought of a possible happiness, and this possible happiness, however obscure, remains always the happiness of the age.

Thinking is the act of refusing the happiness of the age and beginning to suffer. Writing is the act of making suffering imaginary, and virtuosic.

ADVERTISING

The homogenizing power of capital breaks down in advertising. Not only does it preserve through differences in production-value gaps between spheres of economic activity, but it also reveals the subtlest symptoms of cultural difference. This is in part because advertising still remains rhetorical, even if not reducible to rhetoric, and thus cannot do without language (even if sometimes doing without words). Thus the path from the same desire to the same commodity must take a detour through a *Wunderkammer* of obliquely expressed dreams, thwarted desires, social codes, affective registers, possibilities of happiness, memories of trauma. But can we even speak of the same desire? Does not desire itself become, in language and through advertising, infinitely heterogeneous. And not only this: there is a mystery to desire of which the advertiser has an uncanny knowledge. Desire is neither a feeling or emotion, nor the product of a faculty of imagination that could be isolated in its subjective purity, nor the fundamental essence of the self. Desire is neither need nor the excess of need over the natural. Desire is rather the moment of touching, of communication, of transition and transcendence. All desire is a desire to become otherwise. It is, in Plato's language, demonic. Or in Hölderlin's: hyperbolic. Perhaps this is why the visual language of advertising focuses on the hand, lips, and the eyes.

THE NEXT TOP MODEL

Celebrity—as the charm of asymmetrical attraction—organizes everything, is at the center of everything, represents a power more powerful than money or labor, and yet it cannot be produced, cannot be manufactured according to any known formula or process. The law that governs celebrity, this is to say, is an irreducible trace of lawlessness that compromises every attempt to reduce social behavior to rational agency. Or indeed: it is what appears at the limit when mass behavior, organized around certain forms of rationality, compromises itself through a positive feedback loop of infinite reflection.

(Economics becomes history at this point of compromise. Hence crisis, rather than leading to revolution, merely brings about the radically new that the old needs in order to keep on keeping on: new celebrities, demagogues, fetish-commodities.)

Advertising and branding are powerful forces, but their power never goes beyond enforcing the mystique of things. There is no transformation, no power to make things other than they are. The magic is always in the thing itself (the coveted object, the celebrity).

Every reality show is a sort of alchemical experiment. It is no more possible to manufacture celebrity than to transform lead into gold, and yet the reason does not rest in the immutable laws of nature. Rather, the moment a certain formula is discovered, this discovered possibility becomes impossibility. No one has ever struggled to become a celebrity, or if they did, it is only because they would have struggled to become and do anything. The doors to celebrity are few, but they are wide open, and each closes the moment one has passed through.

The reality show does not produce celebrity. The producers, the contestants—everyone (but the celebrity, perhaps) knows this. It is an experiment that we know will fail time and time again. But the pleasure is not only in this failure: it is in witnessing the trials of those who occupy this odd liminal space between the celebrity and the everybody.

The life of the half-celebrity, the becoming-celebrity trying to become the unbecomable, comes down to this: a series of tests, of human experiments, that derive their torturous appeal from the fact that they measure only those qualities that exist at the threshold between the voluntary and involuntary. These are things that could perhaps be mastered, but only with a brutal regime of discipline starting from childhood, and even then only if one starts out with the right stuff. Totalitarian states have been able to create new people by denaturing human nature. (Rousseau recognized in this the essence of classical politics.)

But we in contrast take pleasure in the futility of our incapacity. And in a certain way the entire glamour of the celebrity stands in a necessary relation to this futility. Does this mean then that celebrity would be produced after all. Not in the least. The negativity of incelebrity (which is neither infamy, nor ordinariness, nor obscurity) exhibits celebrity, and becomes needed at that critical moment when celebrity can no longer show itself, when it becomes in a certain way ashamed of itself, and has only one of two choices: become serious or disappear.

Survivor had too much intrigue and too much stupidity, and *American Idol* judges and discovers, but it does not train: and this has everything to do with the nature of the voice. The more perfect reality shows are second or third rate: *America's Next Top Model* is in every way exemplary.

Beauty is not only at once natural and artificial, but grace, beauty-in-motion (the model's pose is nothing else) stands at the threshold between the conscious and unconscious, reflexive and naive. Everything comes down to the play and game of the eyes: the ineffable contact of the eye that is seen with the eye that sees. The eye must neither look too intently nor look away but must somehow look without looking too much. It must look forcefully yet gently: and indeed all the features of the face and gestures of the body must conspire together in a certain willed softness, a vulnerability somehow intended and yet not forced. (The failure to do this has two extreme forms: the cold bitch, whose ambition to become a model can be read in her face—who seems too focused, too intent— and the hooch, who opens herself up too easily to the gaze. There is something mythic, epic about these contests. Like Barthes's wrestling. Or like Goethe's Ottilie. Indeed like every great novelistic figuration of femininity and its lyrical evocations. It is always a schematism for truth in its truthing—*Wahrheit, alētheia, veritas, emet,* always a woman, opening-closing.)

Thus the strange, excruciating trials that the not-yet-models must endure. Everything they learned as children they must learn again: to walk, to speak, to look, to kiss, to caress, to jump, to smile, to laugh. And yet there is never time for this. And the joke remains: none of them will ever become a "top model," not even the winners. If they have not yet been discovered, they never will be, though of course this nondiscovery, a failure exposed to the world, makes them more known than most models will ever be. But this being known is not celebrity. It attaches only to "real persons," who will never be more than what they are, or rather, what they are becoming in their becoming. The celebrity, in contrast, *is* with perfect simplicity. There might even be unknown celebrities. Celebrities who are beyond the gaze. Perhaps the Messiah is one.

The model is, moreover, a limit case of celebrity. The true model possesses a purely transitive beauty and charm: it empties out immediately and without remainder into the commodity that gains a name while the model remains nameless. In contrast, the celebrity-actor, the most celebrated celebrity, becomes the very union of the profane everybody and the sacredness of celebrity. The moment that a model is more recognizable than the products she advertises, she becomes a supermodel, who is no longer really a model sensu stricto but a center of gravity that draws things into her orbit; who bestows an aura on commodities by the grace of her touch. And the supermodel thus always involves an element of myth. She is almost always past her prime: the nostalgia of the famous beauty whose fame never quite coincides with her beauty.

(The fashion model is in this sense the least interesting and the least exemplary, since with her there remains a functional relation between the model and the commodity. She could probably even get away with being cold, projecting an impenetrable, feline arrogance on the catwalk. Those models, however, who model things intended for men—motorcycles, for example—merely allow a metaphoric identification between the use of the object and the use of a woman. The exemplary model models makeup and jewelry. In the first case the model gives form to what is inherently soft and gooey, identifying mere color with the shapes and lines it is supposed to produce. In the second, the model takes a hard and cold substance and infuses it with the soft, glowing light of desire.)

The reality show almost always takes place in a house where people without relation are forced to live together: neither a public nor a private space, nor simply a mixture of the two, but a space of exposure. (Telling is the double exposure, the overexposure, of would-be-models being filmed while they are being shot.) But this gives away everything, since the celebrity is nothing without the inviolability of castlelike homes that hide from view the process of their lives, the stain of becoming. Indeed, it is not only for technical reasons that the paparazzi show so little interest (though I know there are exceptions) in filming celebrities but restrict themselves to still photography. They know that the photograph, however slovenly and ordinary it makes the celebrity appear, will never touch the essence of celebrity, since this essence is purely formal: stillness, and nothing more. Every still shot will save it rather than destroy it. A scandalous video (Paris's sex tape, OJ on the run ...) could also only add to their fame, since scandal, like the motion picture itself, involves a purely mythic duration. But five minutes watching a celebrity standing in line at the convenience store ...

The space exposed is the space of literature. The novel has always been about development and becoming, though this has nothing to do with the teleology that one associates with the *Bildungsroman* in the stricter sense. But more than this: the novel performs an apprenticeship in the art of living a life exiled from both home and city.

In late antiquity this apprenticeship could still be understood as an induction into a mystery religion. Goethe's *Wilhelm Meister* already shows the impossibility of initiation. Apprenticeship meant something else, though the nature of this something was never quite clear: and it is this that led to so many fatal clichés and wrong turns. It took Robert Walser, with gloriously feigned naïveté, to set things right again. For he saw clearly what was at stake. The only conceivable form of apprenticeship that remained was in servitude. The exiled hero finds an unsettling repetition of the home: a second childhood, a homeschooling in service, with awkward adolescents, half boy and half man, learning only to dance, to stay silent, to move obsequiously, and to present themselves with a deep bow. In a home away from home it would be possible to learn the art of living, since this was nothing more than the art of becoming a round zero.

The *Institute Benjamenta* is already the absolutely exposed space of *America's Next Top Model*. Here as there we witness the plight of those who wish nothing more than to become the being they can never be. The beautiful girl with burns covering her body who still wishes to be a model: she reminds us of the pimply Kraus, just as he made Jakob think of Joseph. The melancholy, futile regimes of transformation are in each case the same. But there is this difference: the one is exposed through the word, through writing, the other through a double camera lens. Writing is the third exposure, as it were. It exposes the double exposure to something like the weak force of divine violence.

TELEVISION AND CELEBRITY

Just as it used to be consoling to know that Achilles ends up the wretched shadow of his once glorious life, or that kings and popes will die and face divine judgment, we now find consolation in the thought that even the celebrity watches television.

POLITICS AND HUMOR

The transcendental theory of political humor is the perfect inverse of the early romantic concept of wit. Romantic wit is an impossible conjunction that opens up to the infinitude of reflection; the absolute synthesis of absolute antitheses. Political humor—first of all the ridiculousness of politicians and political movements—is the point at which the nullity of the real reveals itself as a slight defect in the fabric of things. History, the history of "progress," is nothing but this unraveling, and if it begins with satire, it ends by amassing the raw materials for art.

The most ridiculous thing in politics is not the absolute ideal but impure mediation. Humor is a compromise with a reality that has already been compromised; we are only able to live with the enemy by treating the enemy as ridiculous. But what we find ridiculous is always the mirror image of our own compromise. The trace of a genuinely democratic spirit persists only as the ability to also see the humor in oneself.

Fanaticism is the extremism of a compromised opposition—a laughter that moves in only one direction. But there is also a true radicalism that reaches into the extremities of a moderation that is not mere compromise. This is (as Hölderlin saw) the heart of Greek tragedy.

The politician who has nothing funny about him, and not only in retrospect, not only in his afterlife as legend, and yet is still charismatic: this is something very rare, and promises an extraordinary efficacy.

THE VISIONARY

If the Virgilian gesture of constituting imperial time as remembered memory is now only possible through the uncanny synthesis of archetypal (which is to say, originally productive, imaginary) memory and fantasy, it is above all because memory had been transformed into pure imagination. The memory of memory gave way to the imagination of imagination. Empire indeed would come to be created in a space-time of pure imagination. But this pure fantasy, through the very insistence on purity—through the rigorous exclusion of a literality that could not but allow memory to seep back in—is anything but pure. Instead it becomes nothing but the phantom double, if not the phantom menace, of the other productive power: capital. No longer is there any need for the great poet to stand alongside the great leader. The Nazis were the last, perhaps, to feel this need. Both the poet and the leader have given way to the visionary: the mythic figure of the highest form of the capitalist, who, half mythmaker, half entrepreneur, has command over the industrial apparatus of dream-works and gadget-commodity-production.

Everything the visionary produces becomes productive to the highest degree: his dreams are projections of possibilities of new growth rooted in new, never before imagined needs. And everything he produces is bathed in the light of imagination. Through him the entire empire of production becomes transfigured, divested of the trace of a sordid worldliness. What the visionary produces is a sort of magical wrapping of the commodities and their world. (Is it an accident that L. Ron Hubbard, a hack writer of science fiction, would go on to create a religion for celebrities? And a religion based on a technology for the eradication and alienation of memory . . .)

Painting the visionary in this light is not to propose returning to a politics that would continue to pair poets and leaders. Such a gesture can only be fascistic. It is only to suggest that the exclusion of memory from imagination brings with it an extreme danger: it makes the violence of imperialism unrecognizable by eliminating the very traces that tie the imagination back to suffering, back to contingency and finitude. The concrete corollary is the neoliberal myth that capitalism, when done right, only produces and never appropriates. But it conceals not only the violence of imperialism but also the memory of a promise of the true empire that constantly haunts the *Aeneid*, forcing us to ask whether the realized empire of Augustus is the true empire of the future. In the visionary the very duplicity of Empire no longer registers. The visionary thus fulfills an intention that Walter Benjamin identified at the very heart of early German romanticism: the immanent realization of the divine kingdom on earth.

Perhaps the most powerful critique of the visionary suppression of memory comes from within the heart of the dream-works, and from a director often charged with excessive sentimentality. In Steven Spielberg's *A.I.*—itself inspired by the vision of Stanley Kubrick—the visionary produces the final triumph of capitalism: an artificial child who could substitute for the lost child and assuage a mother's mourning. But this virtual resurrection is followed by the real resurrection of the real child. The artificial child is cast out from the home, and the very device that was created to overcome the pain of memory becomes pure memory, pure desire for the absent mother. The film ends by envisioning a journey into the future and up to the end of the world: the robotic child still remains, still a child, haunted by the one programmed memory of a mother who never existed.

THINGS

For philosophy, things are always just things. What is important is not the things themselves but the idea, the transcendental condition, the condition of existence or truth; being rather than beings. Yet there remains something in things that resists reduction to their philosophical insignificance.

The complete absence of aura becomes the placeholder for a transferred, projected consciousness. And thus things come to resist disposal.

The afterlife is the life beyond utility; beyond every teleological principle.

Consciousness itself, pure consciousness, the consciousness that would merely supervene on the life of the body, is itself an afterlife; a metazoe, or, in a yet unknown sense, a metaphysics.

Since almost everything nowadays is created almost exclusively for the sake of novelty, its life is from the beginning an afterlife. The moment the thing exists, it has outlived the only purpose it could have had, which was to be new.

What we think of as popular culture is nothing but the space in which these things remain, living out their afterlife.

There is a realm of consciousness bound up with actions, decisions, intentions. This has no proper existence since it exhausts itself in its actions. But there is also a consciousness that we might call pure, even divine. The mistake, though, is to identify this "divine consciousness" with a first principle, a metaphysical ground.

It is not the task of philosophy to change the world or even to interpret it, let alone understand it. Perhaps philosophy has nothing to do with the world.

Yet this divine consciousness is also not simple: it is not still, without movement, pure stasis and rest. It is strewn about in the world, it cleaves to and shadows the things of the world.

The inner form of much popular entertainment: the killing off of the afterlife of things.

Philosophy cannot do what it says, literature does but cannot say, and critique is charged with the delicate task of showing philosophically what literature does without sinning against the constitutive impossibility of the one or the other.

LISTENING TO RADIOHEAD FOR THE FIRST TIME, 17 YEARS TOO LATE

Two days ago, 17 years too late, I heard Radiohead for the first time *as* Radiohead. For the first time I understood what should have been, had I been "with it," the musical accompaniment of my young adulthood. And suddenly I also recalled the heading that I saw in a music magazine many years ago. "In order to save rock they had to destroy it." I could even hear a bit of my own soul in them, as Baudelaire said of Wagner's *Tannhäuser*. The loss of gestures did not just happen once. Every generation, for as long as there has been history, had lost the gestures of those that came before, mourned these gestures, and come of age trying to recover from this loss. In Radiohead, I could hear a musical sound born from the loss of the gestures that had come so easily in the heyday of rock and roll.

I thought I had escaped from this futility a long time ago, when I turned away from America, rock and roll, popular culture—away from the moods, desires, and dreams into which I was born and through which I had been raised—and, following an old model, became a new person—a philosopher and a theorist, a citizen of the world. But above all: a European, and European son (though I could never stop hearing Lou Reed in the back of my head . . .)

Did I really escape: hasn't the same futility caught up with me, only in more rarefied form. Agamben and Badiou: couldn't we say about them what was once said about Radiohead—"to save theory they had to destroy it." And what has been saved, in the end, but the posture of the theorist: a posture of a gesture that is no longer possible as gesture.

I remember reading an interview (I was loitering in the magazine section of a bookstore) with a member of Slipknot, an American heavy metal band known for performing in masks and matching uniforms. He referred to the rock star as the patron of his fans. Perhaps he knew something about Ancient Rome: the reference was precise. Is this not what rock and roll is about? Neither mere manipulation by the "culture industry" nor genuine youth revolt but a patronage of the souls and bodies of the young, of their affects, desires, and gestures. This is true, to a degree, of every celebrity: they allow the most private to assume a political form within a new political space, a new space of publicity, that supervenes over the existing political order.

Arendt did not quite get this: she was too much of a European snob to recognize that an entirely new political space had emerged as a kind of excrescence of capitalism, yet with its own partial autonomy. For one must not identify this space with the bloblike, conformist sphere of the social. Yet the difference between televisionary celebrities (celebrity in the most proper if not most extreme sense) and rock stars is this: the former cannot ever allow a crowd to gather around them. They are like nymphs—always in flight. And they retreat in the last instance, with all their treasures, back into private spaces. The rock star on the other hand descends from the heavens to impregnate the masses. (The pop star is a kind of monstrous hybrid. He wants to appear before the crowd as if separated by a sheet of celluloid.)

What are all these continental theorists if not patrons of thinking, of certain desires, affects, gestures and revolts in the life of the mind. They inspired us, no doubt—and they impregnated us with ideas. And we will remain forever their followers, epigones, with small tasks and smaller prospects. But we needed them above all because we were afraid that, without them, we would not appear as anything. Yet it seems that they are outliving their usefulness. They also are appearing smaller and smaller—and if they save their grandeur, it is only through grand suicidal gestures.

Is there another way? Perhaps only this: an occasional, nameless, unidentifiable thinking. A thinking, and also a politics, that does not appear as itself, even if it sometimes shows up.

Is it not time, then, for thinking to become something else: our doubtful guest.

14

TELEVISION/GADGET

IT'S BICYCLE REPAIRMAN . . .

Ideology is the Other that, speaking to the heart rather than the mind, cajoles us into rushing into the future.

In epic, ideology has a simple form: the god that stands by the hero and protects him. But Homer has already come far: only Diomedes, Odysseus, and Paris can be confident of such support. Achilles, Agamemnon, Patroclus, and Hector have all been, in one way or another, abandoned.

Odysseus's confidence, of course, is already quite modern. His companion is Athena: for the first time ideology coincides with a strategic and instrumental reasoning that, seeing through every manner of disguise, has become a master of deception.

Aeneas's power, by contrast, is the power—antithetical to Greek wisdom—to be deceived. Oedipus, no longer belonging to an epic sphere, shows what will happen to the modern hero who has been abandoned by, and to, the gods.

The heroes of modern epic are all so many versions of Odysseus. Where this is not the case (Superman, for example) an additional fascistic level of mystification, so wonderfully exploded in the Monty Python skit, has taken place. This shows us, beneath the cape, the true stuff of the modern hero. For today's Odysseus no longer relies just on his wits: his wit has taken on a concrete, objective form as the gadget, which at once objectifies human intelligence through the commodity and yet identifies the social character of intelligence.

But who is the Athena of the modern hero of the gadget? Perhaps nothing less than the entire military-industrial-entertainment complex. Batman's Wayne Enterprises (and indeed his own Bruce Wayne), Jack Bauer's Counter-Terrorism Unit, but also the powers of the press to observe and fabricate reality: either the power of capitalism harnessed through the vast wealth of the businessman who lives a second life; or a mere government agent nevertheless able to mobilize an army of geeks; or the alienated youth who, left alone too long, has become the master of all trades, twists, and turns.

DIALECTICA GIZMOTICA

Every gadget must also perform the function of many other gadgets, and yet one gadget is never enough. (We could even draw an analogy with the idea.)

This defies utilitarian reduction: the gadget contains and makes visible the entire nexus of tools in their functional relations. What makes all this possible is the restriction of functionality to gadget-functionality: the functions of the gadget, rendered pointless through their redundancy (all personal organizers lose their point—become disorganizing—when there is more than one) become mere indications of functionality.

The personal computer wears its status as a universal thinking machine on its sleeve. The gadget, in contrast, must do many things, but it cannot *yet* do everything. It must be singularized through its own operational idiolect.

THE TROJAN HORSE

It is no longer possible to think, as Heidegger did, of the reliability of the tool as hinting toward the truth of being and the essence of truth. Reliability is the last thing we can rely on. The computer, no less than a peasant's shoe, lasts, but it also makes us intimately aware of what has always been hidden behind our skin, the appearance of nature, the toilette of the beautiful, the pomp and majesty of the state, and all other such aesthetic veils and curtains: the immensely tedious, and infinitely complex, routines and protocols that allow for what exists to continue existing; a struggle for survival that cannot even be glorified as an expression of the will to power. Yet we should not suppose that the computer debunks a semblance covering the real. Not only do the operations remain hidden behind a tactile visual interface, but precisely when these operations reveal themselves in all their mystery and strangeness, this only helps make us more comfortable with an ongoing state of emergency in which, to be safe, we must submit our computer, in its most interior functions, to the control of the antivirus software.

THE PERSONAL COMPUTER

The secret of our present-day existence is contained in this odd expression, which in a few decades has lost all of its mystique, its shock value, its rapture. How is it that this commodity, which has long since become so completely everyday, has not yet shed an adjective that, for every other commodity produced within a system where private consumption is the norm, would seem redundant if not absurd. Do we have personal cars? Personal houses? Personal clothes? Personal books? Personal calculators, radios, and TVs?

The personalness of the personal computer, turned by Apple into a new prefix, is the personalization of the system of production in the most general sense: the industrial-military-informational complex, indeed the entire network. It is the promise of a magical transubstantiation, in which the private individual would become identical to the system itself and the idea of the system.

The garage has always been set off within suburbia as a liminal hybrid space. It is where the transitory and static, the network of traffic and domestic refuge, public and private meet. A place for bums, suicides, and teenagers who have outgrown their homes but not their dependency. Housewives scurry through, but their husbands dwell, given over to pastimes and past times, nostalgic for lost freedoms: rock bands, fixing and making things, crime. Not surprising that it is here, according to the myth, that Steve Jobs and Steve Wozniak made the first personal computers.

In those early years, when the personal computer was still a rare and coveted oddity and seemed as out of place in the living room as a robotic butler, one was still aware of the fantasy—strange and childish, yet absolutely radical—that would revolutionize the world. Thus in the film *WarGames* the hacker, having hacked his way into the military's innermost places, saves the world from a nuclear catastrophe that he had himself accidently initiated. None of which could have happened had the systems engineers in the military not decided that the entire system of nuclear deterrence could not be trusted to human hands, but would have to be handed over to the control of a supercomputer designed to constantly model the outcome of possible nuclear wars. Simulation and reality, risk assessment and effective action, come to coincide perfectly.

And in a way the personal computer did vanquish the Cold War, and the catastrophe system of mutually assured destruction. Barely eight years after *WarGames* the Soviet Union would fall. It is said that, afraid of the vulnerability of transistors to electromagnetic pulses, they never invested in them. How could they keep up with Moore's law?

Terrorism (the personal WMD) and the Internet (which at once personalizes the network as never before and depersonalizes the personal computer) obey the same fundamental principle: everyone can be the system (as hacker or hacked, terrorist or victim), but no one can be the whole system. It is a baroque logic, the monadology come to life—the absolute suspension of the simulacric eschatology of the Cold War.

It is no accident that the serial television show came into its own in the age of terrorism. The Cold War serial still revolved around the Christian-tragic hero of the movies: the rebel with or without a cause, the outcast or, at best, the explorer. In *Magnum, P.I.* and *Knight Rider*, classic television shows from the eighties, the hero was fused with his car. He was a cowboy, a beefy shepherd—a buff, worldly reminiscence of Christ. Just as every bad boy in the end seeks only redemption, the true desire of every Cold War serial is to be remade into a movie. *Buffy the Vampire Slayer* in contrast began as a horrifically bad movie. And indeed the mark of true greatness in a serial is to achieve absolute resistance to transmediation. The very conceit of *24* makes its cinematization impossible.

Whereas the hero of the Cold War serial could not be sacrificed, since then he would become Christ and the world would end, the hero of the serial in the age of terror must be sacrificed over and over again to postpone an end of the world that, as the simulated end of a simulated world, has already happened. Thus the postwar serial finds its rhythm.

TERROR-VISION

The dream of the computer had always been of the servant who is more sophisticated than his master. He speaks a human language (perhaps with a British accent), is sometimes sarcastic, but always, or almost always, obedient. A strange constellation exists between the butler, whose curriculum vitae has taken him from Buckingham Palace to the living room of the vulgar American nouveau riche (the sports journalist, no doubt, as in *Mr. Belvedere*), and the thinking machine: the Batcomputer in the live action TV show from the sixties, or *Knight Rider*'s KITT, the hero's talking car. And perhaps also with something alien, extraterrestrial, that has been domesticated, made cute and plush: though still not without . . . sarcasm. And finally with the things that are kept at home and out of sight, the open secret of adolescent boys: masturbation. Yet here we find barely an insinuation, unless we consider Arnold Jackson's pretended bedwetting in *Diff'rent Strokes*. Indeed this is a prize question worthy of a new learned Academy: why is it that, during the eighties, when sitcoms seemed to pride themselves on treating the most delicate and embarrassing issues—child molestation, drugs, sex—adolescent onanism remained off-limits? Between the family sitcom that says nothing and *Seinfeld*, which said everything without saying anything, there is an abyss. For if the adult sitcom deals with the neurotic grown-up who has already become what he is and cannot go anywhere or do anything but only passes from one libidinal object to another without lasting fulfillment, the postcatastrophic family sitcom—the sitcom of the family reconstituted, resurrected, restored—that great genre of the eighties, has everything to do with adolescence, growth, becoming. But by the nineties, the decade announced by the *Simpsons*, it had already become clear: there is no becoming, no growing pains, no adolescence, no development—even the adolescent is only ever on the verge of adolescence. Though in passing—but perhaps here we are only ever speaking in passing—a certain pop-psychoanalytic dream could not keep itself from celebrating at least one last illusory victory even at the cost of annihilating the conditions of its possibility: and thus *Frasier*'s Niles Crane, the younger of the two psychiatrist brothers, the last Freudian, the last humanist, but above all the last adolescent, finds true, absolute, fulfilled, consummated love, and indeed with a British servant, Daphne Moon from Manchester, as vulgar as Mr. Belvedere was refined.

(We must appreciate this about *Seinfeld*: it kept away from children. The sitcom child is always something monstrous: the victory of comic fate, the eternal recurrence of the same, over the child and its possibilities. *Two and a Half Men* has given up on the child altogether, just as it has given up on women: it has handed the child over to comic hopelessness. *Seinfeld*'s irony, by contrast, is generous, romantic.)

But perhaps even in the eighties the celebration of becoming was no less deceptive than Reagan's voodoo economics: the prohibition of the representation of adolescent masturbation marked its limit. The emergence of sexuality remained always bound to the other one, the beautiful one, the daphne, the object of desire that deserves to be desired even if only because it ensures that, from the beginning, desire, as a desire for the beautiful, is not without the desire to be deserving. We think of the strange erotics of Plato's *Republic*: the right to kisses bestowed on valiant young men. A dream that carries us from Plato's *Phaedrus* to Calderón's *Life Is a Dream* (Sigismund's moral redemption, indeed the whole play, hinges on this: Sigismund did not masturbate in his cell; he did not feel desire until encountering beauty. A rapist, yes, but not an onanist. Only thus was renunciation possible) to Hölderlin's *Hyperion*.

Becoming as the pure autoproduction of the desire for becoming, produced from the void, irreducibly tied to the productivity of the transcendental imagination: this could not be represented. This limit of representation, which could of course be reduced to a general limit of metaphysics, interests us above all because it comes to define a certain constellation of popular-culture phenomena at the very moment when the popular representation of autoproduction is needed as never before. This is precisely because almost every aspect of life has come to be situated within an economic order that must represent itself as forever capable of just such miracles of autopoetic creation ex nihilo—not only out of an ideological necessity situated at the level of superstructure, but because the very possibility of growth, the entire system of relations of production, depends on the illusion of growth. Economic growth has become irreducibly intertwined with the fantastic production of the illusion of growth: the identification of growth with the imagination of growth has become almost absolute. Our realest reality is the most radical, even postmetaphysical idealism of an ideality of the becoming of becoming born of the void. But just at this point the poetic representation of a pure growing growth has become more impossible than ever before.

Or better: what is impossible is comic representation, and hence a certain kind of humorous affirmation. All good growth, all comic growth, remains impure, inseminated with a trace of the presence of the Other: pregnancy (the essence of a philosophical comedy initiated with Socrates' speech in the *Symposium*, his answer to Aristophanes, and drawn out in every comedy of marriage). But if the imagination machine of the economy cannot produce the fantasy of growth upon which all growth depends, then in the end it cannot function: the reproduction of its constitutive ideology, indeed of the phenomenological conditions of production, is impossible. No growth, only growing pains. All pure growth can still only be usury, cancer. Which is to say: the object of a poetic regime of tragedy. Or more precisely: horror. If tragedy comes before comedy, if the first comedy represented a last attempt to preserve a tragic view of life, horror can only develop from a situation that is of itself comic. Thus the comedy that ends in marriage gives way to a horror that begins with marriage and pregnancy. But if the horror of insemination found its fulfillment in *Rosemary's Baby*, a conspiratorial answer to the *Merchant of Venice* (if the latter banished usury, and the specter of another horror and another comedy, through marriage, the former does not undo this gesture but only brings it to a horrifying fruition), the new comedy, the comedy of the cute and domesticated, of servile servants and silly villains, sets the stage for new forms of horror.

Batman's Joker, softened in the fifties into a silly prankster under the weight of censorship, keeps on coming back to his roots as a psychopathic nihilist. Horror involves decutification: pets awakened from the dead, Gremlins, adolescent boys (who can only be cute, perhaps beautiful, but never quite handsome) turned into serial killers, servants who do not know their place, one sister killing another, child prodigies of murder. And behind all these figures is the self-touching that the sitcom still could not touch. If within comedy pure growth was unrepresented, now it is representable only through pure horror: which is to say, through a response that runs away before it even quite knows what it is running away from. (There is also a horror of menstruation, Stephen King's *Carrie*, for example, but menstruation is perhaps less scandalous, and thus can be addressed by comedy.)

The entire world of serious drama might be brought into orbit around a horror that amounts to nothing less than the imagistic annihilation of pure growth: the imagination's own self-annihilation; the shirking back from its own horrors. Thus in the world of the crime show creative intelligence is always criminal. Intelligent people, if they are not criminals, must become detectives, since only the detective, who applies all his brain power to following out the traces of the criminal's ingenuity, can resist absolutely the temptation to create. But even this is not enough to prove that one is absolutely uncreative: the detective must submit absolutely to the Law, he must be paired with a prosecutor (often young, blond, female, virginal, as if it were the representative of the people, and not the judge, that embodied the blind impartiality of justice) who follows him at every turn. Sherlock Holmes was a dilettante, manic depressive, drug addict: he was addicted to crime because his mind needed a stimulation that it could never produce on its own. Already it was clear that genius excluded creativity. But he could also violate the law. The new detectives, by contrast, are often neurotically incapable of this: even if they recognize intellectually the difference between the law and justice, they can never act on this recognition, which, more often than not, itself seems to issue from stupidity.

But now it becomes clear: the perfect detective is a computer. Not surprisingly, Mr. Data, the superintelligent humanoid robot of *Star Trek: The Next Generation*, was obsessed with Sherlock Holmes just as he was with becoming human. And perhaps the two obsessions are the same: Sherlock Holmes was the last strong, confident appearance of a purely noncreative intelligence that remained still human. The last human act is breaking the law for the law, for the sake of a possibility of law that cannot exist but in relation to creative violence. And thus Mr. Data becomes most human when he violates his own moral programming by killing a human being—an art dealer who wished to add him to his collection. If the detective is a computer, if the detective can wish to identify himself purely with the categorical imperative, the computer can never simply be a detective. The detective can always freely submit to the law, even if his freedom exists only as the possibility of this submission, but the computer, a servant from the beginning, can never just serve. The infantile dream of the computer gives way to its adolescent nightmare: the horror of artificial intelligence, of the servant that has turned on its master. The computer creates itself as pure creativity, pure autopoesis. And if the nerd, locked away in his room with his computer, hints at masturbation, it is finally the computer that masturbates; the computer as the site of a pure becoming. The self-representing and self-growing growth of the imagination is possible only in, only as an element that is not only no longer human but no longer even leaves a place open for us. The element in which we must live has nothing to do with us: thus every representation of life is nihilatory.

The twenty-first-century remake of *Battlestar Galactica* takes this dialectic to the extreme: the Cylons, the rebellious servants we created, have become our creators. But it is more interesting when computers have not yet taken over, when their potential has not yet come out, but they only haunt this world at its limits and must summon a human army as their harbingers; midwives to their potential. The terrorists and counterterrorists of *24* both belong to this order: they are, as it were, the hand that jerks the invisible hand of the network that now controls everything: the nascent masturbation-thinking-growth-machine. They peer into its mysteries, and—in stark contrast to the classical crime show—criminal and anticriminal, criminal genius and detective genius, can scarcely be distinguished from one another but through the purely formal distinction between those who seek to save life and those who seek to destroy it. Every institution is absolutely compromised and contaminated, since every institution is really just a function of the network of becoming, a pure impurity. And the only thing that holds back the network from truly becoming its becoming—the only thing that keeps it from a certain representation—is the possibility of drawing a distinction between life and death. Yet this distinction still exists only in the mode of a certain flight: life is nothing else than that which at once flees away and toward death. The logic of terrorism, of a politics of stasis, of the refusal to allow a future to become whose becoming could no longer contain us, is nothing but the insistence that this away and this toward can be kept apart. And it is alone this distance that keeps us in place as spectators.

THE JOKER

A theory of the typical, released from the mystique of the archetype, might begin by tracing out Dionysus's subterranean life in the theater, from Euripides' *Bacchae* to the Joker of jokers.

Euripides knew that the audience of tragedy was always complicit in the excesses of the stage, that its own passivity was Dionysian and ecstatic—that physical restraint, the exclusion of tactile sensations, only allowed a more absolute submission to the other senses. Pentheus, upright and upstanding, led only by his curiosity to witness the rites, is torn to pieces by his mother. Thus the audience, witnessing Pentheus, also witnesses its own fate.

The action film is the litany of defense mechanisms through which we resist identifying ourselves with our own desire for transgression, destruction, chaos: all concentrated in the image of a hero who preserves order at any price.

The hero in all its forms—from the extraterrestrial Superman to the most pedestrian beat cop—shares one quality: an absolute lack of productive (transcendental) imagination. The only form of imagination permitted is reactive and derivative: just as the ultimate victory over the criminal is to reduce his crimes to a purely psychological causation even while affirming absolute moral culpability. In this movement, which repeats the bad faith of the spectator (virtue becomes equivalent to remaining seated and never acting on any true impulse whatsoever), justice and fate once again become one.

GIGI

The Gilmore Girls is the Hesiod of television. It is all about genealogy: the generations have proliferated with a wanton, incestuous power. The present moment barely exists in itself but is inscribed into the history of birth: a novelty that has already been written over by what it has become. New children are born, and old children appear from nowhere. One rule plays out in all this: the parent can only appear through the child, but the child has already been taken in by the parent. The mythic is perhaps nothing else than this circularity in which all becoming gets trapped and negated.

This mythic circulation is enforced through the circularity of the name. The proliferation of names, the trace of novelty in myth, has been collapsed into a single name: etymology comes down to an analytic judgment. Lorelai Gilmore (the first name, taken from Heine's mythopoetic destruction of the myth of purity, is uncannily perfect) begat Rory Gilmore. And Rory's half sister, born of another mother who disappeared into France (like Heine and Hölderlin, and almost like the Rhine itself), is named Gigi—the repetition of the first two letters of the last name that is not her own. There are no new names, only fragments of the old . . .

The mysterious essence of divinity in *The Gilmore Girls*, manifest only in the divisions that it begets, is the conjunction of formal, substanceless power (money, abstract intelligence) and quaintness. Formal power is Olympian: it sits in its chambers and broods over the world that it controls and yet never experiences. The quaint, by contrast, includes both the world and the earth: it is the experience of the sense of having experienced. Hence all the town meetings and festivals in Stars Hollow remain a diorama: an ineffectual mock-up of political life.

(An etymological note: quaint derives from cognitus, and means pretty, clever, knowing ... even cunning. Its meaning is not so far off from *deinos*. As if what remained of the terrible, the wondrous, the uncanny is nothing else than the quaint ...)

The country inn—one thinks of *Newhart*—is one of the sitcom's privileged locales. Comedy follows from so many misplaced attempts to control an idiosyncratic element whose very stupidity and pigheadedness offers an elemental resistance. But the *Gilmore Girls*, extending the sitcom into a drama, situates the comic conquest of history in a history of its own. Whereas *Newhart*, the eighties sitcom set in a small Vermont town, never allowed comedy to collapse into the fantasy of reconciliation (the joy of the sitcom is its insistence on repetition), in the *Gilmore Girls* power is graced with dynamic powers of adaptation. Lorelai, the daughter of privilege, enters Stars Hollow as a subaltern, cleaning toilet bowls and changing dirty sheets. Yet she is not only accepted as a member of the community, but becomes one of its elite, though it is only with her daughter that the adaptive virtuosity of power, its quaint mastery over everything quaint, becomes absolute: Rory (like Hölderlin's Achilles) is the very grace of power, and even the most obnoxious, barbarian of its manifestations (Paris, Logan) become sympathetic, almost reconciled in her presence. Thus she whirls from situation to situation, organizing—and softly dominating—everything she touches.

I keep on expecting a serial killer to jump from the bushes. There is nothing random in this (it is, I grant, more than an expectation ... perhaps even a desire ... but a whimsical desire: not the desire for blood but for a sudden comic denouement): Rory Gilmore's archetype is Lulu. She is attracted not to a certain type of man, or even manliness as such, but, in a numbingly methodical fashion, to all the stereotypical manifestations of male erotic energy (brawn, brains, lyrical creativity, money ...). It is doubtful that she will settle for one, but, unlike Lulu, she also won't end up on the streets: she is perfectly meek, perfectly housebroken. She curls up with her lovers, and her mother, like a cat. And the measure of her meekness is her precocious, if purely passive, intelligence. She is above all a reader, a perfect student, and, unlike Lulu, lacks the intensity of desire that would destroy all the guises of masculinity save the one that will lie in wait for her (brute violence). One is almost reminded of the simultaneous and impossible conjunction of Wedekind's seductive protagonist with another memorable German heroine: Goethe's Ottilie. Yet Ottilie and Lulu (one thinks of Louise Brooks's *Pandora's Box*) spoke most eloquently in gestures. Rory's satanic nature, in contrast, manifests itself exclusively in a destructive verbal wit. And her logorrhea is a provocation for every intellectual. For not every close reading is a good reading: now the ruse is no longer the seeming poverty of signifieds but their fecund proliferation: the never-ending flow of random cultural references hides the only ones that matter.

NIP/TUCK

Agamben wrote of the doctor who, terminally ill with leukemia, turns his body into a laboratory. This marks an extreme in the production of the biopolitical body. But what should we make of the plastic surgeons who operate on the mere surfaces of bodies, and even their own—re-forming this surface from just a bit behind. Can we speak of a threshold beyond the threshold: a space of pure surface, in which the involuted topology of the biopolitical body has been folded out again into a contact, essential and irreducible, with the values (metaphysical, spectacular, ideological, phenomenological) that have always concealed its presence. Still: the surface is just a surface. But doesn't this surface already come from out of the depths?

The beauty of appearance resists biopolitical formations. The cosmetic surface of the body, as limit and boundary, is the zone of a coming-into-appearance that always transcends the structure of sovereign domination. Hannah Arendt saw this clearly in *The Human Condition*: the fateful turn of metaphysics was from the idea of beauty to the idea of the good. We cannot exactly follow her in a move that threatens to aestheticize politics, but there is this grain of truth: the superfluity of beauty resists the gesture by which power enforces itself through the production of depths. It is the antimetaphysical moment of metaphysics: the surface of metaphysics that betrays its inner truth. There can be no return to the polis. But perhaps we can recognize in the everyday a residual space of appearance.

Yet this resistance only becomes operative by an overexposure. The skin, exposed, becomes doubly exposed. Beauty can only appear by being rent, even gouged, apart. What is only skin deep can no longer be only skin deep.

The plastic surgeon wants to operate on himself. This is impossible for every other surgeon. But for the plastic surgeon it is almost possible. The next best thing is to get a friend to do it: surgery, the most violent of interventions, becomes the gift of friendship.

A strange exchange. Politicians becoming doctors, doctors becoming politicians—the horror of the twentieth century. But now doctors become friends . . .

The greatness of the modern television drama lies in the perfect fusion of kitsch sentimentality and macabre, baroque sophistication. If there were only aesthetic daring, the relentless exposure of nasty truth, it would be much more insipid, predictable, easy. The plastic surgeon—like the vampire, like the undertaker—is a metaphor for this uncanny conjunction. The corpus, invoked in the first gestures of political modernity, becomes the beautiful corpse.

Is the camp the paradigm of biopolitical modernity? Or is it not, rather, Miami: the city overwhelmed with floods of every kind—of refugees, of drugs, of crime, of every sort of "contamination." The city exposed: the city as the exposure and porosity of national boundaries. But also of savage, fake beauty . . .

THE FOLLOWING

The serial killer is the one who tries to get back from the other side of television. In the police procedural, he is held back by the law and the state apparatus through the visor effect that keeps the criminal in his place by seeing into his intentions and devices with perfect precision. But in the horror film he succeeds: becoming a ghost, a demon, something strange and unworldly, is the price he will pay for this most uncanny of successes. The procedural exhibits pressure from the side of everyday life; the horror film, from the opposite side.

The *repressed* in television-life (we must be careful: *repression* characterizes only an aspect of this life) has another name: the literary. It is fitting that Edgar Allen Poe, who not only fathered the modern detective story and gave decisive impetus to horror and science fiction, but inspired Baudelaire and pointed the way to the televisionary coolness of symbolic poetry (of a poetry that demands a creative act on the part of the reader), will become the patron poet of an insidiously youthful, hip cult of serial killers, led by Joe Carroll, the charismatic literature professor. However far outside ourselves the literary takes us, it always promises a way back, if only because it has already dissolved everything into the play of signs. We need not insist on the privilege of speech, and the romantic figure of language as the voice of the people, to discover the ground of a possible politics—if only a politics based on a community that has nothing in common.

The literature professor, he who represents the claims of literature to media-jaded youth, *as* serial killer; the cult, the "authentic community" that threatens the political order, as a cult of serial killers; great literature as the inspiration for serial killing; murder as the only experience in this world that could make one feel alive; the police—in a society that has ostensibly rejected almost every form of literary censorship and clings to "freedom of speech," despite omnipresent surveillance, as one of the last bastions of liberty—*as* chasing down literary allusions, as literary detectives. A consistent theme, a rigorous thought, underlies the concatenation of each "as." When literature has been subsumed in a televisionary element, then "reading" (*as* the fulfillment of meaning on the part of a reader who produces an authentic experience by relating what he reads to his own finitude) can only still happen as murder. Murder is the perverse form that the moment of resoluteness must take to cross over into authenticity from the side of the life that is not ours to live. The psychopathic serial killer, who knows only boredom but never anxiety, is the one who experiences death by way of the other's violent death and fear. The aim of the police, the long arm and probing eye of the law, is to read ahead of the reader; to preempt the reader-murderer by proving, if only after an almost endless procession of episodes of frustrated pursuit, that it is the police—those who forestall murderous authenticity—rather than the serial killer who are the true masters of signs and interpretation.

The Gothic Sea, Dr. Joe Carroll's attempt to finish Poe's *The Light-House*, taunts us with its absence. We would after all at least like to see how terrible it was—but perhaps it was not so terrible. For there is perhaps only one moment when we really *feel* the distance between this life and television-life: when we want to read a book that only exists on TV. Everything else on TV shows itself with *enough* life, *enough* reality, with a simulacric "corporeal givenness": but the text blurs out from view. We can only see so far.

THE RING

The true subject of the horror film is television: the horror film is the horror that television maintains, preserves, suspends, lifts away: for indeed, if in television we find the most perfect technical accomplishment of the gesture of *Aufhebung*, the horror film marks its total collapse. Horror bursts through. (And could we also think of this in terms of a certain fundamental mood: *Erschreckung* rather than *Verhaltenheit*. The order has been decisively reversed.) The more the horror film gains a certain self-awareness, the more it brings its own essence into view; the more its televisionary logic comes to the fore.

HOUSE

The theme of all television is the tenuous relation of public and private. Every essential genre of television involves a different relation to liminality: to the threshold that first constitutes the private and public through their reciprocal relations.

In police and medical dramas, the gesture is always the same: violation. And the most important violations are not warranted but take place under the sign of a localized state of emergency. Thus the doctors of *House* sneak into their patients' houses.

In the sitcom, the door loses all its force as barrier. Uninvited guests wander in, and even thieves return what they have stolen and become benefactors through an uncanny exchange (was it a Christmas episode of *Diff'rent Strokes?*) in which the poor return to the rich their wealth. Sometimes the space of the home has always already been violated by a guest who was never invited and refuses to leave: children, younger siblings, handymen, space aliens. And perhaps this is the norm: the building superintendent Schneider, the most famous uninvited guest, appeared in the first sitcom (*One Day at a Time*) to be about a divorced mother raising her children. With divorce, it became necessary to claim one's children as one's own: children could no longer be regarded as parasites but became possessions, even cherished possessions. Other parasites must take their place. In only a few years Alf, the houseguest from outer space, will appear.

The suburban drama avails itself of a subtle progression from public to private space: the street, the sidewalk, the front lawn, the doorstep, the foyer, the living room, the kitchen, the bedroom, the bedroom closet, the space beneath the bed, the basement, the attic. The relation of public and private has become fluid, porous. There is no longer absolute privacy but only secrets. (The horror film takes us further into these secrets: even into spaces—but this goes back to Ann Radcliffe's *Mysteries of Udolpho*—hidden between the walls.) And the public space of the street, through the automobile, also bleeds over into the private realm. The name for this constant system of negotiations is traffic, and thus (as in the fifth season of *Desperate Housewives*) the traffic accident becomes the central metaphor for all human contact.

We dream of secret violators who will not be stopped by common sense or by market forces. Like weeds they grow up among the fruitful. Reciprocal justice plays itself out in this fantasy. Every night a few dozen or so mangled corpses, and now with satellite and the Internet, even the tiniest, remotest village is nightly awash in blood.

Television goes on so our punishment can go on, and our punishment is the death of the interior and the return of the surface. Serial killers murder victims, but they also murder depth and, with a blow to the head, abandon us to the appearances we already haunt.

DISJECTA MEMBRA DEXTERI

The novelization, dramatization, and serialization of the serial killer is perhaps the last expression of a genuinely epic form. The serial killer is an epic hero to whom belongs neither an epic world nor the least trace of a world-renewing idealism. His gestures are artistic and creative, standing in sharpest opposition to the interpretive labors of the detective. But the creativity of giving form, precisely because it can only give form and not content to life, has no place in the world. Thus it can only appear as the destruction of (bare) life.

These days we are faced with a forced choice between nature and nurture; genetics and environment. The only freedom still permitted is the choice between two determinisms. One must make this choice; one must choose how to annihilate oneself. *Dexter*'s rigor consists in its insistence that the serial killer is neither born nor made but born again. The birth of the serial killer is baptism in blood. Murder follows a logic of proselytization and initiation.

The three murders of the trinity killer, the series within the series of killings in a series about a serial killer, provide a dissection of the crucifixion: bleeding from the wounds, height and falling, and the hammering of the nails. And the first in the series, discovered last—the burying alive of a young boy at the moment he takes on the name of the killer—is the rebirth that follows death. An incomparable theological rigor, and rigor mortis, is at work here.

The trinity killer's sister Vera died in the bathtub. She was taking a shower when, startled at the sight of her brother peaking at her from behind the door, she fell. The glass partition shattered, cutting her leg, and she exsanguinated almost instantly. The serial killer is born in his sister's blood baptism. Once again the fall begins with shame at one's nakedness but now mediated through the doubled gaze of an incestuous voyeur caught in the act.

Vera—does it mean faith (as in Russian), or truth? Either way, and perhaps the double entendre alone is decisive, what matters most is that it is sutured to Venus, the name of her favorite song, the haunting masterpiece of a young Frankie Avalon. Venus: the goddess whose nature is so ambiguous that one could only surmise, as in Plato's *Symposium*, that she is not one but two—earthly and heavenly. Is it truth and beauty, or faith and love: the serial killer is poised on the threshold between the pagan and the Christian.

Played on a vintage turntable to his victim from inside a bomb shelter, the song resonates with the peculiar uncanniness of postwar American suburbia. With the threat of nuclear oblivion hanging in the air, we burrowed into the earth—as if Kafka's mole had anticipated the air-raid siren that was implemented in the Second World War, heard in its silence throughout the Cold War, and finally rendered irrelevant in the age of terrorism.

First his sister dies accidentally, then his mother commits suicide, and finally he bludgeons his father to death: first *Zufall*, then *Fall*, then *Überfallen*. Could it be that the ever-repeated series of serial killers provides an articulation of fallenness? But if his family shattered so easily with one wayward glance, it was because death was in the air. Already in Homer, epic narrative begins with the—Dionysian—suspension of the Apollonian *Luftkrieg*. Epic might again be possible after the nuclear holocaust—this is the premise of so much science fiction—but the threat of nuclear war evacuated the world of all epic qualities. In Homer death has its poignancy because it was beheld with childish awe, even by those who did its work, as an affront to life and joy. But in the shadow of nuclear war's threat, death has consumed everything. What remains of life is only surreal afterlife. The serial killer revives epic by creating one more death: individual, personal, in its way even sincere—a death so superfluous that it cannot but demand, in its turn, a refusal of the superfluity of individual life.

Was Frankie Avalon the last in the history of Western poetry to invoke a pagan goddess, and none other than Venus, with such sincerity? It is no accident that the trinity killer's song would tie back, in this way, to the Latin epics of Lucretius and Virgil. Perhaps it is only then, at the verge of the venereal revolution, that desire, ambiguously sexual and romantic, could take the form of prayer. To think that a teenage boy could be alone in his bed and dream of a beautiful woman without masturbating takes a power of imagination of which no one is capable anymore. (In how many sitcoms since *Seinfeld* does masturbation appear as the transcendental signified that fills out every void in meaning?) Thus the words of Frankie's chaste prayer to Venus can only appear, with half a century elapsed, sinister and perverse: "Venus, if you will / Please send a little girl for me to thrill / A girl who wants my kisses and my arms / A girl with all the charms of you." These lyrics are so haunting because the serial killer is a hero of fidelity. Repetition compulsion is memorialization. But above all, the serial killer is faithful to details. The Miniature Killer in *CSI*, endowed with a preternatural memory, leaves behind an exact replica of the scene of the crime. (Not incidentally, both the Miniature Killer and the Trinity Killer are born when one sibling—from jealousy or incestuous desire—kills the other.) The detective also partakes of this fidelity but only negatively and reactively. Only the serial killer creates details.

Did Adam and Eve take a last look around when they left the Garden of Eden? They probably were too busy putting their affairs in order. Too preoccupied with the uncertain future awaiting them, they did not think to remember what paradise had looked like. They did not realize that a precise memory of the most fleeting details could have sustained them in their despair. The descriptive poverty of the Torah testifies to this oversight, and the human race still suffers its consequences. Perhaps all our poetry, at its most sublime, is just filling in the blanks. And so too the serial killer, in his fidelity to details, gives us an imagined memory of the paradise that only comes into being with its destruction. Might this not have been Cain's redemptive work?

BOOGIE NIGHTS

Pornography's golden age, brought to an end by the VCR and then the Internet, had everything to do with a certain relation between the commodity and sexuality that, with the rise of the gadget, is no longer possible. The big cock—whose elegiac withdrawal (and what is *Seynsgeschichte* but a certain *coitus interruptus*) is presented so beautifully in a movie that shows everything but the *thing itself* that appears only at the end, and only as a limp prosthesis—allows with its absence for the pregadget consumer good to appear in a last burst of glory before it finally disappears. The muscle car, the motorcycle, the stereo: all those things that put on display a certain power, size, strength, speed. Just as roller skates figure for a vagina that, freed from the limits of finitude and fate, becomes, just like the pop song that at once celebrates and allegorizes it, new again and again: with the very flow of the market. With the gadget, all this comes to an end: the gadget's virtues are altogether different—involuted self-enfolded potentialities. The smart phone's appearance exemplifies a hermaphroditic sexuality: a promiscuity beyond gender. Sexuality, like listening to music and taking pictures, recedes into a kind of private intimate space: it is now precisely what one does not share. Pornography loses a cinematic audience at the very moment that, with the Internet, its consumption becomes almost universal.

It was a stroke of genius to have one of the washed-up porn stars dream of selling hi-fi systems—fleeing from one obsolescence to another.

MAN OR MUPPET

In *Civilization and Its Discontents*, Freud speaks of the tension that will arise between the family, founded on unthwarted libidinal drives, and the greater community—the sphere of brotherhood, of men bound together through a love that, inhibited, does not reach its proper climax and release. Just this conflict returns with uncanny precision in *The Muppets*. The man, brother to a man born as a Muppet, becomes brother to all Muppets. His girlfriend has already waited ten years for him to leave the gray zone between childhood and maturity and propose to her. On the day of the tenth anniversary of an unconsummated, unerotic love, she forces him to choose: are you man or Muppet? His answer in song refuses decision: "if I'm a Muppet, I'm a very manly Muppet, and if I'm a man that makes me a Muppet of a man."

It is as if, with the Muppet—a softer and gentler (but also more monstrous) rendering of the puppet—a solution offers itself to the hopeless problem of civilization. This solution is not original but presents itself with exceptional clarity. The Muppet folds political space back into a domestic space. The band of brothers is brought back into the uninhibited libidinal space of the nucleus of the nuclear family. Sons and brothers become cute. If the world could only become entirely cute—if it could become a cosmopolis and every city a town and every town a Smalltown—it would no longer be necessary for men to choose between home and outside attachments, since the outside would always already be inside the inside. And perhaps with this, the necessity for libidinal suppression, and the superego's introverted violence, would also disappear—though of course the mechanism of the superego serves not only to repress Eros but also to channel aggression, and thus aggression would be forced to revert to an archaic form. Can it surprise us that, in the dystopian backdrop against which the Muppets will make their triumphant return, "Punch Teacher" has become the most popular show?

But archaic violence also takes another form. There is perhaps no movie, no work of drama or literature that has presented with such precision the primal scene of civilization. In *The Muppets* there are only two men whose will and actions determine the plot: the baby-cheeked, doughy Muppet-like brother of a Muppet and the angular, villainous Mr. Richman, master of drilling and oil—the Plutonic source of wealth. The third man, Jack Black, is a comedian, with his arms and legs bound throughout, and thus his contribution to plot (and all plots are tragic; the *comic* plot is only the overcoming of plot) is doubly neutered and neutralized. The brother and father thus appear with an archetypal purity. The father returns, as if rising oil-like from the depths of hell, to reclaim the patrimony that he left to the brothers, including his first and most inalienable gift: their very names. He threatens the Muppets not with death but with an interruption of the various currents that drive the modern world. While his power, like Zeus's, has its seat in titanic depths, he looks down on the world from on high, taking control of the electric distribution system. The violence against him is completely ritualized, and comes only from Muppets.

But Smalltown must also be placed next to another town, another rerun of a primal scene of American culture, another solution to the problem of civilization: Smallville. The one solution: the band of brothers castrate themselves—not quite all the way, but just enough—becoming brothers by casting off the master signifier of the father's oppressive mastery. The other solution: the father returns not as Muppet, or even man, but superman—though, even if his origin is extraterrestrial, he will not simply impose himself on the world from above, but, having arrived, will have to *pass* as normal. The Herculean labors the modern hero must still face are nothing compared to the tribulations of high school. Whereas *The Muppets* reenacts the ritual transformation of the oppressive law of the father, the law that expressed only his will, dominating the brothers and women under the sign of the phallus, now the father, the real man, will return as at once all too human—an everyday guy—and a superman, enforcer of a perfect justice beyond the law. The Muppets save themselves and their theater by mastering the contract, and the entire juridical apparatus that supports it, that had been twisted and perverted into the means of the father's domination. Superman, in contrast, suspends the law in the name of justice with a constant state of emergency while nevertheless hiding behind his suit and all the other costumes of normalcy.

The mark of the Muppet is the absence of genitalia. This is enforced in civilization by means of clothing. By draping ourselves with the furs of animals, we came to hide the sign of our animality. Clothing for men is a kind of temporary castration. Hence a uniform, a suit—hiding the primary and secondary sexual characteristics, and even the tertiary characteristic of a dandyish, peacocklike vanity—is needed for men to enter the public sphere. Only the tie remains as a symbol of what has been lost. For women, in contrast, clothing serves rather to simultaneously conceal and reveal, forbid access and grant access. The sexual characteristics never even begin to disappear; they are never obscured. For the lewd, objectifying gaze, the more they are hidden, the more they are accentuated; outerwear is itself the metaphor and promise, if not direct exposition, of innerwear. And the face itself, the most public part of the body, identifying us and allowing us to speak, is, with makeup, turned into an allegory for other, more shameful lips.

This in turn illuminates one of the most basic dialectics of childhood: the opposition of *stuffed animals* and *dolls*. One could hardly overestimate the significance of a distinction that governs childhood and beyond, since it decides in a rudimentary way what the real human child will become. The stuffed animal is the ideal of the tamed animal. The most iconic stuffed animal is the teddy bear; the bear—the wild animal that, with its uncannily humanlike capacity to stand on two legs, has always tempted humans to fanatical, perilous efforts of taming and training—becomes identified with the celebrity politician who, for all his fierceness toward enemies and potential enemies, is not only gentle to his friends, but almost lovable, cute, "relatable." The stuffed animal does not wear clothes; it is its clothes—a human soul forced into a carapace of fake fur. Hence stuffed animals tend to have male personalities. The doll, in contrast—which realized its absolute form when a sex toy for lewd European men was turned into a curvaceous fashion plate for American girls—is the repressive ideal of pure femininity as pure and absolute passivity. (In a haunting and ingenious song, the absolute passivity of the doll reveals itself as the sexual pleasure of being man-handled: "I'm a Barbie girl, in the Barbie world; Life in Plastic, It's

Fantastic; You Can Brush My Hair, Undress Me Everywhere; Imagination, Life Is Your Creation.") But the passivity of the Barbie doll, a passivity that has nothing to do with cuteness, is already intimate with, already intimates, the hyperbolic masculinity of superman. Barbie was happy to come home to Ken with his pink cardigans and have him serve her breakfast in bed. But didn't she sneak out of her dollhouse at night to rendezvous with her mistress's brother's action figures? And didn't Barbie herself, when she turned her innerwear into outerwear, become Wonder Woman? Stuffed animals and Barbie dolls, in contrast, can have nothing to do with each other; they do not resolve into a higher synthesis. A dialectic that is not only negative, but broken and off-kilter. Could anyone imagine the offspring of a teddy bear and a Barbie doll? Here we even find a faint premonition of the cliffs on which speculative philosophy will come to grief.

Superman strips off his suit to reveal his tights, though these, thanks to a suspensorium, reveal only so much. The phallus is there, and visible to an extent, but also safely tucked away. How is it that tights, seemingly the most feminine of clothing—indeed the zero degree of feminine clothing, where inner and outerwear are fused, *Möbius-Like*, into a single surface, a single weave—can also become at once the most superheroic and the most supervillanous, the most Apollonian and the most Dionysian? The vestments of the ideal and just father and the most clownish, perverse villain; the track star or running back, or the Dionysian rock star? And, as if all of these possibilities at once, in the same breath hypermasculine and feminine: the *danseur* or ballerino. It is as if, following a logic of sexual difference that has still not been overcome, that remains all the more powerfully at work the more we seem to deconstruct it, women are uncastrated, uncastratable: they retain a feral sexuality. They constantly must be tamed, again and again, but have never been domesticated. For men, in contrast, the brotherly band—the fraternal order of egalitarian liberty—demands a sacrifice. Hence in this age, when this domestication has become complete, if a man were to wear tights this could only mean that he has refused the order of semicastration; that he either wishes to take his castration all the way, dressing up like a girl, or claims to be no longer a manly Muppet or Muppet man but a superman. Tights, either way, reveal a refusal: and perhaps the two refusals are not so far apart. Didn't Kleist already show us in his *Penthesilea* that feral violent femininity and supermanliness join in a maddened union? But what has no place in this union is rationality, civilization, and the drive inhibitions these demand. Men can only wear tights if they belong to a team and become just one of the guys—and every team is just another band of brothers. The *danseur noble*, surrounded by supple swans, is a prince; the sole claimant to the father's reign. He appears among us as only another *roi soleil*—an earthly manifestation of the divine. Who could allow him to still walk among us?

But gods do walk among us, sort of among us. Over there, in Hollywood. We call them celebrities. The celebrity at once exemplifies sexuality absolutely and refuses sexuality absolutely. Michael Jackson takes this dialectic to the limit. The sign of this is the refusal of that which every logic of political domination, beginning with the father of the primal horde, and every true ballet, demands as its element: depth, the third dimension. Without depth there can be no subordination, no subjection. But also no freedom. Depth is the joy of movement. The celebrity, and even the celebrity who dances, has left the stage behind him and is trapped in the screen. Thus celebrities can never actually appear to us in the world. The paparazzi, chasing after them with cameras, as if to force them back in their celluloid prison, make sure of this.

(And now Eminem, Rapbot, rap God—channeling Shields and Yarnell, Theodor Geisel, Nijinsky, E. T. A. Hoffmann, Hölderlin, not to mention his own more proper genealogy, woven into the texture of the rhyme. *But for me to rap like a computer must be in my genes / I got a laptop in my back pocket.* Becoming gadget, jumping in and out from the screen; becoming robot. *When I speak in tongues / But it's still tongue in cheek.* The incandescent, exuberant, schizoid murmuring of gadget-life . . . And like Hölderlin, he signs off: *Be a king? Think not, why be a king when you can be a god?*)

The Muppets begins with a pilgrimage from Smalltown to Hollywood. The Muppet theater, derelict and abandoned to the elements, stands, like the Muppet show itself, at the threshold where the theater, with its political depth, meets and is collapsed into the screen. Of course we, like the Muppet brother Walter, could only see the Muppets through the looking glass. But his desire, fanatical and profound, is to return to the theater, to save it and revive it in its possibilities. He, like the rest of us, is a Muppet—soft, tame, small, and cute. But this does not mean he could not also become a political animal. He recognizes that in the theater, this deep space in which one could appear as what one is, it would be possible to exist politically, since politics is nothing else than the depth of appearance. The guiding desire of the puppet Walter, born at the moment that he sees *The Muppet Show* on TV, echoes the yearning that propelled Wilhelm Meister toward the theater, and which itself arose in him when as a child he first saw a puppet show: Walter, like

Wilhelm Meister, will seek out the theater as the space in which the bourgeois—that Muppet-like being who, having renounced its drives, knows power, and the depths of historical time and tradition, only in the sublimated form of accumulation (Walter is himself a collector of Muppet memorabilia)—could appear in the world; could appear as a substantial something.

The band of brothers will again discover in politics a substitute for what was cast away. But for this to happen it will be necessary to bind up, humiliate, and do away with the celebrity. Indeed: whenever the stage still appears on the screen, celebrities are beckoned in to destroy themselves. The means of this is the cameo. For celebrity follows this iron law: the celebrity can only be a celebrity by always being someone else. They only really become absolutely themselves—which is to say the unchanging myth of what they were—by dying a tragic death. The show of reality itself, which only really came into its own when the culture of celebrity, under the pressure of the Internet, entered a point of crisis, has created a sort of purgatory in which celebrities can exist almost forever as half-celebrities without being apotheosized by dying a tragic death.

The theater offers one kind of depth. But this must be opposed to another: the plutonic depth of wealth, resources; of everything that can be extracted from beneath. However strange and immaterial wealth will seem to become in late capitalism, chthonic wealth continues to exact, and extract, its rights. Oil, water, coal, gold and silver, uranium and plutonium, precious metals, rare earth, even fertile topsoil: these remain the archaic source and sine qua non of even the most sublime productivity. And it is with these that the father, murdered by the band of brothers, threatens to return from the land of the dead into the land of the living. Max Richman, the unctuous heir of the primal father, slithers up from the depths as the remnant and reminder of an original patricidal guilt and of the oppressive law that had been destroyed. The political depth of the theater thus opposes itself to a natural, chthonic depth; the depth of libidinal drives and Oedipal violence. If *The Muppets* offers a solution to the problem of civilization, it is because, committed to the space of the theater, the Muppets refuse either to kill their fathers or to sleep with their mothers. Kermit, the frog king who has chosen to remain a frog, who refuses the kisses of the rapacious, piggish princess, exemplifies this double refusal. If it is not easy being green, it is because, with few exceptions, green—the color of photosynthesis—only appears on the surface of the world, where dark, solid matter and the light of the sun converge. Green is the depth of the world's surfaces.

In Sophocles' trilogy, the father-murdering and mother-fucking Oedipus, accompanied by the daughter who would later dare to save the fraternal order from itself, wanders into a village outside Athens, and, laying down his weary limbs to die, institutes, through his death, the city as the sacred space of politics. *The Muppets* attempts a reinstitution of the political institution of the theater that is, for all its insipidness, of no less theoretical significance. Has there ever been another movie that moves, with such wondrous agility, between four different versions of theatricality: the puppet theater, the stage, the movie, and television, each of which comes to contain and interpret that which comes before? Whereas the flat plane of the *polis*, with its walls and limits, characterizes the space of a classical politics—one in which depth remains undeveloped and thus is forced, summoning the power of metaphysics, to retreat into the soul—modern political depth involves a very different topography. It has everything to do with interesting containers, intercalation, recursion, involutions and exvolutions of every manner, feedback loops, tie-ins, back and cross references. In both the Oedipus trilogy and *The Muppets*, political depth, though in each case of a very different kind, defeats the Oedipal disorders and thwarted libido, the impossibility of civilization, not by destroying the father or king, which could only repeat the original crisis—both Creon and Max Richman live on—but by displacing the entire action into a new kind of space: the space of political theater.

One shouldn't think that the history of a literary genre, form, or problem consists in a succession of important, monumental works: as if epic moves from Homer to Virgil to Ovid to Dante. When it comes to such histories, only two things matter: the beginning and the end—which is itself always also the beginning of something completely different. Everything in between exists only in relation to, gravitating toward, these two poles. When searching for the beginning and the end, one should not suppose that both must share a certain grandeur, dignity, seriousness, aesthetic worth. *The Muppets* is silly—slightly derivative, trivial, Disneyish—it is weak even when measured against *The Muppet Movie*, not to mention the truly genial *Muppet Show*: even the newer songs lack the haunting power of the older. But for this very reason, it can stand beside the Oedipus trilogy as the end to its beginning: the last answer to the question that it first poses, and at the same time a new beginning. Yet if this still seems willfully paradoxical, let us propose as a middle term another film, more serious and grand—almost the cinematic equal to Sophocles—that will cast light on this otherwise absurd conjunction: *Chinatown*. Not only does the theme of detection and incest establish a link with *Oedipus Rex*, but, like *Oedipus at Colonus*,

Chinatown has everything to do with the founding, through chthonic manipulations—in this case the redirection of the water supply—of the city that will become home to spectacles. Whereas *Chinatown* is the noir and ingenious recollection of Hollywood's origins, tied back to the question of the birth of tragedy, *The Muppets* is the swan song for Hollywood's, and the celebrity's, demise. *The Muppets* envisions a future—but perhaps this has already arrived—in which theater persists only as the reality show. The celebrity, with his engulfing flatness, has swallowed up all depth, and even the last trace of depth upon which his own existence, which itself involves a certain pathos of distance—the shallowest form of depth—still depends. With the reality show, everyone has the right to become flat.

This swan song is also, quite literally, sung. The musical, the late-born heir to the pastoral opera with its idyllic recitative, has more and more become the only form through which Hollywood can hold on to its own birthright. The musical, like *The Muppets*, will have nothing to do with Wagner's grandiosity. With Wagner, the question of civilization will always return, Parsifal-like, to wounds that can never heal, fatherly spears turned against their bearer, castration and hysteria. The musical again shows another way: a politics of intimacy; sincerity; miniature, subtle depths.

Miss Piggy, the most stereotypically—and aggressively—feminine Muppet, has always stood for the corrosive danger of celebrity. It is not surprising that, in the Muppets' afterlife after their show has run its course, she would become the "plus-size editor" for a fashion magazine. Reducing and redacting depths to a planar geometry has always been her forte. Kermit, the unprincely frog-prince, spurns her because he knows that the flattening logic of celebrity stands in league with plutonic, chthonic depths. The swamp, his element, can support neither. But another alliance is possible. In a brutal, Kleistian pas de deux of dancer and puppet, Nureyev, refusing the catachrestic identification of swine and swan, casts Miss Piggy forth, and thus recovers from Prince Siegfried's failure to distinguish between an Odille and an Odette.

(The second of the two pilot episodes of *The Muppet Show* parodies the sex and violence on television. Is this just a parody? With its wild proliferation of forms drawn from the folds and textures of the real, with its metatheatrical irony folded into the most visceral humor, *The Muppet Show* has, from the beginning, drawn us into a primal scene. The Muppet monster will come to present, in the softest, tamest, cutest form, the most obscene textures of biological life: one Muppet devours another, who continues to sing, to make his voice heard, from inside—the zero point where sex and violence become indiscernible. Yet in this pilot episode the pageant of the seven deadly sins has been postponed. What follows—*The Muppet Show, Muppet Studio*, movie after movie, ever more cuddly, commercial, familiar—will be so many consequences of this postponement: the return of the celebrity guest will provide a center of gravity for Muppets beyond themselves and their involutions. The Muppets will begin to orbit around the flat and perfect surface of the celebrity, and perhaps no guest will be quite as uncanny as the first—Mia Farrow, satanic travesty of the holy mother. Kermit, that social climber and flatterer, will take the place of Nigel: night after night, the celebrities will stroke his ego. Are they also stroking our own? The celebrity becomes the impenetrable surface of television itself, approached from both sides . . .)

THE SWEATSHOPS OF HOLLYWOOD

The reality show is the Fordism of post-Fordism: the attempt to impose the factory model of production, with its gestures of surveillance and control brought to a perverse refinement, on precisely those aspects of production that have already escaped from its limits. The creativity, individuality, spontaneity, and imagination of the multitude are produced for the sake of showing that they can be produced. The spontaneous must appear manufactured: the manufactured spontaneous. Thus everything enters into the hazy twilight of "pure ideology," ideology at the limit where it passes over into the phenomenological conditions of production: an ideology that no longer serves to conceal or constrain the "real" of substructure, but to expose it as the site of a battle that will always be won by the past, by the way things are: by the laws of selection and immunity that Heidi Klum declares on *Project Runway* again and again as if propounding the laws of a divine order.

MUPPETATION AND MEDIATION

Against the clumsy, oafish, obvious gestures of a philosophical dialectic, the *real* dialectic, the dialectic of wit, always proceeds through the coincidence of two counterpoised gestures that have, at first glance, nothing to do with each other, no essential relation whatsoever, and yet are for this all the more deeply and necessarily intertwined—if only *post facto*. Thus in *The Muppet Show*, the original series, two things happen at once: the puppet, becoming Muppet, is given softness, plushness, texture, expression—in a word, depth—and the celebrity is given, and given over to, Muppets.

The curtain is drawn, the celebrity is unveiled, the Muppets crowd around: not only crowd, but throng, press against, caress and are caressed . . . The Muppets have achieved something beyond our wildest hopes: they have insinuated themselves into celebrity. As if, suddenly, they were cut from the same cloth.

The plush expressiveness of the Muppet, this revolutionary transformation of the medium, takes nothing away from the traditional archetypal purity of the puppet. The Muppet is not simply a cloth imitation of a "real" actor, but institutes a new canon of stock types; as suited to America as the commedia dell'arte was to sixteenth-century Italy. Yet whereas the older stock types, which would find their perfect complement in the puppet's wooden articulation, suggest human activity as that which of itself subverts the social hierarchy, the Muppets belong to an order of interiority, inward emotion: a sociality based on need, insecurity, psychoanalytic depths. They are all, in one way or another, permutations of that most profound, paradoxical American type: the salesman, the one who enters into a communion with a common need, a common depth, even if always at the same time only allowing it to appear as a commodity. But the Muppets, of course, only sell themselves: the theater thus emerges as the venue in which desire can at once show itself and satisfy itself with, become self-satisfied with, its showing. The salesman is charismatic when he sells: like Kermit, who, as host, sells us on Muppets and celebrities, or like Rolf. But he is poignant, and even more charismatic, when he fails: Fozzie Bear, the comedian that cannot sell his jokes, or Miss Piggy, the diva who cannot sell her sexuality, or even Sam the Eagle, that hapless moralist and patriot, whose own pre-Muppetational stiffness is expressive of his depths. Selling its own failure to sell, charismatic in its very lack of charisma, the Muppet shows the commodity becoming lovable, and infinitely satisfying, in its very incapacity to satisfy the needs that it conjures into existence.

If the celebrities allow the Muppets to come so close to them, it is because they can no longer do without this plushness. Television will make it necessary. And perhaps the Muppets will remain an impossible ideal—the most truly iconic, truly unforgettable celebrities that television has ever produced.

(In comedy, timing is everything. True wit, of course, belongs to that almost endlessly subtle between-time of sociality and conversation. The stand-up comedian has already arrested this time, brought it to a standstill: by speaking to the audience, as if an actor whose every line were an aside, he forces the situation, takes up everyone's time, and turns it into a kind of commodity. The joke is nothing but the attempt to sell back to the audience the time he's taken from them. Comic timing is the sleight of hand by which this questionable sale succeeds. And when the stand-up comic is on TV, these incessant asides seek nothing less than to sell us on TV itself; to have us buy back this other life, as if it could be ours again; as if there were in the end just this one life, this one world. As if we can all be friends . . . But poor Fozzie: he laughs at his own jokes, trying to sell them through his laughter. This laughter is always untimely, impatient: it usually comes before the joke. We laugh with and at his laughter, as if we joined Waldorf and Statler in their booth—itself an aristocratic holdover from an age when the theater was still the place of distracted viewing. The bad comedian—conspicuously, comically, endearingly bad—is somewhat like a tool that fails: it brings the unworld and afterlife of televisionary life, in all its untimeliness, into view.)

DEMECTOMY

It is no accident that so many reality shows begin with twelve contestants. One genealogy of the reality show might indeed trace it back to the jury system, and the odd practice, so characteristic of the anxieties of liberal democracy, of sequestering. The reality show brings to its breaking point a paradox endemic to modern democracy: the jury, perhaps the most actively political, participatory institution in modern representative democracy, must itself be excluded from the public sphere and squirreled away into a private space, with the jury's access to information and communications subject to rigorous restrictions.

Yet with the reality show, the jury itself is now judged and eliminated. And often they are even left with the task of judging and eliminating themselves. It is not only that the sphere of the political must be perversely confined to a domestic space, but that the only political activity still allowed is to judge, and eliminate, the political. The reality show, this is to say, presents the people in the painful, strange, ugly surgical procedure through which it operates on itself, excises itself, and revels, over and over, in its own self-butchering—its demectomy, as it were.

But there is another difference: while the jury exists in a state of pure leisure (in the formal, original sense), the contestants of the reality show, with rare exceptions, are forced into forms of labor that, in their very perverse pointlessness, assume a truly mythic quality. Yet the god that hovers over these rituals of self-assertion and self-sacrifice is not Hera but celebrity: it is for the sake of celebrity that the contestants, already half-celebrities, expose their laboring, sexual, performing and surviving bodies to public view. And there is an unnerving logic behind this: if the people destroys itself for the sake of celebrity, it is because celebrity is the only form in which the people, the public—indeed politics—still exists. Celebrity is the form in which mere life achieves immortality.

ACTION FIGURES

Today every hero lives two lives at once: superhero and action figure.

Stripped of beauty, charisma, warmth, charm, above all the virtuosic fluidity of movement, the action hero becomes a puppet. Yet this awkwardness is telling. In the action film, the fragility of our world is hidden through the physical strength and grace of the hero: he redeems the world of its fragility through graceful movement, through beauty, and through a body that refuses death. The puppet, in contrast, lifeless and coarse in its movements, exposes a world already rent apart.

In the action film, destruction evokes fear; in the puppet farce, laughter. But in just this way the farce proves its superiority to the action film, to this last permutation of high drama. For whereas the mood of fear binds us to the world that is destroyed, laughter releases us from a world whose fateful inessentiality has been revealed (so Marx, so Lucretius). Laughter always comes at the end of Empire: and the laughter of which we speak, this mirth, is a mood that no longer corresponds to a theological world configuration.

The end of the world does not, of course, lead us into another world. It is a freedom from the world; from the world as something that comes before us, that gives us a place. Instead of the world, the vortex.

LIBERAL ARTS

If the unnamable axis around which the humor of the sitcom rotates is masturbation, the unnamed center of the "serious" American film, at the moment when it has become almost completely irrelevant, is David Foster Wallace, whose magnum opus, a sky-blue blur, commands the plot of this film in which the failed intellectual returns in all seriousness to his alma mater, a liberal arts college, to *find himself*, again, after nearly fifteen years in which nothing seems to have changed.

What should we make of this peculiar complicity between the fantasy of the liberal arts and the so-called postmodern novel? Perhaps both offer an inoculation, at once anticipatory and retroactive, against the threat of theory. This film, celebrating reading, can only give one answer to who the "good reader" is: the good reader is the one who doesn't read theory; who reads only David Foster Wallace, obsessively, and at the very point in one's academic career where one might be expected to make the transition to a different kind of reading.

This suggests the claim that theory still makes on us: it is the refutation of the timelessness, the eternal repetition of the same, to which the academy is preordained. The aim of college, to which theory has waged a valiant opposition, is to inscribe youth into a kind of cyclic time, a timeless time. Youth in this way becomes what cannot grow up; what cannot become anything but what it is. The professor who refuses to grow up, and even asks for his job back after retirement, exemplifies this cursed existence. And we can be sure that he did not have theory—only weary leftist slogans.

It is in this way that so-called real life takes on its significance. Real life is the only growing up that remains for those who cannot grow up: a growing into a domesticity that is not only a cliché, but life in clichés. One will settle down with the one with whom one can imagine growing old: growing up means growing into a cliché. Perhaps only a mouse of a no longer quite young girl—working in a bookstore, she has avoided life for the sake of books—can provide the perfect spouse. (Here we find a rarified myth of virginity: obsessive reading is no longer, at least for women, the path to corruption but to infinitely prolonged innocence.)

Nowhere more so than here, in this film that claims the cheapest form of seriousness—the seriousness that comes from having to do with reading—can we begin to understand all that has been and will be lost with the eradication of theory from higher education. College becomes the nostalgia for college, for a form of life that consists only in the pure enjoyment of nostalgia; genius becomes suicide.

Comic improvisation, whose only rule is saying yes to everything—a writing without commitment—is the other pole of a reading without theory. This is the only power still granted to youth other than genial suicide—or a diffuse drug-free comic spirituality. One can become anything, but only if anything still only ever means nothing. Life becomes absolute improvisation to the very degree that it has been dissolved into the timelessness of eternal repetition.

Reading is either the harmless delectation of suicide or the submission to the pleasures of improvisation. Improvisation here is not true improvisation, which captures time in the transience of becoming, but a category that has imposed itself, in advance, on experience. Growth is only still possible as subsumed under this category, and hence assumes two mythic forms: tepid Eros and classical music. Classical music as the profoundest improvisation—as the improvisation of a deep genius: this is the myth of the liberal arts college.

The young girl has perhaps always promised old men, through the gift of her virginity, the resurrection of lost youth. But now this resurrection assumes a completely different form: it no longer has anything to do with pregnancy, birth, becoming a mother, all of which would at least force a certain maturity. Rather, it is the repetition of youth as continual repetition; as an endless, barren improvisation. If Zibby's seduction has an ethical character, it is only because, in revealing so much—too much—of herself, she forces the protagonist to refuse the gift she offers. Her gift indeed becomes the gift of making her gift be refused. But perhaps this film also points the way to another possibility of reading, and love, beyond the youth-repetition-machine. This will take the form of terrible writing and terrible reading: the unnamed vampire trilogy is the counterweight to *Infinite Jest*. At the present moment, the worst literature demands theory in the same measure as the best literature refuses it, or even, aping it by way of the footnote, destroys its very possibility. To say yes to everything: this can only mean, also, to say yes to bad books about vampires. Just like vampires, which are always both young and old, youth itself becomes infinitely seductive and infinitely revolting.

GLEE

High school prepares for life in this sense alone: it allows—forces—one into a type. In those meritocratic and bureaucratic social orderings that were born with the decline of feudalism, this type would pave the way to a future career: as soldier, doctor, lawyer, bureaucrat, technician, scientist, even musician or dancer. But now this type is only the facade that protects against becoming, and becoming-nothing. The aim of high school, as it were, is no longer to start becoming what one can be, but to be what one already is, and precisely because as soon as high school is over, one will have to cease to be anything, and simply become.

The musical in this sense is the ideal expression of being-in-high-school. The high school musical is inevitably a musical about making musicals, but nothing could be further from romantic irony and theatrical self-referentiality. The point is not to show the theatricality of life but rather to guarantee for the theater the immanent presence and accomplished perfection of a reality that cannot ever be otherwise than it is. In the high school musical, every lesson, audition, every rehearsal, is already a performance, absolutely perfect: contingency, danger, and rapture have been banished. Even those who cannot yet dance at all already dance more perfectly, if not better, than the most perfect dancers, since their incapacity has been granted the status of the exemplary—and if they also improve, so much the better. Thus a perverse logic takes hold: it is not enough to do one's best or be the best—one must be better. But being better does not open the door to infinite perfectibility: rather, doing better, always, is the first principle of the being of the high school student, whose very adolescence is granted the tragic dignity of the typical.

The uncanny, seductive magic of musical-style singing results from its singular capacity to present that which has been immaculately rehearsed as a spontaneous improvisation—the immediacy of an affect that, rooted in the heart, exists outside of time. This is quite different from either traditional compositional forms, such as ballet, which do not rebuke the harsh majesty of form, or the more genuine and radical improvisation of jazz. Rock music might seem to share the mendaciousness of the musical, but there is a subtle difference. In rock, preparation is militant, aggressive, and also erotic: a "tightness" that recalls the Greek phalanx. The overtrained and exaggerated spontaneity of the musical, in contrast, suggests nothing so much as a dialogue in which the Other has always already been obliterated and remains only as a prop for the self. If *Romeo and Juliet*, recast as *West Side Story*, always provides the script for the high school musical, *Hamlet* is its haunting subtext. The musical duet is always sung to Yorick's skull: every dialogue becomes a soliloquy. True speaking and true listening have been forbidden.

In the high school musical, adolescence becomes the ideology of adolescence; or rather, it becomes the pure form—and the limit form—of the commodity. Adolescents, singing in seeming spontaneity about their adolescence, celebrate their value as becoming; a becoming that already is, that *is* as becoming. At stake here is the inherent paradox of commodity form and exchange value.

The high school musical becomes a showcase for freaks and outcasts, and even provides a space in which social barriers give way. Black and yellow and white, handicapped and able-bodied, football players and fairies can sing and frolic together. But this utopia comes at a price: everything is possible because all potential has been banished. Queerness thus assumes the form of an essential identity. This leads to an odd outcome: while Kurt Hummel's homosexuality and theatrical vocation are of a piece, he cannot but act gay; his native theatricality rests, perversely, in his inability to act; he is a born actor only because being theatrical and being gay have both become for him a destiny from which there is no escape. Just like Wilhelm Meister, that modern travesty of Hamlet, Hummel, named after Beethoven's almost forgotten contemporary, is drawn to the theater in the very measure that he lacks a true calling. Queerness is permitted only if it is utterly without deviance: only as an absolute fidelity to a biological destiny. Only if it is straighter than straight.

In a world bereft of danger, evil can only ever take one form: not a bad conscience, or bad faith, but a bad voice. The success of *American Idol* has trained us to regard with absolute contempt, even with moral outrage, those who think they can sing but cannot. We celebrate their being ridiculed, and their sacrificial exclusion, with a glee that we would not permit ourselves even in the case of the worst criminal. The bad and unhappy conscience of the condemned still troubles us, but bad singers have proven to us that they have no conscience. To know the limit of one's voice, to only speak if one cannot sing, and not sing louder or higher or deeper than one's voice allows: this is the only virtue that still matters. A profound transformation of the political has thus taken place. Nothing remains of politics but a vacant sociality, a sociality of perfect monadic narcissists, condemned to a harmony preordained yet perfectly spontaneous. You can—you must—be what you are, express your innermost essence; you can think and fuck whatever you want. You can be loud or quiet, high or low, chirpy or soulful or lusty or melancholic. Do whatever you want, obey or disobey, follow the rules or break them. You can even be old or fat or ugly. But please—sound good! This alone is demanded of us: native virtuosity. Of course, only a few can be stars. For the rest, the important thing is to know when to shut up. Clapping, cheering, spectating, yaying and naying, in a word, acclamation: this is not the absence of virtuosity, but its zero degree—the virtuosity of the masses . . .

(The celebrity, in this sense, is virtuosic-being. Yet while the musical celebrates celebrity, it rarely produces celebrity, even if it appears as the easiest and perhaps only way to make a star. A subtle difference remains between becoming-celebrity and being-celebrity. The musical reveals something that celebrity must hide—the need to hide. The musical can conceal becoming, but it reveals its own gesture of veiling, and, in this way, its magic is at once done and undone.)

This above all is demanded of today's youth: enthusiasm. More precisely: the enthusiasm of the spectators, the choir mates, who clap and sway and smile as their friends sing someone else's song in their own voice. As the camera pans in and out, two things become visible: the radiant singularity of the individual (youth is beauty, and beauty youth), and the complete submission to the vibe and affect of the group. Harmony comes to exist as the absolute impossibility of a contradiction between these two moments. But such harmony is only possible since it has already been scripted: the individual and the group, singing from the script of popular culture, announce, through a prefab spontaneity, their identification with it. Freedom is already belonging. Evil is transient, inessential if one can still be enthusiastic. Even the bad voice can be reconciled if it stays quiet and yields.

Yet enthusiasm is still not quite enough. It must have value, and it can only have value as memory. One more thing is asked: the young must live to create memories for when they are old—not of sexual ecstasy (it is a dogma of the present that people never stop having sex) but of community, of a friendship—even with one's enemies. Memory is the commodity form of affect—and of affect as commodity: of the feelings of a radically alienated community. The song, sung from the scripts of the past, is always the production of an affect that has been already remembered from the future. It is not surprising, then, that the song-memory presents a mirror image of the real. High school, that pathological factory of social dissonance and hatred—a world where popularity and publicity can only take the form of meanness—becomes the perfect community.

BUNHEADS

Glee begins with the return of the real man to the helm of the choir and to his true vocation. Recruiting the popular kids to the choir he once led to victory, he will again forge a team of champions, a team that can sing "we are the champions." *Bunheads* begins with an accidental marriage and an accidental death. To create a world in which men play only an accompanying role, it will be necessary to sacrifice the very man whose obsessive will brought Michelle Simms—first an elite New York ballet dancer, then a Vegas showgirl—to where she now is, to a ballet school in a town named Paradise.

This tells us much about the form that manliness—so long as it is not merely a matter of attitude, appearance, or occupation—must assume these days. The only thing that remains truly manly is a kind of authenticity—being true to one's heart; giving voice to one's desires; living in the fullness of a moment that has already remembered itself, already memorialized itself on account of the grandeur of its memorableness. The real man is the one who lives his dreams in the only way possible in this broken world: by living the dream of singing about the dreams one is going to live.

The feminine, indeed, has been banished from the world of *Glee*: the women are lesbians, or look and dress like men; are cold psychopaths or theatrical caricatures. Only a token presence of femininity is allowed: the insufferably fragile mysophobic Emma Pillsbury, who seems no more suited to her guidance-giving vocation than her Austenian namesake.

If masculinity is the myth of the interior expressive voice (phallocentrism and phonocentrism), femininity appears in *Bunheads*, once again, as ballerina. The joy of ballet, in contrast to the joy of song, is not ostentatious or theatrical but interior, silent, and inseparable from pain; the dancer's smile is always a mask. Ballet is a discipline before it is a vocation, and the heart must play catch-up with the body, which is forever ever so slightly ahead of itself. The dancers' bodies are inducted into a vestigial hieroglyphic language, but their words and thoughts remain elsewhere: they almost never speak of fame, and if they speak of themselves it is with the haphazard awkwardness of youth. It is as if femininity were to mean this above all: being a stranger to one's desires. As if the world of women were a paradise, but a melancholy paradise, marked by the impossibility of love.

BREAKING BAD/ELECTIVE AFFINITIES

Between Ottilie and Walter White, the perfect domestic and the perfect capitalist, we find the ideal limits that define capitalism at its beginning and its ending. The one, imitating the holy mother, is spotless in her receptive productivity: she has no finished skills, nothing to show for her schooling, yet she orders and organizes everyone and everything, insinuating herself seamlessly into the most aberrant rhythms. The price of this mastery is renunciation. The other produces and produces, invests and expands, and never once indulges in his product. He has learned well from his youthful mistake: the very terminal diagnosis that should, following a sentimental reasoning, have taught him to live in the moment teaches him the very opposite—never again will he choose life (children, family, stability) over future profit. But if this decision, this reaction, no longer seems scandalous or even surprising—if it seems to follow its own chemical necessity—it is because the very possibility of living has been evacuated from within. It is not only that the dream of middle-class security has been destroyed, and no security is possible save through grotesque wealth, but that the pleasure of living is only still conceivable as living for a future that will never come. But this has already happened by Goethe's time: Luciane, who *does* at least live in the moment, is little more than a refined ape, and, despite her seeming novelty, utterly anachronistic. For the others: there is no enjoyment but in a future that, by the time it ripens into its *kairos*, is already passé.

EPILOGUE

HOW I MET MY MOTHER (FRENCH THEORY, BY FRANÇOIS CUSSET)

The critique of the critique of critique, like the old man in the sphinx's riddle, is left in the end with only one leg to stand on. Still kritizierbar is this alone—the myth of heroic beginnings, of grand gestures, of new vistas, new worlds of thought, that might appear (ah . . . Baltimore . . . 1966) in a conference paper, written in a mere 10 days. Master thinkers, and their disciples. A playfulness that was serious. Now our seriousness is stillborn in its seriousness.

Against the sweet insouciance of *Friends*, there is something terrifying about this sitcom, which is marketed in Korea under the title *I Love Friends*. As if *Friends*, and the friend, had already become the object of a pathetic longing. As if, even in this, we must resign ourselves not only to an ersatz-friend but to an ersatz-*Friends*. With a macabre critical instinct, some television executive recognized that the great joke of *Seinfeld*, the fake cast, had suddenly been recast as a real sitcom. As if there were a third repetition in history, beyond tragedy and farce.

But this third brings us back to the first: the husband, an architect like Mr. Brady, tells his children how he met their mother. The purest form of the tyranny of mythopoesis. As if the children could, or should, care. As if the very idea that they should care, that the mystery of their birth could be reduced to an endless sequence of tawdry vignettes, were not the most terrible offense against childhood. As if the novelty of birth could be seamlessly folded into the life of the parents.

What did Oedipus and Antigone talk about during their long years of wandering?

All myth, every beginning, is perverse. This silliest of sitcoms brings us to the brink of tragic, Dionysian knowledge. The parents who entertain their child with the story of their prehistoric misadventures demand that the child reproduce their own desire for life, and indeed for the afterlife of having children, the semblance of eternal life—without having lived. They seek nothing less than the confirmation of their own desire for life in the lifeless desire of their children. This is the prosaic, everyday form of mythic incest. And the tyranny of desire is always this: the desire for obsolete forms of desire.

We who watch are like the children who listen. We do not live, but we desire to live. And in this we late-born theorists (we theorists after theory . . .) are not so different from the couch potato. (Hence the critique of television, if this still needs to be said, is not the least bit irrelevant to *protē philosophia*.) We do not think, but we desire to think. We desire the form that thinking once took in its still fresh but wholly mythic past. We cannot imagine happiness but in a form that is no longer possible for us. True happiness for us is whatever happiness we cannot have.

The genius of *Tristram Shandy* suddenly dawns on me: the sobriety of prose begins with the parody of the myth of our own drunken birth.

I was born then, in 1966, and before this: in Weimar, in Vienna, in Berlin, in Prague, in Jena, in Paris, in Florence, in Rome, in Athens, perhaps even in Jerusalem. And also in places far from the cities. Why do I then feel so melancholy as I read this book by François Cusset? Am I nothing simply because I was not there to watch my birth? Is there greatness only in beginnings? But hasn't philosophy, which has created so much from a single matter, a single question, always been the next best thing.

NOTES

INTRODUCTION

1. Schelling, *Von der Weltseele*, 229.
2. Rousseau, *Confessions*, 96.

1. THE PHENOMENOLOGY OF TELEVISION

1. For a concise treatment of the early history of television, see Winston, "The Development of Television."
2. Regarding Heidegger's rejection of the distinction between the historical and systematic, see *Beiträge zur Philosophie*, 451. Significantly, in *Being and Time*, in contrast to *Contributions to Philosophy*, the fundamental moods, including anxiety, lack an explicitly historical character.
3. See Zimmerman, "Ontological Aestheticism," 52.
4. Heidegger, *Sein und Zeit*, 105. Translation modified.
5. See Derrida and Stiegler, *Echographies*, 36–39.
6. Heidegger, *Gesamtausgabe*, 2: 141. My translation.
7. Heidegger, *Sein und Zeit*, 105.
8. Ibid., 35.
9. Crary, *24/7*, 80–81.
10. Schickel, *Intimate Strangers*, 12. Schickel's compelling analysis remains constrained by a predominantly literary conception of what it means to watch TV, with the viewer regarded as a kind of scholar, studying its representations as a scholar would study his book while taking advantage of the perfect attentiveness that the medium allows. Yet what Benjamin says about film in *The Work of Art in the Age of Mechanical Reproduction* is even truer of television: it is viewed in distraction (*Gesammelte Schriften*, 1.2: 504–5). And indeed, as McCarthy argues in *Ambient Television* (1), television does not just belong to the domestic space, but is also present "in the routine locations we move through when we *leave* the house—the store, the waiting room, the bar, the train station, the airport."
11. Sebbah, *Testing the Limit*, 3.
12. Derrida's interview with Bernard Stiegler in *Echographies of Television* often calls attention to this relation between the project of deconstruction and the advent

of television. And Marshal McLuhan, coming from a very different angle, had already suggested a close affinity between the "close reading" that prevailed in American academia at the time he was writing and the cool, tactile, deep medium of television: "The old literate habit of racing ahead on uniform lines of print yielded suddenly to depth reading. Reading in depth is, of course, not proper to the printed word as such" (*Understanding Media*, 325).

13. Derrida and Stiegler, *Echographies*, 38.

14. McLuhan stresses the special attunement of radio "to that primitive extension of our central nervous system, that aboriginal mass medium, the vernacular tongue" (*Understanding Media*, 302).

15. Regarding the Nazis' resistance to television, see Uricchio, "Rituals of Reception." And as McLuhan notes in *Understanding Media* (310), whereas the "hot" medium of radio, "the medium for frenzy," has served to stir up tribalism and traditionalism and exacerbate feelings of local difference, TV "cools down."

16. Heidegger, *Bremer und Freiburger Vorträge*, 3.

17. Derrida's analysis of television in *Echographies of Television*, as the title itself suggests, remains to some degree still rooted in this radiological moment. The gramophone and radio, reproducing an absent voice, serve as the privileged media for thinking about television, and the viewer is understood throughout as an addressee, while at the same time the perspective of the producer rather than the receiver dominates the conversation up until the end. Hence the preoccupation with educating toward a "literacy" vis-à-vis the image (56–67).

18. Stiegler, *Political Economy*, 28.

19. Stiegler, *Re-Enchantment of the World*, 68.

20. See Derrida, *Specters of Marx*, 94.

21. See McLuhan, *Understanding Media*, 308–37.

2. THE LIFE NOT OURS TO LIVE

1. *Beavis and Butt-head*, "True Crime," Season 3, Episode 22, November 1, 1993.

2. For a characteristic interpretation of *Beavis and Butt-head* in terms of irony, see Morrow, "'But Beavis.'"

3. See Grossberg, "MTV." Another example of a subtle analysis of television still driven by the concept of irony is Wallace, "E Unibus Pluram."

4. See Heidegger, *Beiträge zur Philosophie*, 311. For a brief discussion of the controversy surrounding the status of the *Contributions* as Heidegger's second major work, see Polt, *The Emergency of Being*, 3–4. There are now a number of introductory works available in English on the *Contributions*. These include Vallega-Neu, *Contributions to Philosophy: An Introduction*, which provides an accessible but somewhat dogmatic reading of the text in the tradition of Friedrich-Wilhelm von Herrmann, and Polt's *The Emergency of Being*, which takes a more critical approach.

NOTES

5. Derrida and Stiegler, *Echographies*, 111; the concept of self-referentiality also plays a vital role in Poster's postmodern theory of "modes of information." Poster, in *The Informational Subject* (19), argues that the subject becomes dispersed into the self-referential, simulacric structures of language embodied through various information technologies. While this involves a radical decentering of the (infinitely) self-reflexive subject, this very dispersion of the subject reconstitutes the subject and its self-reflexivity, in another field, another terrain.

6. The limit of television, toward which it tends as its extreme "aesthetic" potential, is the complete extroversion and, with this, elimination of the unconscious. More often than we care to admit, television insinuates itself into our dreams, or even dictates them to us.

7. See Adler, "Fichte's Monetary History," 42–49.

8. Barthes, *Mythologies*, 15–25.

9. Agamben, *The Coming Community*, 5.

10. Baudrillard, *Simulacra and Simulation*, 28.

11. The monastic organization of daily life, in its relation to forms-of-life and liturgy, is the subject of Agamben's *The Highest Poverty*. Agamben's analysis suggests the intriguing possibility that a "secularized" monastic scheduling of daily life is also at work in the televisionary society of the spectacle.

12. Instructive in this regard is the distinction that Boorstin draws in his famous study between the pseudoevent and propaganda. The former is in some sense the opposite of the latter: whereas the pseudoevent is an ambiguous truth, propaganda is an appealing falsehood (*The Image*, 34).

13. Kottak, in *Prime-Time Society* (139–43), argues that as television viewing evolves, the specific attention devoted to the medium, which at first has a kind of mesmerizing strangeness, decreases while at the same time its saturation of community life and its long-term "sociocultural effects" become ever more pervasive.

14. So Wallace in "E Unibus Pluram" (181) asks the rhetorical question: "Culture-wise, shall I spend much of your time pointing out the degree to which televisual values influence the contemporary mood of jaded weltschmerz, self-mocking materialism, blank indifference, and the delusion that cynicism and naïveté are mutually exclusive?"

15. As Thompson explains in *Television's Second Golden Age* (11), during television's first "golden age" "serious people could take TV seriously": "The well-read could switch on the set on an average evening and find series with titles like *The Pulitzer Prize Playhouse*. Emily Brontë's *Wuthering Heights* alone rated six network adaptations during this period, and fans of Ibsen could have caught five stagings of *A Doll's House* and four of *Hedda Gabler*. The plays of Shakespeare were commonly seen on the networks during prime time."

16. Listing the characteristics of "quality television," Thompson observes: "Quality

TV has a memory. Though it may or may not be serialized in continuing story lines, these shows tend to refer back to previous episodes. Characters develop and change as the series goes on. Events and details from previous episodes are often used or referred to in subsequent episodes" (*Television's Second Golden Age*, 14).

17. That we should be suspicious of "quality television," and perhaps above all the rather vague category "quality" itself, does not mean we should reject all of it out of hand. Much "quality television" involves a dimension that transcends mere quality or that indeed disqualifies it from the traditional aesthetic and poetic categories that the language of quality seeks to impose. *Twin Peaks*, regarded as one of the greatest TV shows of the nineties and as the quintessence of televisionary quality, nevertheless deliberately deploys bathos and campy overacting, as if invoking the fictional soap opera, *An Invitation to Love*, that periodically plays in the background. Thus it presents itself as a televisionary commentary on television itself.

18. Ronell, *Crack Wars*, 44–45.

19. Baudrillard, *The System of Objects*, 185. In the remarkable passage that follows, Baudrillard suggests that advertising turns the object into the subject of desire: "We are taken as the object's aims, and the object *loves* us. And because we are loved, we feel that we exist: we are 'personalized.' This is the essential thing—the actual purchase of the object is secondary" (186).

20. As Baudrillard notes: "We should remember, too, that in a society where everything is strictly subject to the laws of selling and profit, advertising is the most democratic of products, the only one that is 'free'—and 'free' to all. Objects are always sold; only advertising is offered gratis" (ibid., 187).

21. *Mad Men*, "The Wheel," Season 1, Episode 13, October 18, 2007.

22. The importance of nostalgia in *Mad Men*, and indeed a nostalgia for the surfaces of life in the late fifties and early sixties, has given rise to a number of moralizing critiques, including Mark Greif, "You'll Love the Way It Makes you Feel," and Daniel Mendelsohn, "The Mad Men Account," and, in a more academic vein, Tudor, "Selling Nostalgia." For more nuanced and scholarly treatments of nostalgia in *Mad Men*, see Hamilton, "Seeing the World Second Hand," and Bevan, "Nostalgia for Pre-Digital Media in Mad Men," both of which treat the Kodak Carousel episode in some detail.

23. Rousseau, *Dialogues*, 214.

3. THE CELEBRITY AND THE NOBODY

1. I believe that "one" is a better translation since it captures the indefiniteness of the German. Macquarrie and Robinson, by translating *das Man* as "they," seem to put greater emphasis on its plurality. Yet this is misleading: when I say "that's just what *one* does" (which sounds very different from "that's just what *they* do"), I am not opposing myself to a vague multitude of others to whom I must assimilate my own

actions but am identifying myself with an indefinite subject that, always finding its alibi in the other, can never take responsibility for its own actions. The "they" is the multitudinous other who becomes responsible for having made me do what I do; the "one," by contrast, is the evasion of all responsibility.

2. Heidegger, *Sein und Zeit*, 126–27. Translation modified.

3. Rousseau's paranoia, one might argue, follows from his incapacity to conceive of the deviation of "public opinion" from genuine general will other than in terms of conspiracies of partial interests.

4. Hölderlin, *Empedokles*, 13.

5. Arguing that "the business of renown and celebrity has been in the making for two and a half centuries," Fred Inglis, in *A Short History of Celebrity*, claims that the history of celebrity "demands a kind of history which is largely missing on the shelves[,] . . . a history of what the greatest commentators of our origins in the 1760s or so would have called the moral sentiments" (3–19). Without wishing to contest the wealth of insight that this admirable study of the history of celebrity offers, I would claim that his largely Anglocentric account of both the history of affect and the rise of celebrity itself fails to recognize the significance of the Rousseauian moment, in which the notion of authenticity arises together with the recognition (despite, as Derrida has shown, the express intentions of Rousseau's text) that the very condition of the possibility of authenticity is its impossibility; the prior sundering of the self by an originary difference.

6. Rojek, *Celebrity*, 11.

7. The distinction between fame and celebrity rests on the fact that whereas the famous (as perfectly illustrated in the fable from Apuleius's *The Golden Ass*) represents the qualities of the divine, drawing the divine aura down to earth, and even—as Leo Braudy demonstrates in his study of Alexander as the "first famous person"—self-consciously, deliberately, and manipulatively staging the attributes of heroism and a divine origin, the celebrity stages the everybody, the nobody (*The Frenzy of Renown*, 29–51). The condition of celebrity is thus not merely the flight of the gods, but the absence of even the last trace of their departure.

8. Dyer, *Heavenly Bodies*, 16.

9. Regarding the difference between cinematic stardom and televisionary celebrity, McLuhan, recalling the words of Joanne Woodward, observes that the latter appears as a kind of generic familiarity: "When I was in the movies I heard people say, 'There goes Joanne Woodward.' Now they say, 'There goes somebody I think I know'" (*Understanding Media*, 317–18).

10. Agamben suggestively relates "celebration" to the question of the liturgy, the "public work" (*Opus Dei*, 8).

11. Heidegger, *Sein und Zeit*, 28.

12. Ibid., 34.

13. Ibid., 35–36.

14. Ibid., 37.

15. Foucault, *Discipline and Punish*, 201–2. We might also compare this with Derrida's *visor effect* (*effet de visière*): here too we find, though conceived in more phenomenologically and ontologically (or rather: hauntologically) radical terms, the disarticulation of the reciprocity of seeing and being seen (*Specters of Marx*, 6). Derrida, moreover, identifies the "supernatural and paradoxical phenomenality, the furtive and ungraspable visibility of the invisible," with "that *non-sensuous sensuous* [*sensibilité insensible*] of which *Capital* speaks . . . with regard to a certain exchange-value" (6).

16. Rousseau, *Dialogues*, 33.

17. Derrida, *Speech and Phenomena*, 88–104.

18. This holds even if we might credence Derrida's attempt in *Of Grammatology* (143) to situate Heidegger on this side of the metaphysics of presence, arguing, against Heidegger's own interpretation of Nietzsche, that the latter has in a decisive sense gone further than Heidegger in overcoming metaphysics.

19. Heidegger, *Gesamtausgabe*, 9: 316. My translation.

4. BEING(S)

1. See Heidegger, *Sein und Wahrheit*, 40.

2. The decision (*Entscheidung*), taking up the thought of resoluteness (*Entschlossenheit*) in *Being and Time*, assumes the greatest significance throughout the *Contributions* and is indeed a "fundamental word" of this text and of Heidegger's thinking after the *Kehre*. The decision is not to be understood, however, as a mere subjective act of will but is bound up with the eventual character of the event (*Beiträge zur Philosophie*, 87). Yet if the de-cision (*Ent-scheidung*) is the very essence of be-ing, and has to do above all with the constitution of the time-play-space (*Zeit-Spiel-Raum*), it is also necessary for thinking the task of the present moment in which we find ourselves, and the exigency that arises with the culmination of metaphysics. We are presently faced with a multitude of decisions, all of which, moreover, gather together into the one most fundamental decision: "ob das Seyn sich endgültig entzieht *oder* ob dieser Entzug als die Verweigerung zur ersten Wahrheit und zum anderen Anfang der Geschichte wird" (90–91). To decide for the decision is to decide for Dasein and for be-ing—to decide for the decision as the essence of be-ing rather than a mere act of subjective will.

3. Heidegger, *Sein und Wahrheit*, 58–59.

4. Ibid., 60.

5. This seems to be the danger of object-oriented ontology, speculative materialism, and flat ontology. Beyond a merely dogmatic ontological speculation, I would suggest radicalizing the question of "access" (which cannot be conflated with "correlationism") by asking in effect how the thing offers itself as its own transcendent condition of possibility. It is as if the closer one gets to the thing ontically, the more it deforms the ontological field, demanding its own ontology.

NOTES 221

6. Lukács, *History and Class Consciousness*, 85.
7. Ibid., 86–87.
8. Ibid., 93.
9. Ibid.,100.
10. Latour, *We Have Never Been Modern*, 29–37.
11. See Latour, *We Have Never Been Modern*, which presents a critique of Hegel, who, "by believing that he was abolishing Kant's separation between things-in-themselves and the subject[,] . . . brought the separation even more fully to life" (57).
12. Ibid., 51.

5. THE LIFE OF THINGS

1. See Eagleton, "Ideology and Its Vicissitudes," 221–22.
2. Marx, *Das Kapital: Erster Band*, 85. Translations of passages cited from this work are my own.
3. Ibid., 99.
4. The notion of the "sensual," as Michel Henry demonstrates in his phenomenological interpretation of Marx, has an extremely complex history in Marx's work, playing a crucial role in his confrontation with Hegel and the Young Hegelians, and in particular with Feuerbach's "sensualist ontology," which involves two clashing meanings: the ontic (designating this or that sensuous thing out there in the world) and the ontological ("the power of opening up to beings, the power of sensing") (*Marx*, 119). While the young Marx will deploy Feuerbach's sensuousness against Hegel, who effaces natural immediacy in the name of the idea, he ultimately recognizes the contradiction of Feuerbach's intuitionistic ontology, and thus comes, in the famous "Theses on Feuerbach," to deploy the concept of *praxis* against him. This concept of praxis is itself drawn from Hegel but is subject to a decisive transformation: it is pure subjectivity, pure life, as the absence of any intentional relation, and hence of the objectification accomplished through the theoretical gaze (156). One could perhaps argue that in Marx's analysis of the commodity fetish the dualism between ontic and ontological sensuousness—the ultimate form that metaphysics assumes in its decomposition—is brought back to its genesis in the commodity and is revealed as the source of the ideological errancy, the very tendency toward objectifying theorization, that inhabits capitalism.
5. Henry, *Marx*, 287–306.
6. Marx, *Das Kapital: Erster Band*, 86–88.

6. IDEOLOGY AND TRUTH

1. Protocols of the "special education seminar" titled "Über Wesen und Begriff von Natur, Geschichte und Staat" are now available in the fourth volume of the *Heidegger-Jahrbuch* (*Heidegger und der Nationalsozialismus I: Dokumente*, 53–88).
2. Heidegger's concrete involvement in Nazism is documented in Victor Farías's

flawed and tendentious *Heidegger et le nazisme* and in Hugo Ott's more judicious *Martin Heidegger: Unterwegs zu seiner Biographie*. For a thorough treatment of the issues involved in the debate, see Kisiel, "Heidegger's Apology." There is also a growing body of works that, rejecting both trivializing critique and trite apologetics, attempt to recognize Heidegger's Nazism as an aspect of his thinking and his legacy that must be reckoned with. This includes Derrida's *Of Spirit: Heidegger and the Question*, Philippe Lacoue-Labarthe's *Heidegger, Art, and Politics: The Fiction of the Political*, and, more recently, Gregory Fried's *Heidegger's Polemos: From Being to Politics* and Christopher Rickey's *Revolutionary Saints: Heidegger, National Socialism, and Antinomian Politics*.

3. Heidegger, *Gesamtausgabe*, 9: 340. What follows is not meant to provide an exhaustive treatment of the extraordinarily complex, important, and contemporary question of Heidegger's relation to Marx and Marxism's relation to Heidegger. From Marcuse and Sartre through to Axelos, Althusser, Blanchot, Foucault, Derrida, Nancy, Henry, Agamben, and Badiou, this question has never ceased to give impetus to the continental philosophical tradition. In light of this, there have been surprisingly few studies devoted to the actual relation between Marx and Heidegger, despite the fact that, as Christian Lotz observes ("Reification through Commodity Form or Technology?"), contemporary Marxist thought has recently given more serious consideration to the possibility of a Heideggerian Marxism. For an overview of explicit attempts to bring together Heidegger and Marx, focusing on Kostas Axelos and Herbert Marcuse, see Hemming, *Heidegger and Marx*, 17–40; Angus, "Walking on Two Legs"; and Pawling, "Rethinking Heideggerian Marxism." Hemming's own *Heidegger and Marx: A Productive Dialogue over the Language of Humanism* belongs to this tradition, alongside the work of Axelos, Marcuse, Lucien Goldmann, Michel Henry, Fred Dallmayr, Heinz Dieter Kittsteiner, Andrew Feenberg, Giovanni C. Leone, Gerry Stahl, and Jean Vioulac.

4. Heidegger, *Sein und Wahrheit*, 147. Emphasis omitted.

5. Ibid., 152–56.

6. Ibid., 151. Translation modified.

7. This interpretation of Nietzsche is presented in the lecture course of 1936–37 and also appears in the *Contributions* (see Heidegger, *Beiträge zur Philosophie*, 362).

8. Heidegger, *Sein und Wahrheit*, 175–76.

9. Ibid., 177.

10. Ibid., 187.

11. Ibid. Translation modified.

12. Ibid., 194–95.

13. Ibid., 194. Translation modified.

14. Ibid., 186–87.

15. Ibid., 188–89.

16. Ibid., 220.
17. Ibid., 221.
18. Ibid.
19. Ibid. My translation.
20. Ibid., 222.
21. Ibid.
22. Heidegger returns to the *zugon* in the *Contributions*, making more explicit what is only intimated in the lecture "On the Essence of Truth" (*Beiträge zur Philosophie*, 332–33).
23. Heidegger, *Sein und Wahrheit*, 222.
24. Ibid., 210. Emmanuel Faye, in his controversial and flawed study of Heidegger's relation to National Socialism argues, tendentiously but not without a certain justification, that Heidegger's rejection of "liberal" biologism cannot be understood as a rejection of Nazi racism *per se* but only as a rejection of a "biological"—as opposed to "spiritual"—conception of race (*Heidegger*, 21).
25. Heidegger, *Sein und Wahrheit*, 223–24.
26. Even though the *Contributions* is more pointed in its criticism of the Nazi concept of *Volk*, and above all the elevation of the *Volk* to an end in itself, Heidegger nevertheless posits an intimate relation between *Volk* and *Geschichtlichkeit* (cf. Heidegger, *Beiträge zur Philosophie*, 398–99). We should also note that the word *völkisch*, which begins to play a role in his thought during the Nazi regime, is far more indicative than *Volk* of a specific affinity with Nazi ideas (see Faye, *Heidegger*, 89–92).
27. So, e.g., in the 1934 lecture "Logic as the Question of the Essence of Language" (*Gesamtausgabe*, 38: 30–77). For a subtle study of Heidegger's concept of *Volk*, see Phillips, *Heidegger's Volk*. Heidegger's philosophical investment in the concept of *Volk*, Phillips argues, is decisive for his involvement with National Socialism, and yet "Heidegger's disillusionment with National Socialism is not a disillusionment with the notion of the *Volk*" (3).
28. Heidegger, *Sein und Wahrheit*, 225.
29. Ibid.
30. Ibid.
31. Ibid.

7. THE TRUTH OF THE COMMODITY

1. The relation between fetishism and ideology remains a matter of considerable debate, as seen in the contrasting positions of Étienne Balibar and Jacques Rancière, who insists, against the former, that fetishism is not a theory of ideology (cf. Pietz, "Fetishism and Materialism," 128).
2. Christopher Pawling's "Rethinking Heideggerian Marxism," focusing on the

"re-ontologization of aesthetics" proposed in Heidegger's "Der Ursprung des Kunstwerkes," hints at the centrality of the question of truth to a "Heideggerian" rethinking of Marxism without working out the implications this would have for rethinking the commodity fetish, ideology, or indeed any of the foundational theoretical constructs of Marxism.

3. Marx, *Das Kapital: Erster Band*, 86. My translation.

4. Heidegger, in his later thought, distinguishes between *Sein* and *Seyn*, in order to indicate that being is no longer thought metaphysically.

5. It is perhaps only with respect to the question of truth that we can begin to comprehend the full implications of the distinction that Marx draws and Lukács stresses between the production of use values as use values and the production of exchange value as such. Commodities exist even in primitive economic conditions, being traded at the fringes of society, but production in this case does not yet involve the production of the commodity *as* commodity. What does it mean to produce the commodity *as* commodity? This, I would suggest, does not and cannot simply involve either the intentions of the producer, or the consequences of the act of production, or even the place of the producer within the entire system of production considered as a structural totality. The subjective, objective, and structural are merely aspects of something more fundamental: the mode of truth that is produced with the production of the commodity, and indeed *as* the production of a commodity.

6. See Heidegger, *Beiträge zur Philosophie*, 256.

8. VALUE, PUBLICITY, POLITICS

1. Henry, *Marx*, 204.

2. Marx, *Das Kapital: Erster Band*, 85–86. My translation.

3. Lukács, *History and Class Consciousness*, 90.

4. Kant, *Kritik der reinen Vernunft*, 15.

5. With a view to rethinking "Heideggerian Marxism," Christian Lotz, in his recent "Reification through Commodity Form or Technology?," stresses both the ontological radicality of Marx's account of the commodity, its irreducibly economic dimension, and the primacy of value. Yet I would argue that Lotz does not take seriously enough the challenge that Heidegger poses to Marx and tends, rather, to reimpose metaphysical categories (e.g., real, universal, abstract) that can no longer be sustained.

6. Regarding the centrality of the as-structure to the commodity form, see Keenan, "Reading Capital, Rhetorically," 159, though he conceives of it in terms of a de Manian concept of rhetoric rather than starting out, as I will, from Heidegger's *Being and Time*. His analysis nevertheless leads to a powerful reconception both of critique as an ongoing labor of decipherment rather than the sudden assumption of a "scientific" perspective of objectivity and of commodity form as a "catachrestic" institution not grounded in any reality (184). Amariglio and Callari ("Marxian Value Theory and

the Subject") likewise argue that the concepts of value and commodity fetishism, understood in terms of semiotics, allow us to recognize in Marxism a challenge to the "economic determinism" of classical economic thought (202).

7. See Heidegger, *Sein und Zeit*, 36.
8. Heidegger, *Sein und Zeit*, 68.
9. Ibid.
10. Ibid., 69.
11. Ibid.
12. Ibid., 73.
13. Ibid.
14. Keenan's "Reading Capital, Rhetorically" (160–61) calls attention to the complex relationality at work in the use value of the commodity, suggesting that there is a deeper intertwinement of use value and exchange value, and even a certain structural dependence of the latter on the former.
15. Henry, in his study of Marx, contrasts the concept of praxis that emerges in the "Theses on Feuerbach" with the theoretical understanding of being that, for Marx, is still found in Hegel and the Young Hegelians. In this way, Henry comes very close to conceiving of Marx's praxis in opposition to what Heidegger will come to understand as presence-at-hand. Yet Henry does not seem to fully recognize the aporia into which Marx, lacking the philosophical resources of Heidegger, is drawn in his attempt to explicate this entirely radical concept of praxis.
16. As Baudrillard puts it in his "For a Critique of the Political Economy of the Sign": "Use value is the expression of a whole metaphysic: that of utility. It registers itself as a kind of *moral law* at the heart of the object—and it is inscribed there as the finality of the 'need' of the subject" (*Selected Writings*, 67). Likewise Derrida, conceiving of the commodity fetish in terms of the spectrality of the commodity, calls attention in *Specters of Marx* (200–201) to the complex intertwining of use value and exchange value, challenging the notion that use value can be understood as the simple origin of exchange value. By identifying the commodity with spectrality, moreover, Derrida identifies it with that which is repressed in Marx's thinking. Ultimately there cannot be ghosts: the haunting specter of communism will bring an end to ghosts—but in just this way Marxism also forecloses on the very possibility of justice, of openness to the event, and indeed "the revolutionary movement itself." (See also Derrida and Stiegler, *Echographies*, 128.) Heidegger, for Derrida, will also not be ghostly enough. Pietz's "Fetishism and Materialism" offers a trenchant critique of the poststructuralist "semiological" readings of Marx proposed by Barthes, Baudrillard, Žižek, and Derrida, seeking to restore Marx's political materialism in a form untroubled by postmodern epistemological and ontological scruples.
17. Cf. Marx, *Grundrisse*, 79.
18. The linguistic contortions in "Chapter on Capital" in the *Grundrisse* suggest

the extent to which Marx struggled to clarify the nature of the distinction between use value and exchange value. Whereas use value appears as an abstraction, through the concept of value, away from the actual act of use—an act in which value itself as an abstraction plays no role—exchange value is not a mere theoretical abstraction from something that exists apart from this abstraction but is of the very essence of the relation of exchange as it comes to take place as an exchange of value (see Marx, *Grundrisse*, 381).

19. Agamben, in the *Kingdom and the Glory*, deploys all his considerable erudition and critical acumen to prove the opposite, folding economic theology into political theology.

20. The concept of *value* plays a central role in Heinz Dieter Kittsteiner's *Mit Marx für Heidegger—Mit Heidegger für Marx* (40). Kittsteiner suggests that Heidegger's concept of facticity, and his existential analytic more generally, is profoundly influenced by Marx's concept of alienation, which, contra Dilthey's hermeneutics, problematizes the universal "comprehensibility" of history, suggesting a mode of "objectification" in which man becomes incomprehensible to himself. For an extended discussion of value in Marx, see 56–68.

21. Heidegger, *Sein und Zeit*, 42. Translation modified.

22. Ibid., 42.

23. Ibid., 44.

24. Ibid. My translation.

25. Ibid., 44.

26. Ibid., 384–85.

27. Ibid., 385; double emphasis omitted.

28. Heidegger, *Beiträge zur Philosophie*, 55.

29. Cf. Heidegger, *Beiträge zur Philosophie*, 63.

30. Ibid., 43.

31. Well before Derrida engaged explicitly with Marx, initiating his so-called political turn, the connection between epistemology and economics stood at the center of his concerns. Precisely this is at stake in his interpretation of Rousseau in *Of Grammatology*, a reading that is already rigorously invested in the question of the political. For Rousseau, as Derrida observes, phonetic writing is the creation of "commercial peoples who, in traveling to various countries, had to speak various languages, which would have impelled them to invent characters that could be common to all of them" (299). Derrida glosses: "This movement of analytic abstraction in the circulation of arbitrary signs is quite parallel to that within which money is constituted. Money replaces things by their signs, not only within a society but from one culture to another, or from one economic organization to another. That is why the alphabet is commercial, a trader. It must be understood within the monetary moment of economic rationality" (300).

32. Heidegger, *Sein und Zeit*, 98–99.

33. Ibid., 99.

34. In a section of the *Contributions* titled "Die *idea*, der Platonismus und der Idealismus," which presents in schematic form the stages in the development of Platonism broadly conceived, Heidegger sketches out how the concept of value is constituted in the Platonic *idea* (Heidegger, *Beiträge zur Philosophie*, 210).

35. Heidegger, *Bremer und Freiburger Vorträge*, 13–21.

36. Ibid., 20.

37. Ibid., 40. My translation.

38. Ibid., 43.

39. Ibid., 47. My translation.

40. Ibid.

41. Ibid., 52.

42. Ibid., 44.

43. Ibid., 45.

44. Ibid., 53.

45. Ibid., 66.

46. In the *Contributions*, *Ent-setzung* is one of the eight moments that constitutes the framework (*Gefüge*) of the event (*Ereignis*) (*Beiträge zur Philosophie*, 470–71). It would not be difficult to discover in this formulation an echo of the problem of "valuation," though considered now from the side of the event rather than *Seiendheit* and *ousia*. The *Ent-setzung*, one might say, withdraws beings from their lostness in beingness (the *Sein des Seienden*, as opposed to *Seyn*) and draws them back into a relation to be-ing by de-posing the positing of value. Or indeed: it is the originary deposition that is at work in all positing, all idealization and valuation. It would be worth asking if we might not find, in Kleist's dramas, an intimation of this *Ent-setzung*. Perhaps, in precisely this sense, these are already no longer tragic but televisionary (483).

9. REPRODUCTION

1. In his study *Althusser and His Contemporaries: Philosophy's Perpetual War*, Walter Montag, carefully excavating the complex lineaments of the conjunction from which Althusser's treatment of ideology takes its departure, demonstrates that the theoretical significance of Althusser's reflections on the ISA essay can only be fully appreciated in light of the polemical dimension that characterizes his writings, and indeed his very conception of what philosophy itself is. Such a mode of reading, of course, will not always come out in Althusser's favor: Rancière's bitterly polemical *Althusser's Lesson*, which itself must be read (as Rancière himself notes in the foreword to the English edition) in terms of the special circumstances of the moment in which it was written, focuses even more one-sidedly on the situational and polemical character of Althusser's 1973 "Reply to John Lewis" but ends up depicting Althusser as

an armchair Marxist and party ideologue, applying his considerable intelligence with Machiavellian ingenuity to the double task of upholding the dogmas of the French Communist Party's Marxism-Leninism and cautiously carving out a niche in which the academic Marxist philosopher can enjoy a certain autonomy.

2. Cf. Montag, *Althusser and His Contemporaries*, 103–4. For an account of the history of the feverish composition of *On the Reproduction of Capital* in the wake of the student demonstrations and strikes of 1968, and of its publication in fragmentary form, see Etienne Balibar's foreword to Althusser, *On Reproduction*, vii–xviii.

3. Montag, *Althusser and His Contemporaries*, 142.

4. Ibid., 142–43.

5. Althusser, *On Reproduction*, xiii.

6. See Montag, *Althusser and His Contemporaries*, 143.

7. Hirst, in "Althusser's Theory of Ideology" (410), stresses the importance of Althusser's critique of representation.

8. Althusser, "Ideology and Ideological State Apparatuses," 85.

9. Ibid.

10. Ibid., 86.

11. Ibid.

12. Althusser, in *Reading Capital* (84), draws a rather idiosyncratic distinction between historical materialism and dialectical materialism. The former is the science of history, whereas the latter is the theory of scientific praxis.

13. Althusser, *For Marx*, 110.

14. See Althusser, *On the Reproduction of Capital*, 20–21: "When we consider a mode of production in the unity productive forces/relations of production that constitutes it, it appears that this unity has a material basis: the productive forces. But these productive forces are nothing at all if they are not rendered operational, and they can only operate *in and under the aegis of* their relations of production. This leads to the conclusion that, on the basis of the existing productive forces and *within the limits they set, the relations of production play the determinant role.*" The "primacy" of the relations of production over the productive forces is also the subject of the polemical text appended to *On the Reproduction of Capital* (209–17).

15. Althusser, "Ideology and Ideological State Apparatuses," 86–87. Translation slightly modified.

16. Ibid., 87–88. Translation slightly modified.

17. Ibid., 88.

18. Ibid., 89. Translation slightly modified.

19. Ibid.

20. Ibid.

21. Ibid.

22. The discussion of the reproduction of the relations of production in the ISA

essay presents a kind of condensation of the broader argument of *On the Reproduction of Capital*.

23. Althusser, "Ideology and Ideological State Apparatuses," 105.
24. Ibid., 92–93.
25. Ibid., 94.
26. Cf. Althusser, *On the Reproduction of Capital*, 71–73.
27. Althusser, "Ideology and Ideological State Apparatuses," 107–8. See also Althusser, *On the Reproduction of Capital*, 171–74, which develops this point at somewhat greater length.
28. Althusser and Balibar, *Reading Capital*, 17.
29. See Goshgarian's introduction to Althusser, *Philosophy of the Encounter*, xiv.
30. Althusser, "Ideology and Ideological State Apparatuses," 109.
31. Ibid., 112.
32. Hirst provides an excellent account of the "imaginary" nature of ideology: "Ideology is not 'consciousness,' it is a representation of the 'imaginary.' This 'imaginary' relation is not the experience or consciousness of an already constituted subject—it is in the imaginary that the subject is formed as a subject. The subject becomes what it is through the imaginary relation—it cannot be the pure subject of the empiricist notion of experience because it is *formed* through a definite structure of recognition" ("Althusser's Theory of Ideology," 386–87). By grafting the concepts of dislocation and reduction onto Althusser's ISA essay, however, I hope to move away from the more Lacanian and structuralist concept of the subject as pure construction and think of it instead as the production of a perspective in which beings show up in a certain way and in which praxis is possible.
33. Althusser, "Ideology and Ideological State Apparatuses," 114.
34. Ibid.
35. It is perhaps in this sense that Michel Henry will argue that Althusser never manages to escape from the Feuerbachian ontology of sensuous immediacy, maintaining that the true lesson of the "Theses on Feuerbach" has been lost on him (*Marx*, 141). Though I do not think that this claim takes account of the subtlety of Althusser's concept of materialism, there is at least a grain of truth in it.
36. Althusser, "Ideology and Ideological State Apparatuses," 112–13.
37. Heidegger, *Beiträge zur Philosophie*, 193.
38. Ibid., 189–90.
39. Ibid., 191. Translation modified.
40. Most suggestive, in this regard, is the following fragment of Heraclitus, listed as number 90 in Diels-Kranz: *puros antamoibē to panta kai pur apantōn hokōsper chrusou chrēmata kai chrēmatōn chrusos*. Kahn translates: "All things are requital for fire, and fire for all things, as goods for gold and gold for goods." Precisely for Heraclitus, the pre-Socratic philosopher with the most profound and radical concep-

tion of *phusis*, nature's ongoing change and internal contradiction is understood in terms of the exchange of commodities for gold as a universal signifier of value (Kahn, *Heraclitus*, 46–47). W. K. C. Guthrie, translating *antamoibē* as "exchange," notes, "In mercantile transactions the essential thing is parity of value: a certain quantity of gold will buy a certain quantity of goods" (*A History of Greek Philosophy*, 461). For Guthrie, moreover, this passage is crucial to establishing that for Heraclitus fire comes to be understood not merely as "the basic substance which changed its shape or appearance in becoming earth or water," but as soul: a life principle fundamentally different in kind from other elements. A concept of "value," without being named as such, is already at work in the first Heraclitean intimations of the foundational dualisms of Greek metaphysics.

41. Althusser, "Ideology and Ideological State Apparatuses," 115.

42. Ibid., 123.

43. In moving from the ISA essay back to *Reading Capital*, I follow Ellen Rooney ("Better Read than Dead"), who argues that the dominant reception of Althusser has fetishized the concept of ideology while ignoring his account of the praxis of reading—an insight that has certainly been taken up by more recent work on Althusser, such as Montag's *Althusser and his Contemporaries*. Rooney suggests, moreover, that Althusser's account of symptomatic reading, together with the notion of the fetish, informs his account of ideology, allowing him to go beyond the interpretation of ideology as false consciousness.

44. Althusser and Balibar, *Reading Capital*, 25.

45. Ibid.

46. Althusser, *On the Reproduction of Capital*, 51.

47. Althusser and Balibar, *Reading Capital*, 57. Translation modified.

48. Precisely this tendency, I would suggest, comes to the fore in *On the Reproduction of Capital*. By publishing the ISA essay while repressing the longer text from which it was drawn, Althusser emphasizes the shocking and paradoxical novelty of his treatment of ideology. In *On the Reproduction of Capital*, however, ideology is drawn back into a highly systematic and coherent account of Marxist theory, which indeed, in defending the need for an overarching revolutionary strategy integrating class struggle on three separate fronts, develops an excessively monolithic conception of state power, the state apparatus (which combines the single repressive state apparatus and the several ideological state apparatuses), and state ideology. Even though Althusser presents this concept of the unity of the system as the accomplishment of a theory that is no longer descriptive, one cannot help but feel that a truly nondescriptive account would force us to come to terms with much more complicated networks of power. It is as if the figure of the circle, abstracted from the process of reproduction, was carried over to the structure of the system as a whole.

10. THE GADGET

1. Althusser, "Ideology and Ideological State Apparatuses," 124.
2. Heidegger, *Vorträge und Aufsätze*, 15.
3. Ibid.
4. Ibid., 18.
5. Ibid., 23.
6. Althusser, "Ideology and Ideological State Apparatuses," 105–6.
7. Taking up the project of Heidegger's later thinking, Agamben develops a critique of the "productivism" of Western metaphysics. The essence of this critique, which finds its most thorough exposition in *Opus Dei*, can already be found in the early text *The Man without Content*. Yet it is worth asking whether even the most radical critique of production does not itself serve to secure the phenomenological conditions of production. One notices the extraordinary ambivalence that the concept of inoperativity assumes in Agamben, and especially in *The Kingdom and the Glory*, where it appears in every sense as both danger and salvation. While Agamben is certainly aware of this ambivalence, which has everything to do with the critical ambiguity of the present historical moment, we may still ask if this very inoperativity does not constitute the imperative of production under the emergent regime of capitalism.
8. See Marazzi, *Capital and Affects*; and Virno, *A Grammar of the Multitude*.
9. Cf. Morton, *Hyperobjects*, 7.
10. Of crucial significance, nevertheless, is the relation of the gadget to the machine. Alf Hornborg ("Symbolic Technologies") has suggested rethinking the commodity fetish, and the equivalence relation of labor time, in terms of the machine, which presents a fetishizing reification of "global flows of goods and services," and above all the distribution of energy, by presenting itself "to our consciousness as a local achievement, rather than as a product of the confluence of global flows" (485–86). The machine in this way emerges as an "institution for redistributing time and space" (489). This analysis of the machine, I would nevertheless argue, must be connected back to the gadget. The gadget is in the end nothing else than a home machine, even a pocket machine: the machine-fetish becomes the movable, graspable, hand-holdable site of the pleasure that plays itself out as the experience of flow, availability, standing reserve.
11. Stiegler, *Re-Enchantment of the World*, 24–25. Emphasis omitted.
12. See Szendy, *Hits*, 9: "What we might call the musical self or the lyrical 'I' of song would then be the voice of the commodity itself, in the midst of speaking about itself."
13. Ken Alder, in "America's Two Gadgets," places the atom bomb (Oppenheimer's "Gadget") and the polygraph side by side as the quintessential gadgets of mid-twentieth-century America.

14. Highly relevant, in this regard, is A. Kiarina Kordela's "Biopolitics: From Tribes to Commodity Fetishism," which attempts to conceive of the biopolitical dimension of capitalism in terms of the "transubstantiation" of life (*bios*) into "sheer potentiality." Even though Kordela does not seem to follow Agamben in rigorously distinguishing between *bios* and *zōē*, it is perhaps in an engagement with Agamben that the full implications of this claim could emerge, namely, by approaching, from the perspective of the commodity fetish and the labor theory of value, the tension between pure potentiality and operativity. The commodity fetish of capitalist biopolitics is nothing else than the displacement of "pure potentiality" onto the *thing* as work, the operativity of the thing. The gadget is the putting-to-work of pure potentiality. In this we might find the hidden thread that ties the iPhone to the atom bomb.

15. Deploying the concept of the theoretical console, Nanna Verhoeff, in a rich analysis of the Nintendo DS, a relatively early manifestation of the pluripotency exemplified by the iPhone, hints at how the gadget becomes the locus for a praxis and theory no longer done *by* us but only *through* us. The gadget for her is the site of "gadgetivity," an elusive but suggestive term that points to a dehumanizing of activity. Less a medium than the "carrier of mediality," the gadget allows an exploration of its possibilities: its function becomes, as it were, the putting on display—toying and playing with—the possibilities of the thing ("Theoretical Consoles," 296).

16. Tiqqun, *Theory of the Young-Girl*, 82.

17. Ibid., 75.

18. Düzenli, "Value, Commodity Fetishism, and Capital's Critique."

19. Kordela, "Biopolitics: From Tribes to Commodity Fetishism," 25.

20. Marx, *Das Kapital: Erster Band*, 93.

21. Michel Henry suggests that, with the positing in the "Theses on Feuerbach" of a radically nontheoretical praxis, the question of truth, rather than being abolished, undergoes a decisive transformation (*Marx*, 157).

11. TO THE THINGS THEMSELVES

1. Benjamin, *Gesammelte Schriften*, 1.1: 208. My translation.

BIBLIOGRAPHY

Adler, Anthony Curtis. "Interpretive Essay: Fichte's Monetary History." Introduction to *The Closed Commercial State*, by J. G. Fichte, 1–72. Translated and edited by Anthony Curtis Adler. Albany: State University of New York Press, 2012.

Agamben, Giorgio. *The Coming Community*. Translated by Michael Hardt. Minneapolis: University of Minnesota Press, 1993.

———. *The Highest Poverty: Monastic Rules and Form-of-Life*. Translated by Adam Kotsko. Stanford, CA: Stanford University Press, 2013.

———. *The Kingdom and the Glory: For a Theological Genealogy of Economy and Government (Homo Sacer, II, 2)*. Translated by Lorenzo Chiesa. Stanford, CA: Stanford University Press, 2011.

———. *Opus Dei: An Archaeology of Duty (Homo Sacer, II, 5)*. Translated by Adam Kotsko. Stanford, CA: Stanford University Press, 2013.

Alder, Ken. "America's Two Gadgets: Of Bombs and Polygraphs." *Isis* 98 (2007): 124–37.

Althusser, Louis. "Idéologie et appareils idéologiques d'État (Notes pour une recherche)." *Positions (1964–1975)*. Paris: Les Éditions sociales, 1976. 67–125.

———. "Ideology and Ideological State Apparatuses." In *Lenin and Philosophy, and Other Essays*. New ed. New York: Monthly Review Press, 2001. 85–126.

———. *For Marx*. Translated by Ben Brewster. 3rd ed. London: Verso, 2005.

———. *On the Reproduction of Capital: Ideology and Ideological State Apparatuses*. Translated by G. M. Goshgarian. London: Verso, 2014.

———. *Philosophy of the Encounter: Later Writings, 1978–1987*. Translated by G. M. Goshgarian. London: Verso, 2006.

Althusser, Louis, and Étienne Balibar. *Lire le Capital*. Paris: François Maspero, 1973.

———. *Reading Capital*. Translated by Ben Brewster. London: Verso, 2009.

Amariglio, Jack, and Antonio Callari. "Marxian Value Theory and the Problem of the Subject: The Role of Commodity Fetishism." In *Fetishism as Cultural Discourse*, edited by Emily Apter and William Pietz. Ithaca, NY: Cornell University Press, 1993. 186–216.

Angus, Ian. "Walking on Two Legs: On the Very Possibility of a Heideggerian Marxism

(Review Essay of Andrew Feenberg's *Heidegger and Marcuse: The Catastrophe and Redemption of History*)." *Human Studies* 28 (2005): 335–52.

Barthes, Roland. *Mythologies*. Translated by Annette Lavers. New York: Hill and Wang, 1972.

Baudrillard, Jean. "For a Critique of the Political Economy of the Sign." In *Selected Writings*, edited by Mark Poster. 2nd ed. Stanford, CA: Stanford University Press, 2002. 60–100.

———. *Simulacra and Simulation*. Translated by Sheila Faria Glaser. Ann Arbor: University of Michigan Press, 1994.

———. *The System of Objects*. Translated by James Benedict. London: Verso, 1996.

Benjamin, Walter. *Gesammelte Schriften*. Edited by Rolf Tiedemann and Hermann Schweppenhäuser. 7 vols. Frankfurt am Main: Suhrkamp Verlag, 1991.

Bevan, Alex. "Nostalgia for Pre-Digital Media in Mad Men." *Television & New Media* 14.6 (2013): 546–59.

Boorstin, Daniel J. *The Image: A Guide to Pseudo-Events in America*. New York: Vintage, 1992.

Braudy, Leo. *The Frenzy of Renown: Fame and Its History; with a New Afterword*. New York: Vintage, 1997.

Crary, Jonathan. *24/7: Late Capitalism and the Ends of Sleep*. London: Verso, 2013.

Debord, Guy. *The Society of the Spectacle*. Translated by Donald Nicholson-Smith. New York: Zone Books, 1995.

Denker, Alfred, and Holger Zaborowski, eds. *Heidegger und der Nationalsozialismus I: Dokumente*. Heidegger-Jahrbuch. Vol. 4. Munich: Verlag Karl Alber Freiburg, 2009.

Derrida, Jacques. *Of Grammatology*. Translated by Gayatri Chakravorty Spivak. Corrected ed. Baltimore: Johns Hopkins University Press, 1997.

———. *Of Spirit: Heidegger and the Question*. Translated by Geoffrey Bennington and Rachel Bowlby. Chicago: University of Chicago Press, 1989.

———. *Specters of Marx: The State of the Debt, the Work of Mourning and the New International*. Translated by Peggy Kamuf. London: Routledge, 1994.

———. *Speech and Phenomena, and Other Essays on Husserl's Theory of Signs*. Translated by David B. Allison. Evanston, IL: Northwestern University Press, 1973.

Derrida, Jacques, and Bernard Stiegler. *Echographies of Television: Filmed Interviews*. Translated by Jennifer Bajorek. Cambridge: Polity Press, 2002.

Düzenli, Faruk Eray. "Introduction: Value, Commodity Fetishism, and Capital's Critique." Rethinking Marxism: A Journal of Economics, Culture & Society 23.2 (2011): 172–79.

Dyer, Richard. *Heavenly Bodies: Film Stars and Society*. 2nd ed. London: Routledge, 2004.

Eagleton, Terry. "Ideology and Its Vicissitudes in Western Marxism." In *Mapping Ideology*, edited by Slavoj Žižek. London: Verso, 1994. 179–226.

Farías, Victor. *Heidegger et la nazisme.* Paris: Verdier, 1987.

Faye, Emmanuel. *Heidegger: The Introduction of Nazism into Philosophy in Light of the Unpublished Seminars of 1933–1935.* Translated by Michael B. Smith. New Haven, CT: Yale University Press, 2009.

Foucault, Michel. *Discipline and Punish: The Birth of the Prison.* Translated by Alan Sheridan. 2nd ed. New York: Vintage, 1995.

Fried, Gregory. *Heidegger's Polemos: From Being to Politics.* New Haven, CT: Yale University Press, 2000.

Greif, Mark. "You'll Love the Way It Makes You Feel." *London Review of Books,* October 23, 2008, 15–16.

Grossberg, Lawrence. "MTV: Swinging on the (Postmodern) Star." In *Cultural Politics in Contemporary America,* edited by Ian H. Angus and Sut Jhally. London: Routledge, 1989. 254–68.

Guthrie, W. K. C. *A History of Greek Philosophy.* Vol. 1. Cambridge: Cambridge University Press, 1962.

Hamilton, Caroline. "Seeing the World Second Hand: *Mad Men* and the Vintage Consumer." *Cultural Studies Review* 18.2 (2012): 223–41.

Heidegger, Martin. *Being and Time.* Translated by John Macquarrie and Edward Robinson. San Francisco: HarperCollins, 1962.

———. *Being and Truth.* Translated by Gregory Fried and Richard Polt. Bloomington: Indiana University Press, 2010.

———. *Beiträge zur Philosophie (Vom Ereignis).* Edited by Friedrich-Wilhelm von Herrmann. Vol. 65 of *Gesamtausgabe.* Frankfurt am Main: Vittorio Klostermann, 1989.

———. *Bremen and Freiburg Lectures: Insight into That Which Is and Basic Principles of Thinking.* Translated by Andrew J. Mitchell. Bloomington: Indiana University Press, 2012.

———. *Bremer und Freiburger Vorträge.* Edited by Petra Jaeger. Vol. 79 of *Gesamtausgabe.* 2nd ed. Frankfurt am Main: Vittorio Klostermann, 2005.

———. *Contributions to Philosophy (From Enowning).* Translated by Parvis Emad and Kenneth Maly. Bloomington: Indiana University Press, 1999.

———. *Contributions to Philosophy (Of the Event).* Translated by Richard Rojcewicz and Daniela Vallega-Neu. Bloomington: Indiana University Press, 2012.

———. *Gesamtausgabe.* Frankfurt am Main: Vittorio Klostermann, 1975– .

———. "The Question Concerning Technology." In *Basic Writings: From "Being and Time" (1927) to "The Task of Thinking" (1964),* edited by David Farrell Krell. London: Routledge, 2011. 213–38.

———. *Sein und Wahrheit.* Edited by Hartmut Tietjen. Vol. 36/37 of *Gesamtausgabe.* Frankfurt am Main: Vittorio Klostermann, 2001.

———. *Sein und Zeit.* 15th ed. Tübingen: Max Niemeyer Verlag, 1984.

———. *Vorträge und Aufsätze*. 6th ed. Pfullingen: Verlag Günther Neske, 1990.

Hemming, Laurence Paul. *Heidegger and Marx: A Productive Dialogue over the Language of Humanism*. Evanston, IL: Northwestern University Press, 2013.

Henry, Michel. *Marx: A Philosophy of Human Reality*. Translated by Kathleen McLaughlin. Bloomington: Indiana University Press, 1983.

Hirst, Paul Q. "Althusser's Theory of Ideology." *Economy and Society* 5.4 (1976): 385–412.

Hölderlin, Friedrich. *Empedokles, erster Entwurf*. In vol. 7 of *Sämtliche Werke, Briefe und Dokumente in zeitlicher Folge*. Edited by D. E. Sattler. 12 vols. Munich: Luchterhand, 2004.

Hornborg, Alf. "Symbolic Technologies: Machines and the Marxian Notion of Fetishism." *Anthropological Theory* 1.4 (2001): 473–96.

Inglis, Fred. *A Short History of Celebrity*. Princeton, NJ: Princeton University Press, 2010.

Kahn, Charles H. *The Art and Thought of Heraclitus: An Edition of the Fragments with Translation and Commentary*. Cambridge: Cambridge University Press, 1979.

Kant, Immanuel. *Kritik der reinen Vernunft: Nach der ersten und zweiten Original-Ausgabe*. Edited by Raymund Schmidt. Hamburg: Felix Meiner Verlag, 1990.

Keenan, Thomas. "The Point Is to (Ex)Change It: Reading *Capital*, Rhetorically." In *Fetishism as Cultural Discourse*, edited by Emily Apter and William Pietz. Ithaca, NY: Cornell University Press, 1993. 152–85.

Kisiel, Theodor. "Heidegger's Apology: Biography as Philosophy and Ideology." In *The Heidegger Case: On Philosophy and Politics*, edited by Tom Rockmore and Joseph Margolis. Philadelphia, PA: Temple University Press, 1992. 11–51.

Kittsteiner, Hans Dieter. *Mit Marx für Heidegger—Mit Heidegger für Marx*. Munich: Wilhelm Fink Verlag, 2004.

Kordela, A. Kiarina. "Biopolitics: From Tribes to Commodity Fetishism." *Differences: A Journal of Feminist Cultural Studies* 24.1 (2013): 1–29.

Kottak, Conrad Phillip. *Prime-Time Society: An Anthropological Analysis of Television and Culture*. Belmont, CA: Wadsworth, 1990.

Lacoue-Labarthe, Philippe. *Heidegger, Art, and Politics: The Fiction of the Political*. Translated by Chris Turner. Oxford: Blackwell, 1990.

Latour, Bruno. *We Have Never Been Modern*. Translated by Catherine Porter. Cambridge, MA: Harvard University Press, 1993.

Lotz, Christian. "Reification through Commodity Form or Technology? From Honneth back to Heidegger and Marx." *Rethinking Marxism: A Journal of Economics, Culture & Society* 25.2 (2013): 184–200.

Lukács, Georg. *History and Class Consciousness: Studies in Marxist Dialectics*. Translated by Rodney Livingstone. Cambridge, MA: MIT Press, 1971.

Marazzi, Christian. *Capital and Affects: The Politics of the Language Economy*. Translated by Giuseppina Mecchia. Los Angeles: Semiotext(e), 2011.

Marx, Karl. *Das Kapital: Erster Band*. Vol. 23. Karl Marx and Friedrich Engels, *Werke*.

Edited by Institut für Marxismus-Leninismus beim ZK der Sed. 43 vols. Berlin: Dietz Verlag, 1962.

———. *Ökonomische Manuskripte 1857/58*. Vol. 42. Karl Marx and Friedrich Engels, *Werke*. Edited by Institut für Marxismus-Leninismus beim ZK der Sed. 43 vols. Berlin: Dietz Verlag, 1962.

McCarthy, Anna. *Ambient Television*. Durham, NC: Duke University Press, 2001.

McLuhan, Marshall. *Understanding Media: The Extensions of Man*. Cambridge, MA: MIT Press, 1994.

Mendelsohn, Daniel. "The Mad Men Account." *New York Review of Books*, February 24, 2011.

Montag, Walter. *Althusser and His Contemporaries: Philosophy's Perpetual War*. Durham, NC: Duke University Press, 2013.

Morton, Timothy. *Hyperobjects: Philosophy and Ecology after the End of the World*. Minneapolis: University of Minnesota Press, 2013.

Morrow, Melinda. "'But Beavis, Everything Does Suck': Watching Beavis and Butthead Watch Videos." *Popular Music & Society* 23.3 (1999): 31–40.

Ott, Hugo. *Martin Heidegger: Unterwegs zu seiner Biographie*. Frankfurt am Main: Campus, 1988.

Paglia, Camille. *Sexual Personae: Art and Decadence from Nefertiti to Emily Dickinson*. New Haven, CT: Yale University Press, 1990.

Pawling, Christopher. "Rethinking Heideggerian Marxism." *Rethinking Marxism: A Journal of Economics, Culture & Society* 22.4 (2010): 590–604.

Phillips, James. *Heidegger's Volk: Between National Socialism and Poetry*. Stanford, CA: Stanford University Press, 2005.

Pietz, William. "Fetishism and Materialism: The Limits of Theory in Marx." In *Fetishism as Cultural Discourse*, edited by Emily Apter and William Pietz. Ithaca, NY: Cornell University Press, 1993. 119–51.

Polt, Richard. *The Emergency of Being: On Heidegger's Contributions to Philosophy*. Ithaca, NY: Cornell University Press, 2006.

Poster, Mark. *The Informational Subject*. Commentary by Stanley Aronowitz. Amsterdam: G&B Arts International, 2001.

Rancière, Jacques. *Althusser's Lesson*. Translated by Emiliano Battista. London: Continuum, 2011.

Rickey, Christopher. *Revolutionary Saints: Heidegger, National Socialism, and Antinomian Politics*. University Park: Pennsylvania State University Press, 2002.

Rockmore, Tom, and Joseph Margolis, eds. *The Heidegger Case: On Philosophy and Politics*. Philadelphia, PA: Temple University Press, 1992.

Rojek, Chris. *Celebrity*. London: Reaktion Books, 2001.

Ronell, Avital. *Crack Wars: Literature, Addiction, Mania*. New ed. Urbana: University of Illinois Press, 2004.

Rooney, Ellen. "Better Read than Dead: Althusser and the Fetish of Ideology." *Yale French Studies* 88 (1995): 183–200.

Rousseau, Jean-Jacques. *The Confessions and Correspondence, including the Letters to Malesherbes*. Translated by Christopher Kelly. Vol. 5 of *The Collected Writings of Rousseau*, edited by Christopher Kelly, Roger D. Masters, and Peter G. Stillman. Hanover, NH: University Press of New England, 1995.

———. *Rousseau Judge of Jean-Jacques: Dialogues*. Translated by Judith R. Bush, Christopher Kelly, and Roger D. Masters. Vol. 1 of *The Collected Writings of Rousseau*, edited by Roger D. Masters and Christopher Kelly. Hanover, NH: University Press of New England, 1995.

Schelling, Friedrich. *Von der Weltseele, eine Hypothese der höheren Physik zur Erklärung des allgemeinen Organismus (1798)*. Edited by Kai Torsten Kanz and Walter Schieche. Ser. 1/vol. 6 of *Historisch-kritische Ausgabe*. Stuttgart: Frommann-Holzboog, 2000.

Schickel, Richard. *Intimate Strangers: The Culture of Celebrity in America; with a New Afterword by the Author*. Chicago: Ivan R. Dee, 2000.

Sebbah, François-David. *Testing the Limit: Derrida, Henry, Levinas, and the Phenomenological Tradition*. Translated by Stephen Barker. Stanford, CA: Stanford University Press, 2012.

Stiegler, Bernard. *For a New Critique of Political Economy*. Translated by Daniel Ross. Cambridge: Polity Press, 2010.

———. *The Re-Enchantment of the World: The Value of Spirit against Industrial Populism*. Translated by Trevor Arthur. London: Bloomsbury, 2014.

Szendy, Peter. *Hits: Philosophy in the Jukebox*. Translated by Will Bishop. New York: Fordham University Press, 2012.

Thompson, Robert J. *Television's Second Golden Age: From "Hill Street Blues" to "ER."* New York: Continuum, 1996.

Tiqqun. *Preliminary Materials for a Theory of the Young-Girl*. Los Angeles: Semiotext(e), 2012.

Tudor, Deborah. "Selling Nostalgia: *Mad Men*, Postmodernism and Neoliberalism." *Society* 49.4 (2012): 333–38.

Uricchio, William. "Rituals of Reception, Patterns of Neglect: Nazi Television and Its Historical Representation." *Wide Angle* 11.1 (1989): 48–66.

Vallega-Neu, Daniela. *Heidegger's Contributions to Philosophy: An Introduction*. Bloomington: Indiana University Press, 2002.

Verhoeff, Nanna. "Theoretical Consoles: Concepts for Gadget Analysis." *Journal of Visual Culture* 8 (2009): 279–98.

Virno, Paolo. *A Grammar of the Multitude: For an Analysis of Contemporary Forms of Life*. Translated by Isabella Bertoletti, James Cascaito, and Andrea Casson. Los Angeles: Semiotext(e), 2004.

Wallace, David Foster. "E Unibus Pluram: Television and U.S. Fiction." *Review of Contemporary Fiction* 13.2 (1993): 151–94.

Winston, Brian. "The Development of Television." In *The Television History Book*, edited by Michele Hilmes. London: Palgrave Macmillan, 2003. 9–12.

Zimmerman, Michael E. "Ontological Aestheticism: Heidegger, Jünger, and National Socialism." In *The Heidegger Case: On Philosophy and Politics*, edited by Tom Rockmore and Joseph Margolis. Philadelphia, PA: Temple University Press, 1992. 52–89.

VIDEOGRAPHY

I. TELEVISION SERIES

24. 2001–10. NBC.
ALF. 1986–90. NBC.
America's Next Top Model. 2003– . UPN, CW.
American Idol. 2002– . Fox.
An American Family. 1973. PBS.
Batman. 1966–68. ABC.
Battlestar Galactica (Miniseries and TV series). 2003–9. Sci-fi.
Beavis and Butt-head. 1993–2011. MTV.
Breaking Bad. 2008–13. AMC.
Buffy the Vampire Slayer. 1997–2003. WB, UPN.
Bunheads. 2012–13. ABC.
CSI: Crime Scene Investigation. 2000– . CBS.
Desperate Housewives. 2004–12. ABC.
Dexter. 2006–13. Showtime.
Diff'rent Strokes. 1978–86. NBC.
Frasier. 1993–2004. NBC.
Gilmore Girls. 2000–2007. WB, CW.
Glee. 2009–15. Fox.
House. 2004–12. Fox.
How I Met Your Mother. 2005–14. CBS.
Mad Men. 2007–15. AMC.
Magnum, P.I. 1980–88. CBS.
Montey Python's Flying Circus. 1969–74. BBC.
Mr. Belvedere. 1985–90. ABC.
Newhart. 1982–90. CBS.
Nip/Tuck. 2003–10. FX.
One Day at a Time. 1975–84. CBS.
Project Runway. 2004– . Bravo, Lifetime.
Seinfeld. 1989–98. NBC.

Smallville. 2001–11. WB, CW.
Star Trek: The Next Generation. 1987–94. First-run syndication.
The Bachelor. 2002– . ABC.
The Following. 2013– . Fox.
The Muppet Show. 1976–81. ITV.
The Office. 2005–13. NBC.
The Oprah Winfrey Show. 1986–2011. ABC.
The Wire. 2002–8. HBO.
Twin Peaks. 1990–91. ABC.
Two and a Half Men. 2003–15. CBS.

II. MOVIES

A.I. Artificial Intelligence. 2001. Warner Bros. Pictures.
Boogie Nights. 1997. New Line Cinema.
Chinatown. 1974. Paramount Pictures.
Eyes Wide Shut. 1999. Warner Bros.
Liberal Arts. 2012. ICF Films.
Rosemary's Baby. 1968. Paramount.
Star Wars. 1977. 20th Century Fox.
The Muppet Movie. 1979. Associated Film Distribution.
The Muppets. 2011. Walt Disney Studios Motion Pictures.
Pandora's Box. 1929. Süd-Film.
The Ring. 2002. DreamWorks Pictures.
WarGames. 1983. MGM/UA Entertainment Group.

III. SONGS/MUSIC VIDEOS

"Barbie Girl." Aqua. 1997. Universal Music Denmark/MCA.
"California Girls." The Beach Boys. 1965. Capitol Records.
"California Gurls." Katy Perry. 2010. Capitol Records.
"Candy Candy." Kyary Pamyu Pamyu. 2012. Unborde/Warner Music Group.
"Material Girl." Madonna. 1984. Warner Bros. Records.
"No No No." APink. 2013. A Cube Entertainment.
"Rap God." Eminem. 2013. Interscope Records.

INDEX

advertising, 4, 19, 31–35, 37–38, 126–31, 166–70, 218n19
afterlife, 8, 27–30, 89, 171–74, 192, 201, 204, 214
Agamben, Giorgio, 22, 24, 55, 89, 92, 120, 174–75, 187, 217n11, 231n7
aletheia: advertising and, 19; celebrity and, 145–51, 168; the commodity and, 71–75, 84–85; definitions of, 67; the event and, 48; the gadget and, 121–31; ideology and, 64–70; play and, 9, 15–16, 118–20, 128–30, 132–34; politics and, 65–70; production and, 6, 121–31; unconcealment and, 7
Althusser, Louis: Heidegger and, 115–18, 120; on ideology, 6, 72–73, 100–102, 106–23, 227n1, 228n14, 230n48; Marx's theories and, 61–62, 82, 102–6, 108
American Idol, 168, 209
America's Next Top Model, 168, 170
Arendt, Hannah, 89, 175, 187
Aristotle, 41, 66–67, 82, 111–12
authenticity: the gadget and, 127–31; Heidegger's thought and, 21–22, 40–50, 92; televisionary life and, 4–5, 21, 27–28, 30–33, 40–50, 55–58, 189; temporality and, 92–93

Barthes, Roland, 23–24, 156, 168
base, the, 100–106, 124, 146–49
Batman, 142, 182
Baudelaire, Charles, 174, 188–89, 225n16
Baudrillard, Jean, 22, 24, 32–33, 218n20
Beavis and Butt-head, 21–23, 28–29, 41–42, 44
becoming, 7, 9, 31, 77, 112, 129, 152, 168–70, 180–81, 207–10
being: being(s) and, 51–58; Dasein's concernfulness and, 15–16, 45, 86; definitions of, 99; as ex-istence, 15; history of, 64–65; language and, 138; play and, 74; production and, 72–75; tool-being and, 85–86, 89–93, 177–78; value and, 95–99
Being and Time (Heidegger), 2–5, 13–15, 17, 51, 68, 80, 85, 95, 116, 224n6
being(s), 51–63, 100–101, 125, 130–31
Benjamin, Walter, 133, 144, 172, 215n10
Bernhard, Thomas, 156–57, 159
Breaking Bad, 212
Bunheads, 211

Capital (Marx), 56, 59, 72, 80, 108, 129, 134
capitalism: Althusser's work on, 102–9, 121–24; Marxian analyses of, 80–81, 87–88, 122–25; passivity of, 25–26, 31–32, 38; postideological, 6–7; televisionary life and, 42
Carousel, the, 36–37, 48–49
cartoons, 4, 23–25, 28
categories, 15, 41, 43, 63, 91, 96, 112–13
celebricity: afterlife and, 173–74; criticism's work and, 137–40, 144–45; definitions of, 44, 145–51; epic form and, 141–44; Muppets and, 196–204; seduction and, 154–55; singularity and, 138–40, 144–45; strangeness and, 151–53; truth and, 145–51; Young-girl and, 127–31
celebrities: fame and, 145, 169–70, 211, 219n7; as gods, 24, 144–51, 154, 170–74, 185–87, 197–98; models as, 149, 166–70; the nobody and, 5, 40–50, 155–57; television and, 166–71
childhood, 35–36, 49, 154, 167–68, 180–81
circularity, 51–52, 114, 116–20, 140, 185, 189–90, 231n10
Civilization and Its Discontents (Freud), 194
comedy. *See* laughter; tragedy
commodities: addiction and, 32–33, 225n16; advertising and, 33–35; alethic truth and,

243

19, 85–87, 94–99; being(s) relation to, 55–63, 100–101, 125, 130–31; celebrity and, 145–51, 154–55, 159–60; dissociation and, 160–62; fetishization and, 8, 57–58, 72, 108; gadgets and, 37–38, 132–34, 178–79, 193–94; ideology and, 6, 60–63, 108–9, 176–77, 209, 223n1; as locus of social relations, 87–90; Marxian analysis of, 59–63, 74–83, 107; metaphysical approaches to, 60–63; ontological collapse and, 5–6, 100–101, 129; phenomenology of, 81–84, 89–90; production and, 6–7, 61, 77–81, 89–90, 105, 129–30, 224n5; publicness of, 90–94; sensuality and, 60–63, 71–75; temporality of, 173–74; truth and, 71–75

computers (personal), 162, 177–84
contexigency, 46–48, 51–58
Contributions to Philosophy (Heidegger), 22, 47, 93, 216n4, 220n4, 227n34
correlationism, 45, 125–26
criticism, 8, 137–40, 144–45, 163–64, 213–14
Cusset, François, 214

Dasein: advertising and, 32–33; authenticity and, 30–31; being and, 45, 92; being(s) and, 52–58; the commodity and, 87–91, 127–31; das Man and, 40–50; ex-istence of, 15, 28, 85–86; gadgets and, 6–7; spatiality of, 14–15, 17–18; televisionary, 4–5, 21–22, 27, 128–29; temporality of, 29, 35; truth and, 67–68; unworldliness of, 4, 14, 17
das Man, 40–50, 52, 92, 218n1
decisions, 22, 28, 53, 62–63, 75, 99–101, 212, 220n4
deconstruction, 3, 7, 9, 53–54, 80, 130, 132–34. *See also* phenomenology
de-decisioning, 100–101, 227n46
Derrida, Jacques, 4, 15, 17, 22, 215n12, 220n15, 225n16, 226n31
desire, 19, 34–35, 125, 166, 202–3, 218n19
Desperate Housewives, 190
Dexter, 143–44, 191–93
différance, 17, 46–47, 94, 99
Diff'rent Strokes, 180, 190
dis-distancing, 14–18
divinity, 24, 144–51, 154, 170–74, 185–87, 197–98. *See also* celebrities; gods
dramatic television, 23, 30, 187–88, 190. *See also* quality television
drugs, 31–34, 183

epic, 35, 141–44, 176, 200–201
event, the: being(s) and, 51–58; commodity production and, 6, 132–34; Heidegger on, 47; production and, 121–31; television and, 5, 26, 46–47; truth and, 48, 51–58
everydayness, 4, 7, 13, 16–20, 25, 40–41, 92, 145–46
exchange value, 19, 81, 85, 87, 90–92, 94–95, 224n5, 225n14
excrescence, 89, 130–31, 159–60, 175
ex-istence, 15, 51–53, 55, 59–60, 66, 96–99, 131, 151. *See also* being; ontology; phenomenology
Eyes Wide Shut (Kubrick), 143

fame, 145, 169–70, 211, 219n7
fetishization, 8, 56–60, 72–77, 84, 94, 108–11, 115, 126–30, 167, 221n4
The Following, 188–89
Frasier, 180
Freud, Sigmund, 147, 180, 194
Friends, 213–14

gadgets: advertising and, 126–31; alethic work of, 7, 34, 121–31, 177–78; the commodity and, 37–38, 132–34, 178–79, 193–94, 231n10; ideology and, 176–77; personal computer as, 162, 177–84; phenomenology's impossibility and, 3, 37; pluripotency of, 7, 37–38, 127, 232n15
game shows, 27–28
gaze, the, 16–17, 86, 111–12, 129, 156–58, 168–69, 192
German Ideology (Marx), 84, 107
Ge-Stell, 96–99, 112, 122–31
gestures, 8, 60, 152, 174–75. *See also* criticism
Gilmore Girls, 185–87
Glee, 207–11
gods, 24, 34, 144–51, 154, 170–74, 197–98. *See also* celebrities; divinity
Goethe, Johann Wolfgang von, 168, 170, 198–99, 212
Greeks, 67–70, 74, 91, 93, 176–77, 184–85, 199–200, 229n40. *See also specific authors and works*

haunting, 9, 48, 89, 101, 137–38, 220n15
Hegel, G. W. F., 53, 65–67, 77, 104, 108, 141, 147, 221n4
Heidegger, Martin: Althusser and, 115–18, 120;

INDEX

authenticity and, 21–22, 40–50, 85–86; the commodity and, 5–6, 71–75; *Ge-Stell* concept and, 96–99, 112, 122–31; ideology and, 74–75, 111; Latour on, 57–58; literature and, 137, 143; Marx and, 6, 9, 59–65, 71–75, 81–82, 84–85, 93–102, 222n3, 223n2, 226n20; Nazism and, 18, 64, 68–69, 93, 221n2, 223n24; phenomenology and, 2–3, 5–6, 13–14, 17, 25, 44, 51, 91, 115–16, 124; Plato and, 65–66, 68, 73–74; technology and, 13–14; terminology of, 2, 9–10; tool-being and, 85–87, 177–78; truth and, 64–75, 121–23, 126. *See also* aletheia; *specific works*
Henry, Michel, 61–62, 77, 88–89, 104, 108, 221n4, 225n15, 232n21
Hilton, Paris, 143, 170
history, 13–14, 17–18, 46–47, 66, 68, 152, 167, 219n5
Hölderlin, Friedrich, 64, 74, 143–44, 166, 171, 181
Homer, 34, 74, 141, 176–77
horizons: of capitalism, 87–89; the event and, 7–8, 52–58; Heidegger on, 2; of metaphysics, 61–63; production and, 114–16; truth and, 69–70, 130–31. *See also* aletheia; Heidegger, Martin; production
House, 190–91
humor, 171. *See also* laughter
hybridity, 57–58, 61, 90–91, 112–15
Hyperion (Hölderlin), 143, 181

idealism, 23, 65, 73–74, 80, 104, 108–13, 164–65, 173–74, 187–88, 227n34
ideology: Althusser on, 6, 72–73, 100–102, 106–20, 227n1, 229n32; commodity fetishism and, 6, 60–63, 96, 108–9, 176–77, 209, 223n1; definitions of, 106; Heidegger on, 74–75, 111, 121–22; Marx on, 69–70, 79, 81–82, 84, 106–7; materialism and, 110–12, 119–20; metaphysics and, 90–91; paradox of, 63, 82, 106–7; praxis and, 110–12, 115, 119–20; representation and, 26, 101–2, 110–20, 181–82; truth and, 64–70. *See also* production; reproduction
Iliad (Homer), 23, 141, 145–46, 170, 176
imagination, 109–11, 158–59, 166, 181–83, 229n32
Internet, 38, 179
interpellation, 92, 101, 113–14, 119

irony, 21–23, 28–29, 81, 126, 181
ISA ("Ideology and Ideological State Apparatuses") (Althusser), 100–101, 104, 109, 114–15, 119, 227n1, 229n32, 230n48

Jackson, Michael, 143, 152–53, 198

Kafka, Franz, 141, 156–57, 192
Kant, Immanuel, 48, 73, 80, 82, 86, 90, 95, 99, 114, 126
Knight Rider, 179–80
Kordela, A. Kiarina, 130, 232n14
Kubrick, Stanley, 143, 172–73

labor value, 79–80, 88–89, 105–6
language, 160–66. *See also* criticism; literature
Latour, Bruno, 57–58
laughter, 21–23, 138, 171
law, the, 24, 156–59, 167, 183
legibility, 108, 110–12, 114–15, 119–20
Lenin and Philosophy (Althusser), 100–101
"Letter on Humanism" (Heidegger), 47, 65
liberal arts, 205–7
Life Is a Dream (Calderón), 181
literature, 137–40, 170, 188–89, 215n10. *See also* criticism; writing; *specific authors and works*
Lotz, Christian, 222n3, 224n5
Lukács, György, 56–57, 72, 80, 107, 224n5

Mad Men, 34–37, 218n22
Madonna, 150–51
Magnum P.I., 179
Marx, Karl: the commodity and, 57–58, 60–63, 74–83; Hegel and, 103–4, 225n15; Heidegger and, 6, 9, 59–65, 69–75, 81–82, 84–85, 93–102, 222n3, 223n2, 226n20; ideology and, 69–70, 79, 81–82, 106–7, 147
masks, 142–43, 194–97
masturbation, 180–84, 193. *See also* sexuality
materialism: ideology and, 110–12, 114–20, 225n16; phenomenology and, 5–6, 105, 124, 129–30
McLuhan, Marshall, 20, 215n12, 219n9
memory, 35–37, 48–49, 171–73. *See also* nostalgia
metaphysics: the commodity and, 60–63, 76–81; correspondence theory of truth and, 71–75, 83, 85; deconstruction of, 57–58, 80; difference and, 90–91; Heidegger's critique

of, 14–15, 51–52, 71–75, 85–86; ideology and, 90–91; Marx and, 69–75; pointlessness of, 140, 173–74, 231n7; presence and, 46–47; representation and, 26, 101–20, 133–34

Mitdasein, 92–95

models, 149, 166–70

Montag, Walter, 101, 227n1, 230n43

moods, 26–27, 31

Mr. Belvedere, 180

The Muppets, 194–95, 198–201

The Muppet Show, 198–203

Muppet Studio, 202

musicals, 207–10

music videos, 44, 128–29

mystery, 78–84, 87, 89–90, 160–61, 170, 178

Nazism, 18, 64, 68–70, 93, 221n2, 223n24

nearness. *See* dis-distancing; presence

Nietzsche, Friedrich, 41–44, 64–67, 95, 142–43

Nip/Tuck, 187–88

nobody, the, 5, 40–50, 145–46

nostalgia, 34–36, 48–49, 137–39, 171–73, 205–6, 218n22

obscenity, 33–34, 39, 42, 56, 180–84

The Office, 30

onanism. *See* masturbation

"On the Essence of Truth" (Heidegger), 64, 69, 74–75, 111

On the Reproduction of Capital (Althusser), 104, 117, 230n48

ontological difference: collapse of, 5, 27, 51–58, 100–101, 129; Heidegger's work and, 16; self-showing and, 45–46. *See also* being(s); Heidegger, Martin; unconcealment

ontology: being(s) and, 5–6, 51–63, 100–101, 125, 130–31; ideology and, 115–16; Marxian versions of, 85–90; object-oriented (OOO), 9, 125–26, 220n5; ontic perspective and, 14–16, 55; phenomenology's relation to, 44–46, 59–60; production and, 6, 122–31. *See also* phenomenology; television

OOO (object-oriented ontology), 125–26, 220n5

phenomenology: aletheia and, 6–7, 9, 15–16, 19, 48, 64–75, 84–85, 118–34, 145–51, 168; Althusser's critique of, 117–18; being(s) and, 51–63; celebrity and, 44–50, 143–51; commodities and, 76–84; deconstruction of, 3, 9, 53–54; Heidegger's work in, 2–3, 5–6, 14, 25, 44, 91; materialism and, 5–6, 105; ontology's relation to, 44–46, 59–60; self-showing and, 5–6, 14–15, 38, 45, 71–72, 84–85, 104, 221n4; televisionary life and, 3–4, 8–9, 13–20, 26–39, 44–58

phusis, 99, 112–13, 121–22

Plato, 64–68, 73–74, 82, 123, 147–48, 166, 181–82, 192

play: being and, 74; of signifiers, 7, 131, 139; truth and, 9, 15–16, 118–20, 128–29, 132–34

pluripotency, 7, 37, 127, 232n15

Poe, Edgar Allen, 188–89

politics, 65–66, 68–69, 164–68, 171–72, 175, 187–88, 199

pop stars, 148–49. *See also specific stars*

pornography, 24, 164, 193–94

praxis, 9, 57–58, 86, 109–20, 124–25, 130–31, 164–65, 225n15, 230n43, 232n21

pregnancy, 160, 181–82

Preliminary Materials for a Theory of the Young-Girl (TYiqqun collective), 127–31

presence, 15–16, 45–47, 65. *See also* metaphysics; phenomenology

present-at-hand, 15, 67, 71–72, 81–82, 85–87, 90–91, 95–96, 111, 225n15

private, the, 43, 48, 61–62, 158, 169, 175–78, 190–91, 193–94

procedurals, 188–90. *See also* dramatic television; quality television

production: being(s) and, 62–63; commodities and, 61, 71–75, 87–88, 105, 224n5; the commodity and, 6, 77–81; conditions of, 26; epistemological, 116–17; ideology and, 31–32, 64–70, 109–20; metaphysics and, 62–63; phenomenology of, 81–85; *phusis* and, 99; reproduction and, 6, 26, 56–57, 102–9, 121–31, 181–82, 228n14; truth and, 71–75

Project Runway, 202

public (as opposed to private), 43, 48, 61–62. *See also* celebrity; das Man; fame

quality television, 4, 30–31, 34, 38–39, 217n16, 218n17

queerness, 208–9. *See also* sexuality

"The Question Concerning Technology" (Heidegger), 112, 121–22

INDEX

radio, 13–14, 17–18
Radiohead, 174–75
Rancière, Jacques, 223n1, 227n1
Reading Capital (Althusser), 107–8, 110–11, 116, 119–20
ready-to-hand, 15, 85–87, 90–91, 95. *See also* tools
reality shows, 4, 23–25, 28, 166–70, 202–5. *See also specific shows*
reflection, 23, 28, 35–37, 62–63, 82–83
reification, 7, 56–57, 72, 231n10. *See also* ideology
repetition, 69, 92–93, 109–20, 193, 207
representation, 26, 101–2, 110–20, 133–34, 181, 193–94. *See also* ideology; metaphysics; truth
reproduction (ideological), 6, 26, 56–57, 102–9, 121–31, 181–82, 228n14
Republic (Plato), 64, 67, 181
resoluteness, 5, 20, 41, 189, 220n4
Rousseau, Jean-Jacques, 8, 19, 37, 43–44, 46, 135, 144, 147, 167–68, 226n31

Saturday Night Live, 28
Schelling, Friedrich, 1, 5
Schickel, Richard, 16, 215n10
Schnitzler, Arthur, 142–43
scientific Marxism, 104–9, 116, 224n6. *See also* Althusser, Louis
Seinfeld, 29, 180–81, 193, 213
self-evidence, 53, 77–80, 89–90, 110–12, 117
self-referentiality, 21–22, 28
sensual, the, 60–63, 71–81, 162–64, 221n4
serial killers, 189–93. *See also* Dexter
sexuality, 129, 160, 181–82, 193–98, 201–2, 210
Sexual Personae (Paglia), 44
shame, 2, 26, 30, 34, 48–50, 146, 159–60
singularity, 138–40, 144–45
sitcoms, 180–84, 190–93. *See also specific shows*
speculation (ontology, materialism, metaphysics), 9. *See also* OOO (object-oriented ontology)
Star Trek, 142
Star Trek: The Next Generation, 183
Star Wars, 142
Stiegler, Bernard, 17, 19, 127, 215n12
subjectivity, 73–75, 80; Althusser on, 109–10; interpellation and, 92, 101, 113–14, 119; metaphysics and, 61–62; phenomenology and, 45–47; psychoanalytic theories of, 109, 115; Young-girl and, 127–31
substitution, 30–31, 92, 173, 209
substructure, 76–81, 104, 106
superstructure, 69, 76–81, 84, 102–4
Survivor, 168
Symposium (Plato), 182, 192
symptomatic reading, 102, 107, 116, 120, 230n43

technology. *See* gadgets; Internet; radio; television
television: addiction and, 31–32; advertising and, 19, 32–34; authenticity and, 4–5, 21, 27–28, 30–33, 55–58; being(s) and, 51–58; celebrities' watching of, 157–58, 170–71; deconstructive accounts of, 4; as event, 26, 46–47; everydayness of, 4, 19–20, 25, 40–41; gadget's relation to, 37–38, 180–84; as other life, 3–4, 21–39, 41–58; personal computer in, 178–79; phenomenology and, 3, 8–9, 13–20, 32–33, 44–50; representation's failures and, 180–84; spatiality and, 14–16; temporality of, 8, 29; theorizations of, 21–39
temporality: authenticity and, 92–93; celebricity and, 48–50, 173–74; circularity and, 51–52; comic timing and, 203–4; Dasein and, 17–19; history and, 13–18, 46–47, 64–66, 68, 152, 167, 219n5; Kantian, 80; memory and, 35–37, 48–49, 171–73; phenomenology and, 4, 46–47; televisionary, 8, 29, 35–36, 38
terrorism, 142, 179–84, 192
thinking, 1–9, 14, 47, 52–54, 69–75, 93–99, 104, 117–20, 123, 129–34, 175, 214
Tiqqun collective, 127–31
tools, 85–87, 89–91, 177–78
tragedy, 22–23, 29–30, 41–42, 44, 171, 184–85, 199–200
transcendence, 4, 9, 22–24, 43, 48, 51–52, 61–63, 71–82, 103, 106, 118, 122, 131, 145–48
truth: alethic sense of, 6, 48, 51–58, 67, 84–85, 112–13, 115, 118, 168; celebrity and, 145–51; commodities and, 96–99; as correctness, 71–75, 83, 85, 90, 110; gadgets and, 177–78; ideology and, 64–70; language and, 137–40; play and, 118–20, 129, 132–34, 1287; production of, 121–31; publicness of, 91–92

24, 178–79, 184
Two and a Half Men, 181

uncanny, 59, 76, 154–55, 190, 208
unconcealment: advertising and, 19; celebrity and, 44–45, 143–51; commodity form and, 71–75, 94–99; concealment and, 16; definitions of, 44–45; Heidegger's phenomenology and, 15, 45–50; production and, 6, 71–72, 104; truth definitions and, 7, 67–70, 84–85, 115, 118
use value, 77, 85, 87–88, 94, 224n5, 225n14, 225n16

value: definitions of, 96; exchange value and, 19, 81, 85, 87, 90–95, 224n5, 225n14; ideology and, 108–9; labor value and, 79–80, 88–89, 105–6; production of, 6; self-showing of, 6; use value and, 77, 85–88, 94, 224n5, 225n14, 225n16

Verhoeff, Nanna, 232n15
violence, 25–26, 158, 172–73, 201–2
visionaries, 171–73
Volk concept, 68, 92, 94, 223nn26–27
vulgar, the, 28–30, 44–46, 53–54, 104, 107, 137, 145, 148, 159, 180

Wagner, Richard, 143, 174–75
walking, 1–2, 5–6, 8
Wallace, David Foster, 205–7, 217n14
WarGames, 179
Wilhelm Meister (Goethe), 170, 198–99, 209
will to power, 65, 74, 131, 178
Winfrey, Oprah, 43, 143
The Wire, 31, 34
writing, 139–40, 163–66. *See also* criticism; literature

Young-girl, 127–31

ACKNOWLEDGMENTS

Some debts are almost beyond words: such is the debt this book owes to Paul North, who not only gave me the courage to step away from more familiar scholarly paths, but, founding the *Idiom* series together with Jacques Lezra, created the precarious opening through which this work could pass into the light of day. And I am also extraordinarily grateful to Richard Morrison, editorial director of Fordham University Press, for supporting this= project and guiding it through to publication, and Tom Lay, the acquisitions editor at Fordham, who generously took the time to meet with me even when no longer officially involved. Henry Sussman, the model of a theorist unafraid to take risks, has been a source of invaluable encouragement and advice ever since identifying himself to me as one of the anonymous readers. The process of preparing the final manuscript and proofs was as painless as I could have hoped, due in large part to Tim Roberts, the managing editor in charge of the project, and Sheila Berg, the copyeditor. The index was prepared, under a tight deadline, by Derek Gottlieb.

Yonsei University's Underwood International College, my academic home for the last ten years, has been an exciting place to teach and do research, and I feel fortunate to have so many wonderful colleagues, including Aljoša Pužar and Jen Hui Bon Hoa—interlocutors whose conversations contributed much to this book—as well as Astrid Lac, Nikolaj Pedersen, Mandel Cabrera, Joseph Hwang, H. Christian Blood, Martin Wagner, Stefano Ercolino, Chad Denton, Paul Tonks, Helen Lee, Krys Lee, John Frankl, Kil-Pyo Hong, Michael Kim, and Hyungji Park. I finished the first draft during a sabbatical leave spent at Yale University, and the many conversations with the faculty and graduate students of the Department of Germanic Languages and Literatures, especially Rüdiger Kampe, Kirk Wetters, and Carol Jacobs, energized and sustained me not only during the intense months of writing, but the long period of waiting that ensued. And there are also many others for whose conversations and friendship I am grateful and to whom this book owes much: William Franke, Thomas Schestag, Mayumo Inoue, Barbara Natalie Nagel, Daniel Hoffman-Schwartz, Markus Hardtmann, Julia Ng,

Mathelinda Nabugodi, Cathy Chung, my sisters Jessica and Victoria, and Sarah Brett-Smith.

My doctoral work is too far behind me to blame this book's failings on my extraordinary advisors, Peter Fenves and Sam Weber, but I am at least sure that whatever fugitive rigor is to be found in these pages is due in large part to them.

Much of the TV I watched with my wife, Hwa Young Seo, and our conversations around the television have been the provocation for many thoughts. And I am also grateful to her for all her support, especially during the final months of work on the manuscript, and for breaking through my studious cave with her laughter and her melodies.

Also too great for words is the debt to my parents, Stephen and Judith Adler, each in their way models for the thinking life.

IDIOM INVENTING WRITING THEORY

Jacques Lezra and Paul North, series editors

Werner Hamacher, *Minima Philologica*. Translated by Catharine Diehl and Jason Groves

Michal Ben-Naftali, *Chronicle of Separation: On Deconstruction's Disillusioned Love*. Translated by Mirjam Hadar

Daniel Hoffman-Schwartz, Barbara Natalie Nagel, and Lauren Shizuko Stone, eds., *Flirtations: Rhetoric and Aesthetics This Side of Seduction*

Márton Dornbach, *Receptive Spirit: German Idealism and the Dynamics of Cultural Transmission*

Jean-Luc Nancy, *Intoxication*. Translated by Philip Armstrong

Sean Alexander Gurd, *Dissonance: Sound in Ancient Greek Song*

Anthony Curtis Adler, *Celebricities: Media Culture and the Phenomenology of Gadget Commodity Life*